Creation of the Sacred

CREATION
OF THE
SACRED

⊗⊗

*Tracks of Biology in
Early Religions*

Walter Burkert

HARVARD UNIVERSITY PRESS
*Cambridge, Massachusetts
London, England*

Copyright © 1996 by the President and Fellows of Harvard College
All rights reserved
Printed in the United States of America
Third printing, 1998

First Harvard University Press paperback edition, 1998

Library of Congress Cataloging-in-Publication Data
Burkert, Walter, 1931–
Creation of the sacred : tracks of biology in early religions /
Walter Burkert.
p. cm.
Originally presented as Gifford lectures delivered in Feb. and
Mar . 1989 at the University of St. Andrews.
Includes bibliographical references (p.   ) and index.
ISBN 0-674-17569-7 (cloth)
ISBN 0-674-17570-0 (pbk.)
1. Religion.   2. Physical anthropology—Religious aspects.
3. Sociobiology—Religious aspects.   4. Human evolution—Religious
aspects.   I. Gifford lectures.   II. Title.
BL48.B79   1996
95-44787
291—dc20

Acknowledgments

This book grew out of the Gifford Lectures given at the University of St. Andrews in February and March 1989. My thanks, first of all, to the University of St. Andrews and the Gifford Committee for their kind invitation; to the Department of Classics for its hospitality and assistance in the atmosphere of wintry St. Andrews; and most specially to Ien Kidd for his unfailing friendship. The lectures have been revised; their sequence has been changed and additional evidence and arguments have been introduced, but the main contents and the line of approach remain as before. I am grateful to my collaborators at Zürich University, Thomas Kappeler, Eveline Krummen, and Christian Oesterheld, for their help in the elaboration of the text and notes.

Contents

Preface

"Natural Theology, in the widest sense" was proposed for investigation by the will of Lord Gifford in 1886.[1] More than a hundred years later no one will claim that we have come to any firm conclusions in this task. Instead, we find ourselves entangled in widening problems. Does religion come naturally to human beings? In what sense can religion, let alone theology, be seen as "natural?" What is the meaning of nature in general, and in this context?

The concept of nature has long been the domain of the natural sciences, which have made gigantic progress since the time of Lord Gifford. Yet nature itself is disintegrating in the process. As science is revealing the details of molecular biology and unraveling the genetic code, the processes going on in living organisms become accessible to knowledge and manipulation far beyond that delicate harmony established in the evolution of life which had been called Nature by admiring philosophers and poets. At present, no Nature remains to hold hopes for providing the framework for stability, order, and morality; it has been dispelled as a concept and is physically vanishing from our sight under the heap of man-made construction and refuse.

Religion, though, fails to disappear. While all around us generations are growing up factually without religion, the religious forces remain unexpectedly tenacious and impetuous, nay dangerous and sometimes disastrous. We are puzzled by the drawing power of new cults and sects, we are horrified by the passions of religious strife in many contemporary conflicts, we are apprehensive of the growing tide of fundamentalism in different encampments. More than seventy years of well-organized atheistic education and propaganda did not succeed in abolishing religion in the Soviet empire, and its re-emergence is resuscitating age-old battles. It is no less agonizing to observe the failure of religion to deal with such urgent problems of the day as environment protection and population control. Religion still enjoys high moral credit and yet appears thoroughly problematic, a challenge to reason in its theory and practice as it has always been—all the more reason, then, for anthropology to take account of this phenomenon. We must at least try to make sense of the irrational in the hope of gaining some illumination, some insight from the fringes of experience, whether superhuman or subhuman.

It is the process of modernization and the growing achievements of science that make us realize more than before how much we are ourselves part of nature. Even if nature has ceased to exist as an immutable essence or matrix and rather appears as an irreversible process of self-organization in transient patterns emerging from chaos, we cannot escape from being involved in this, formed as we are by the age-old evolution of life. In this sense, biological "nature" is working in each of our acts and thoughts, just as the changes of nature and the threats to nature are affecting our own existence. The study of nature and human self-knowledge should no longer be separated, even if Socrates long ago insisted it was right to do so. And if religion constitutes an integral part of the human world embedded in nature, understanding religion should be part of the same theoretical effort, in a framework of natural (biological) anthropology.

The inquiry concerning "natural theology in the widest sense," including its historical dimension, thus turns into this question: what has been the *raison d'être* for religion in the evolution of human life and culture hitherto? Is there a natural foundation of religion, based on the great and general process of life which has brought forth humanity and still holds sway over it, beyond chance and manipulation, personal idiosyncrasies and social conditioning?

As both nature and theology are assuming a nostalgic ring, there is a new incentive to look farther back in history, to conduct an investigation starting with the earliest forms of religion attested.[2] The most ancient documents bearing on our tradition come from Near Eastern and Mediterranean civilizations: Mesopotamia, Egypt, Asia Minor, Israel, and Greece. The approach based on the earliest written evidence has the advantage of a distanced view, largely exempt from the tensions and anxieties encircling living religions. The ancient gods—with the single exception of Jahweh—are no longer powerful nor represented in living belief; they do not demand cult and no longer spread awe. What is more, pre-Buddhistic, pre-Christian, pre-Islamic religions lack certain forms of systematic reflection, organization, and defense mechanisms which have contributed to the overwhelming success of the so-called world religions. The older models, being more variegated, experimental, and changeable, may still give clues to the original growth or construction of religion through their apparent "primitivity."[3] Contemporary religions have grown out of these, in an evolutionary and sometimes revolutionary process; identical elements still abound. In what sense this can be called natural remains to be seen.

§§

An attempt to tie historical and philological research to biological anthropology requires that one explore fields set far apart, each crowded with innumerable publications, amidst more and more refined and specialized if often conflicting methods, results, and controversies. It is far beyond an individual's abilities to master all the relevant discussions. Yet precisely because historians have become aware of how much of their work, beyond the mere retrieval and accumulation of data, is bound by the special patterns, principles, and fashions of their own civilization, they must look beyond the narrow historical perspectives of the past and take into regard the widening scientific horizons of our own world. General anthropology will in the end have to merge with biology.

Historical studies presuppose some optimism as to the existence of facts and the possibility of correct accounts. This may sound naive vis-à-vis modern or post-modern tendencies to dissolve every object of study into interpretations, to be analyzed in turn to detect their tacit preconceptions and tendentious distortions.[4] Those who cling to a hard core of reality may still claim company with science, which in its most abstract constructs remains tied to empirical data. Biology is exploring the "reality" of living organisms with growing success, from self-replicating molecules to human consciousness. Even in the humanities, interpretations are not just constructs but hypotheses about reality which does not cease to make itself felt. If, for example, the language and symbolism of sacrifice in a specific cultural context prompt a variety of interpretations, real bones remain at the site to prove that real killing took place there. Religion is life-and-death realistic—which keeps it close to nature.

Creation of the Sacred

1

🙵

Culture in a Landscape

SITUATING RELIGION

Beyond Culture

"Neither history nor anthropology knows of societies from which religion has been totally absent."[1] The observation that practically all tribes, states, and cities have some form of religion has been made repeatedly, ever since Herodotus. Ancient philosophers made this "consensus of nations" proof for the existence of the gods.[2] The question is not whether ethnographers may still find a few exceptions to that consensus; it is the universality of the consensus that has to be explained. To be sure, differences in belief and practice are dramatic; indeed, religion can be a most serious obstacle for communication between different groups, producing "pseudo-species" which exclude and may try to exterminate each other; but even this divisive tendency is a common feature.

The ubiquity of religion is matched by its persistence through the millennia. It evidently has survived most drastic social and economic changes: the neolithic revolution, the urban revolution, and even the industrial revolution. If religion ever was invented, it has managed to infiltrate practically all varieties of human cultures; in the course of history, however, religion has never been demonstrably reinvented but has always been there, carried on from generation to generation since time immemorial. As for the founders of new religions, such as Zarathustra, Jesus, or Mohammed, their creative achievement consisted in transforming, reversing, or rearranging existing patterns and elements, which continue to carry an undeniable family resemblance to older forms.

The civilizations that will come into closer view in this book, mainly the Mesopotamian, Jewish, Greek, and Roman, are contiguous and were in contact for a long time. While they developed under comparable climatic, economic, and social conditions, they also present glaring contrasts and revolutionary changes, from monarchy to democracy, from temple economy to monetary systems, from illiteracy to writing. Yet there are impressive similarities in their understanding and practice of religion, their myths and their rituals, temples and offerings. Diverse cultures have proved hospitable to many of the same elements of religion.

Culture has been defined as a "realized signifying system," a social system characterized by standard forms of communication.[3] Anthropologists see not just one system of this kind but an apparently boundless variety of them, although this variety seems to merge into a yet undefined conglomerate today. Hence the principle held by the leading schools of contemporary social sciences: each culture must be studied in its diversity and relative autonomy. In consequence, the very concept of human nature has come under attack. In what has been termed "new dualism," nature is excluded from cultural studies.[4] Humans are defined by culture far beyond their natural makeup: "there is no human nature apart from culture." Likewise, "humanity is as various in its essence as it is in its expression."[5]

This exclusively cultural approach would make any investigation into the natural elements or foundations of a phenomenon such as religion worse than heresy from the start. It is now common to integrate religion into culture, to view it in relation to specific groups and epochs. Religion is thus posed in contrast to nature and cannot be treated as a general phenomenon deriving from human nature.

Some of the most important and influential anthropological

studies of civilizations and religions in our century exemplify this view, exploring the Nuer or the Azande, the Andaman islanders or the Argonauts of the Western Pacific.[6] "Religion as a Cultural System" is the title of a famous paper by Clifford Geertz.[7] In the wake of Émile Durkheim religion has been seen, first of all, as a social phenomenon; Durkheim replaced the concept of religious ideas by that of "collective representations."[8] More recent decades have brought into ever sharper focus the forms and functions of communication within social groups.[9] This line has been followed in the successful development of semiology, structuralism, and poststructuralism.

Important studies along these lines have been carried out in the field of Greek religion, especially by the Paris school of Jean-Pierre Vernant.[10] In these works, Greek religion emerges in the context of the Greek city state, the *polis* as it has evolved beginning in the 8th century B.C. The details of myth and ritual, and especially of sacrifice, are seen as objective agents in their respective contexts marking distinctions and correlations, normality and deviation, within the structure of a particular ancient society. The impulse provided by this approach has been effective far beyond the specialized circles of classical philology.

Yet if cultures remain enclosed each in its own signifying system, what about the interactions of cultures, influences, and traditions that link the present to the past? What about our own chances of transcultural understanding of other civilizations whether past or present? And how do we account for the ubiquity and persistence of a phenomenon such as religion?

An alternative thesis may provide a basis for dealing with such questions. It proposes that there are phenomena common to all human civilizations, *universalia* of anthropology; they may be but need not be called characteristics of human nature. Religion belongs with them. Cultures interact; there are exchanges and conflicts, breaks but also continuities even within historical change. Above all there are basic similarities in all forms of human culture, inasmuch as everywhere people eat, drink, and defecate, work and sleep, enjoy sex and procreate, get sick and die.

There is no denying either the general or the biological character of these processes. Cultural anthropologists will claim they are trivial; it is only the cultural elaborations and differences that make these phenomena at all interesting. But they are there.

What is startling is the ubiquity of certain less trivial phenomena, which are culturally determined in every case and yet not generated nor explicable in isolation. They always appear integrated into specific cultures and take various shapes accordingly, but their unmistakable similarity makes them a general class transcending single cultural systems. They must be presumed to fulfill basic functions for human social life in all its forms, even if it is easy to imagine alternatives. These universals include such disparate phenomena as the nuclear family with a marked role of the father and the special father-son relationship; the use of technology, especially of fire; interactions that include economic exchange but also warfare; and above all language, art, and religion.[11] The last two mentioned may come as a surprise: what are in fact the functions of art and religion? They seem to be much less necessary for human life than the other items mentioned, yet they have been with us for all the time *homo sapiens sapiens* has been in existence.

❦

The worldwide similarity of religious phenomena is easy to point out: they include formalized ritual behavior appropriate for veneration; the practice of offerings, sacrifices, vows and prayers with reference to superior beings; and songs, tales, teachings, and explanations about these beings and the worship they demand. Normally, religion is emphatically accepted. If voices of skepticism arise, it is deemed wise to silence them. "The fool says in his heart: there is no god"[12]—but most are not so foolish as to speak out. Even rhetoricians know that "one has to worship the divine: nobody opposes this exhortation unless he has gone mad."[13]

Nevertheless it is notoriously difficult to define religion in a general, transcultural way. Most attempts work at the level of ideas or symbols. Jan van Baal, for example, defines religion as "all explicit and implicit notions and ideas, accepted as true, which relate to a reality which cannot be verified empirically."[14] This comes close to the older concept of religion as belief in the supernatural, while disregarding the practice of religion which is not necessarily based on so-called true belief. More circumspect is the definition of religion by Clifford Geertz: "(1) a system of symbols which act to (2) establish powerful, persuasive, and long-lasting moods and motivations in men by (3) formulating conceptions of a general order of existence and (4) clothing these conceptions with such an aura of factuality that (5) the moods and motivations seem uniquely realistic."[15] (Note the characteristic paradox that the symbolic should seem "uniquely realistic.") The realistic, that is, practical, aspects of religion may still be underestimated in Geertz's formula: it is not the symbols alone that create this seeming reality; it is the ongoing activity of living people interacting with each other through symbols, exchanging signs and reacting to them while working on their own "reality," which constitutes religion.

Numerous other proposed definitions and pertinent methodological reflections have been offered on the subject of religion.[16] Here, as Benson Saler has recommended, it will suffice to assemble some elements that characterize religion in almost every instance.[17] This attempt to grasp the distinctive features of religion remains at the level of observable behavior; the claims of factual truth or real existence of the gods are not of primary concern in the study of past religions.

The first principal characteristic of religion is negative: that is, religion deals with the nonobvious, the unseen, that "which cannot be verified empirically." Protagoras the sophist spoke of the *adelótes,* the "unclearness" or "nonevidence" of the gods.[18] Religion is manifest in actions and attitudes that do not fulfill immediate practical functions. What is intended and dealt with cannot be seen, or touched, or worked upon in the usual fashion of everyday life. This is why strangers are usually puzzled by religious practice. Conversely, we are tempted to suppose that any-

thing puzzling and not immediately apparent may be religious—
a problem often met in prehistoric archaeology; drastic misunderstandings may of course occur. It is difficult to "get" what is
meant in religious behavior, but some common basis for empathy, interpretation, and translation evidently does exist. The criterion of *adelótes* is insufficient, yet it remains basic.

It is true that this unclearness is often emphatically denied by
the insiders. "The knowability of god is clear among men," St.
Paul wrote in Romans, "for god has made it clear for them. For
the invisible (characteristics) of him are seen by the mind in his
works, from the creation of the world. . . ." In both these arguments, from the mind and from the world *(kosmos)*, Paul was
following Greek popular philosophy.[19] The very emphasis, circumstantial argument, and special pleading of his claims acknowledge the difficulties of access. Even St. Paul's most optimistic formulation retains the "invisible." *Adelótes* can neither
be abolished nor denied; it can be given a positive twist, however,
by proclaiming it a secret.

To get beyond the barrier of unclearness, special forms of experience—meditation, vision, and ecstasy—are commonly invoked; thus the paranormal range of feelings is called upon to
establish direct encounter with the supernatural. Yet the remarkable fact is not the existence of ecstasy and other forms of altered
consciousness; it is their acceptance and interpretation by the
majority of normal people. The ecstatic phenomena are integrated into religion and confirm existing belief, and these manifestations are themselves shaped by cultural training and practice insofar as they become communicable and accessible to
others. In fact, they are judged and selected by an existing religion's own categories: "test the spirits."[20]

The second principal characteristic of religion stands in antithesis to the ineffable: religion manifests itself through interaction and communication. It is thus a relevant factor in the
systems of civilization. Even the lonely ascetic communicates, as
he becomes the object of admiration, propaganda, and pilgrimage. In fact, religious communication always focuses in two di-

rections, toward the unseen and toward the contemporary social situation. Through attitudes, acts, and language certain non-obvious entities or partners with special characteristics and interests are introduced, recognized, and tended.[21] Distinct from humans and still analogous in many respects, they are deemed superior specifically because of their invisibility, the supernatural as such. People give them various names, class them as spirits, demons, gods, or equate them with long-dead ancestors.[22] Religion thus becomes a "culturally patterned interaction with culturally postulated superhuman beings."[23] Communication with these entities interferes with normal relations within society and thus often turns out to be a special form of indirect communication, using the supernatural to strengthen the effect of intended conventional communication. In this sense one might even say the divine is a social tool to manipulate communication.[24] At any rate, it is the practice of interaction, together with its consequences, that makes religion "uniquely realistic."

Implicit in the first two is the third characteristic of religion: its claim for priority and seriousness, for which Paul Tillich used the term "ultimate concern." Religion is thus set apart from other forms of symbolic communication, from play and from art. Although in play as in ritual there is an element that transcends reality, an "as if" structure which creates unseen partners with whom to interact, these playmates can be dismissed at will. In religion there is a postulate of priority and necessity, of certainty that given thoughts and actions are essential and unavoidable. All other plans, projects, predilections, or desires are downgraded, foregone, or at least postponed. Spartans stopped warfare to celebrate their festivals even at crucial moments; Jews decided to die rather than defend themselves on the Sabbath.[25] Even the Roman senate, relentlessly repressing the infamous *Bacchanalia* in Italy, respected the "necessity" some people felt to carry on their ritual according to tradition.[26] Religion is serious; hence it is vulnerable to laughter and derision.[27] But the unseen, in the form of personal partners, calls for submission and veneration, and the ego has to take second rank. As supernatural power spreads to objects, these acquire limits of access or use, whether as taboo or just sacredness. Religion can be deadly serious in the most direct way, sanctioning violence in a terrifying spectrum, ranging from human sacrifice to internecine wars, from witch-burning to an Ayatollah's *fatwa*—and no less shocking acts of self-sacrifice, down to mass suicide.[28] This absolute seriousness, derived from dealing with unseen superiors, is the prerogative of the sacred that characterizes religion.

Religions, both past and present, appear in special cultural, social, and historical settings; they can be elaborated as symbolic systems and interpreted in fascinating ways. Yet this universal and prehistoric phenomenon cannot be explained by or derived from any single cultural system. The search for the source of religion calls for a more general perspective, beyond individual civilizations, which must take account of the vast process of human evolution within the more general evolutionary process of life. This process was once hypostasized as Nature; we may still use it as a metaphor. In this sense the history of religions implies the problem of "natural" religion. Cultural studies must merge with general anthropology, which is ultimately integrated into biology.

Sociobiology?

To introduce biology into cultural studies is to enter a battlefield. For a long time many philosophers, historians, and sociologists, confronted with the success of natural sciences, have been building up defenses against biologism, or biologistic reductionism, as it is called.[29] The other side has been making use of the tremendous progress in molecular biology and genetics. Ethology, the study of animal behavior, was brilliantly developed in mid-century by Konrad Lorenz and has been popularized even in its application to humans. At the same time the study of primates, especially chimpanzees, has expanded greatly and established beyond expectation how close they are to humans. With the refinement of evolution theory, sociobiology was proclaimed as "the new synthesis" by E. O. Wilson. This has not silenced criticism at all; controversies are bound to continue.

Darwin's theory of evolution made a lasting impression on theories of culture in the nineteenth century. Social Darwinism applied the Darwinian principle of survival of the fittest to group selection. Certain social groups would prove to be more successful than others and oust their rivals in the end; morality and religion could be made factors in the process, strengthening or weakening the group's fitness. These theories conceived interaction as a struggle or battle, neglecting the role of cooperation. This school of thought appears unattractive and naive in retrospect.

A new and more specific approach was inaugurated by Konrad Lorenz's book *On Aggression*, first published with the less aggressive title *Das sogenannte Böse* in 1963, a work distinguished by the author's special skill in understanding animals.[30] In establishing homologies in behavior of different species and deciphering the function of their signals, Lorenz insisted on the positive role of so-called evil behavior, or intraspecific aggression, for the preservation of the balance of life. He showed similarities, analogies, and even continuities between animals and humans in the field of anger, fighting, and war, but in particular he described the establishment of bonds of friendship and solidarity through common aggression, symbolized in aggressive display. By extrapolation it would seem possible to explain the success of religious solidarity on the basis of the aggressive acts of hunt and sacrifice.[31]

Lorenz's claim that zoology could throw light on the *condition humaine* immediately provoked critical reactions from sociologists and social anthropologists; the thesis of aggression was met by counteraggression.[32] Critics judged it was dangerous to derive human values from animal nature, to see biological inheritance as determining human practice, and, in particular, to make aggression an inherited and hence immutable trait of the human race. Humanization and the very progress of civilization seemed to be at stake.

The conflict was restarted in a new key through E. O. Wilson's concept of sociobiology proposed in 1975.[33] Its opponents protested again that any thesis about genetic determination of cultural behavior, norms, or values would destroy the hope for progress in humanization.[34] Self-determination, free will, free choice among various possibilities—these seemed the marks of culture. The advocate of what looked like biological automatism was marked as reactionary. Cultural autonomy was the banner raised against biologism.

The basic hypothesis of sociobiology is the "coevolution of genes and culture," with constant feedback between the two. From its Darwinian inheritance sociobiology takes the concept of survival fitness, related to the chances of procreation, and tries to correlate certain institutions or ideas with such fitness. "Cultural success consists in accomplishing those things which make biological success (that is, a high inclusive fitness) probable."[35] Misfits will diminish in number and gradually disappear. Cultural progress and modification of genes go together.

Sociobiology could be called the computerized version of social Darwinism. Whereas Lorenz had still largely relied on observation and empathy, evolution theory now moves along the lines of game theory, models of which can be tested by computer programs. In this context one basic idea of social Darwinism, the principle of group selection, was exploded immediately, by disproving the claim that group solidarity would naturally win in the struggle for survival. It is the genes, not the individuals, that get passed on; hence it is the cheater within a group who enjoys the greatest advantage and by this very fitness will multiply his genes. "The selfish gene" has become a catchword of the new approach.[36] It remains true, however, that certain strategies of behavior within a group will prove to be more successful than others and thus make a difference even in gene selection.

The technical problems of evolution theory and sociobiology cannot be discussed here in any depth. They include the very formulation of the definition of "fitness" in a way that is not circular,[37] and the alternative of continuous evolution amenable to statistics versus sudden and unforeseeable catastrophes or "fulgurations."[38]

The most complicated issue is still how to verify the connection between cultural phenomena and biological preconditions. Even primitive functions of life and simple processes of growth depend upon the interaction of many genes and numerous intermediate stages and agents that make up the phenotype. Behavior is hopelessly complex already at the level of primates. In response to ever changing situations, behavior will always present a mixture of innate responses and learned programs.[39] Even in the realm of animals it is very difficult to isolate one from the other by experiments; at the human level experimentation is not possible.

In addition, in human social life quite different levels and criteria of success come to the fore; these cannot be represented by a single set of numbers in computer games. There is always variety, and seldom extinction. No doubt dominant members of a society have more chances to raise their children successfully; but it appears that again and again special elites rose to power who produced fewer children but, through an elaborate culture, kept control over their inferiors who produced more children. Should this be called a lack of fitness of the ruling class?

Sociobiology has had some success in interpreting rules of marriage and sexual taboos in relation to the probabilities of genetic relationship and hence to the spread of selfish genes. Such studies focus on cultural institutions or patterns directly linked to physical procreation. An alarming study shows that male aggressiveness is deliberately cultivated in a primitive tribal society, so that killers have more chances to beget children than their more peaceful kinsmen.[40] However, it is not possible to run experiments that use neutral test groups to test the validity of these conclusions. And how can we know whether some rule or institution has been in effect long enough, through a sufficient sequence of generations, to produce a marked change in the frequency of the respective genes? How many generations are needed to make a sizable difference?[41]

ေၜၜ

"Religion constitutes the greatest challenge to human sociobiology," E. O. Wilson wrote.[42] No doubt religion has appeared as a new phenomenon in the course of evolution. Chimpanzees, for all their genetic closeness to man, have neither art nor religion.[43] All the same, the practice of religion must be extremely old. It is certain that the basic religious structures had evolved before humans reached America, for despite thousands of years of isolation, the religions of American aborigines remained comparable and similar to their Old World counterparts in many respects. In fact, there are clear traces of religious practice since the Upper Paleolithic that can be brought into line with attested religious phenomena.[44] Still earlier, Neanderthals practiced ceremonial burial of the dead; many think that religious ideas must have accompanied such activities about 100,000 years ago.

In a naive way, an explanation of religion as expression of cultural fitness had already been advanced, on the basis of social Darwinism. Otto Gruppe wrote in 1921: "Individuals who make themselves appear to possess supernatural powers get a great advantage out of this, which is easily seen because they exercise some power on the society in which they live; but they also give some advantage, less easily recognizable but nevertheless quite real, to their own group in the struggle for existence, through their purported powers and by facilitating the growth of a common societal will."[45] Can this be rephrased to mean that religion, once entrenched as a cultural phenomenon, brought definite advantage to certain individuals and thus was likely to multiply their and their adherents' chances of offspring and hence their genes, to the detriment of the nonreligious?

The fitness of religion in the sense of procreation and survival value is not at all agreed upon. Many religions call for renunciation of worldly goods and retreat from competitive struggle, as Buddhism and Christianity notably do. Christianity has extolled martyrs and altruistic self-sacrifice. Drastic examples of self-destroying religious behavior include saints starving themselves to death and sectarian groups committing collective suicide. Still—the very propaganda effect of martyrdom proves that, on balance, even these may be strategies of success. The loss is matched by an increase in acceptance. Propaganda, by its very name, is a form of procreation. "The blood of the martyrs is the seed of the church"[46]—a striking metaphor of biological growth. Self-denial is to result in multiplication; the grain of wheat dies to bring forth a rich harvest.[47] Cases of self-sacrifice occur even lower on the evolutionary scale: some male spiders lose their life at copulation, bees work to exhaustion to feed the queen's offspring. In fact, the individual's sacrifice for the benefit of his or her genetic relatives can be seen as a strategy to multiply the genes shared by the family. This is "inclusive fitness," a concept developed by William Hamilton.[48] In an analogous way, even religions that proclaim self-sacrifice may be basically adaptive.[49] Because on the whole the history of religions has been a story of success, a good strategy for survival in the long run must have been at work. In other words, a certain survival fitness of religion has to be granted.

In contrast to the foregoing, another school of thought imputes to religion the very opposite of survival fitness; we may call it the opium thesis.[50] Religious ideas and practices are accused of fulfilling human wishes in a fantastic, unrealistic, and possibly detrimental way, just as drugs do when they provide the illusion of happiness while misusing and overriding the normal cerebral functions.[51] Not that this would make religion exempt from biology: even the spread of malfunctions is a biological fact. But is illusion dysfunctional? The discovery of endorphins, natural pain relievers in the brain, rather points to the positive biological function of illusive happiness to overcome dramatic crises of stress and pain. A case could be made even for the sociobiological advantage of religious illusions.

Ancient religions normally gravitate to the dominating classes and the representatives of power. After the triumph of Christianity, for many centuries of European history that has also been the situation of the Christian churches. Islam expressly claims to direct law, social order, and political authority. Successful religions tend to use power and even violence to suppress dissident groups or rival religions, both within and beyond their territory. Christianity as well as Islam have become world religions by ousting the more ancient forms of religious polytheism, and they remain adamant in fighting atheism. The same militancy occurs on the individual level: within strictly religious societies a non-religious child, rebellious in feeling and behavior, will hardly have a chance of survival.[52] Yet if the dominant majorities are stabilized by religion, there are also minorities that persist through their religion, some of them retaining special influence just by remaining a religious minority. Some disadvantaged minorities survive in a kind of niche existence for millennia, held together by their religion. The dominant religions of course present advantages to their adherents and disadvantages to their opponents, so they are bound to have momentous effects on selection. Nonetheless, minority groups still survived centuries of Christian and Islamic rule.

It is notable that many religions urgently advocate procreation within the group. Isolation and procreation became the Jewish strategies for surviving the historical catastrophe of the Babylonian exile; in reinforcement, Mosaic law forbade the use of established forms of birth control such as homosexuality, prostitution, abortion, and exposure of children. In effect, a Jewish population explosion occurred in Hellenistic times. A similar sexual morality caused Christian groups to grow beyond proportion within the Roman empire. Until the present day Catholicism and Islam both passionately oppose birth control. Is it a biological instinct, the thrust of selfish genes, that works behind the laws of Moses or Allah?

It is true that different attitudes of competing religions toward birth control can dramatically change majority-minority relations—witness the case of Lebanon, where Moslems came to outnumber Christians; but even the catastrophe of Lebanon did not lead to annihilation.[53] And even if the premise of social Darwinism should materialize in extreme cases, and some religious groups do get exterminated, historical catastrophes, short-lived and exceptional as they are, will not have much effect on the genetic pool within a heterogeneous world society.

Another hypothesis traces religion's success to ecology. One example is Roy Rappaport's study of pig festivals in New Guinea, in which he explained the festal cycle in such terms. The pig population is left to multiply and would grow out of hand, but they are sacrificed and consumed when they are about to become too numerous. Thus the ritual slaughter functions as a homoeostat to prevent overexploitation of the environment.[54] In this way the stability of the social system within the environmental balance is maintained through regulation motivated by religious restraint. Should we assume that, in the long run, only the religious individuals, sensitive to the control imposed by otherworldly regulatory systems, managed to survive in stable human societies? Alas, ecological caution is anything but universal in religions. In the island of Malta, the proliferation of gigantic temples admired by modern tourists seems to have gone together with an ecological collapse and the final decay of the Early Bronze Age civilization.[55]

It is tempting to assume that the very advantage secured by religion is stability and thus continuity of culture. As the "software" of civilization became too precious and too complicated to leave its preservation to individual choice or chance, new institutions had to arise to guarantee social cohesion across long spans of time. Incipient forms of culture observed in other primates, such as washing grain in water or transporting stones to crush nuts, can be lost again without endangering the species. For *homo sapiens,* the technique to preserve fire did need continuous care. But this may be just an instance of the necessity of culture: it cannot be lost without catastrophe; it cannot be put at stake by experiments. The permanent authority of ancestors or immortal gods provides the needed stability.

Yet as provider of continuity, religion remains paradoxical

from the sociobiological perspective. Survival fitness, in the long run, means adaptability to changing conditions; in the cultural systems the key to success is the ability to learn fast and to keep learning in a changing world. Religion, however, strives to teach the unchanging "eternal truths," and to make sure that beliefs and attitudes remain unchanged. What kind of fitness is it that renders people unfit for change, and how can we say that it has been successful?

A final surmise is that the success of religion may be attributed to its providing a heightened endurance in the face of catastrophe, encouraging procreation even in desperate circumstances. This comes close to the "endorphin" hypothesis. We humans are capable of experiencing states described as "loss of reality"—chimpanzees are apparently immune to this—in such diverse manifestations as extreme patriotism, the fascination of games and sports, the scientist's or artist's proverbial distraction or rather concentration, and, not least, the fervor of religious behavior. In such cases the mental system overrides reality, and the invisible gets the better of the obvious. Although religious obsession could be called a form of paranoia, it does offer a chance of survival in extreme and hopeless situations, when others, possibly the nonreligious individuals, would break down and give up. Mankind, in its long past, will have gone through many a desperate situation, with an ensuing breakthrough of *homines religiosi*.

These positive or self-stabilizing functions of religion seem more or less plausible and are not mutually exclusive; it is difficult, however, to find concrete evidence for them, especially since the ubiquity of religion means that neutral test groups are not available. But even if accepted, these functions do not in fact prove any correlation between religion and gene selection. Religions are established by learning, they are propagated both through imitation and through explicit verbal teaching. Traditions developed in this way can evidence a kind of cultural fitness for survival without any genetic basis. The Roman Catholic Church has been working successfully for about sixty generations, led by an elite that explicitly renounces physical procreation. Jews have been living in relative isolation with special marital rules for about 100 generations, yet there are no Jewish genes. The success of particular forms of religion appears to be due to organization, propaganda, power, or fashion, with many different motives determining individual choices or attitudes, rather than to physical procreation.

One religious institution does focus on sexuality; it is circumcision. While this ritual has been strictly practiced for thousands of years, it has no more bearing on procreation than eating or not eating pigs; neither practice will provide a genetic basis for the eventual success of either Judaism, Christianity, or Islam.[56] Circumcision functions as *character indelebilis* of a certain community[57] and possibly as a traumatic, unforgettable individual experience;[58] that is to say, it functions at the social and psychological, not the genetic level.

In contrast to the practice of circumcision, human sexuality as such has a clear biological function and pedigree. During adolescence humans everywhere and at all times will spontaneously discover sexuality along with new feelings and behavior, while cultural and educational efforts to repress them normally fail. Postmoderns have pointed out that sexuality too takes different forms in different civilizations and hence should be considered a cultural construct or even an "invention."[59] But such variations and deviances are slight in the face of overwhelming uniformity. The biological program develops on its own according to predetermined patterns, which reach back far beyond the emergence of humans and have long been inscribed in the genetic code. It has never been shown that religiosity rises spontaneously in such a way; religion depends on the formative impact of cultural learning. The prospect for discovering religious genes is dim.

ᴆᴈ

What remains is an intercultural family resemblance of religious phenomena throughout the world and over the ages. Likewise, the emotional aura encircling religion cannot be easily dismissed.

Biologists hold that each of our spontaneous feelings can be qualified as the reflection of some biological function.[60] "Memoirs most easily recalled, emotions they are most likely to evoke" are invoked by Lumsden and Wilson to testify for biological foundations.[61] Konrad Lorenz has drawn attention to the shudders of anxiety or even of elation that we still experience, shivers running down our backs and arms in appropriate situations, which are nervous reactions intended to raise the mane at the back and head, as they still do among gorillas and chimpanzees. For us, "hair-raising" survives mainly as a metaphor, but once it was part of the aggressive behavioral program.[62] Today, when we speak of the sacred shivers of awe that characterize religion in particular, we may be forgetting that origin.[63] Yet anxiety linked to aggression through biological inheritance manifests itself in our emotions, including patriotic and religious enthusiasm.

In this context, it may help to take into consideration more closely the most important universal of humans: language. Language is learned in childhood in every society, together with the various special phonologies and semantics that make crosscultural understanding so difficult. Language is linked to an uninterrupted chain of historical tradition;[64] it has never—in tens of thousands of years—been reinvented.[65] Language is exclusively human, even if chimpanzees can be taught its rudiments to a surprising degree.[66] But it is no less true that language has a biological foundation, most evident in the development of a vocal apparatus which is missing in chimpanzees and whose presence in Neanderthal man is doubtful. A genetic alteration was critical to its development. Language also has a clear sociobiological function. In fact it has become one of the most important conditions for survival in our social systems: an individual incapable of speech usually drops out. Thus gene selection has been associated with social functions within the evolution of culture. If language is a phenomenon of culture, culture has determined and continues to control the genes in this case, while language still remains to be taught afresh to every generation. Human language thus may be called a hybrid of culture and biology.

It is still unclear to what extent we can be precise about this chapter of evolution. There was a cultural revolution about 40,000 years ago, which manifested itself through new forms of signifying systems and representational thinking. The revolution was the birth of art amidst simpler forms of marking and making distinctions.[67] Art is unknown to other primates; it is found in a less developed form among the remains of Neanderthal man. Art means "to make special" certain objects of perception, producing a characteristic tension between the familiar and the admirable and thus creating new aspects of a potentially common world.[68] The striking fact is that within a few millennia of the creation of art, Neanderthal man became extinct. One may presume that this happened on account of some lack of cultural fitness. Yet there was no genetically new type of man to inaugurate the new stage; it now appears that Neanderthal man coexisted with modern man for about 50,000 years.[69] Thus far, "biology cannot explain the cultural revolution that then ensued."[70] But perhaps sociobiology can. It is tempting to assume that the cultural progress of the rivaling species brought the disadvantaged to extinction. Did human language take form just then? Was Neanderthal man unable to speak in an articulate way?[71] At any rate, the survivor was *homo sapiens sapiens,* who has been *homo loquens* and *homo artifex* ever since, but also *homo religiosus.*

Parallel to language, religion too, as an effective means of most serious communication, can be hypothesized to have arisen at a certain stage in prehistory as a competitive act, a way of gaining an advantage over those who did not take part in it. Religion may well be older than the kind of language we know, insofar as it is bound to ritual, which entails fixed behavioral patterns marked by exaggeration and repetition and often characterized by obsessive seriousness—patterns which are prominent even in most modern varieties of religious communication.[72] In principle, ritual reflects a preverbal state of communication, to be learned by imitation and to be understood by its function. It seems to be more primitive and may be more ancient than speech; it clearly has analogies in the behavior of animals. Although rituals do not

19

necessarily leave archaeological traces, yet funeral practice is well attested for Neanderthal man, while his ability to speak is in doubt.[73] We are free to imagine that a richer palette of rituals existed among hominids at an early stage, such as dances in the context of hunting, warfare, or mating display, but also veneration, even worship, of the unseen.[74] This could be called a complex of prereligion, perpetuated to a large extent in the rituals of religions we know. But it must remain a guess.

The possibility of a sociobiological derivation of religion thus remains shrouded in prehistory. The idea is attractive. There is a vast expanse of time available for the evolutionary process, with tens of thousands, or even hundreds of thousands of generations to fill the hiatus between chimpanzee and *homo sapiens,* whereas in other cases studied by sociobiology the problem of the time span involved seemed insurmountable. Religion, stemming from time immemorial and often characterized by the principle of unchangeable continuity, might well provide a model case for the "coevolution of genes and culture." Yet there is no way of testing this hypothesis, be it through 30,000 or 300,000 or 3,000,000 years, through 1,000, 10,000, 100,000 generations; by scientific standards, the hypothesis loses its point. We can only vaguely reconstruct the decisive cultural conditions. While uncertainties multiply with time, the evidence evaporates. Sociobiology, insisting as it does on precise parameters in mathematical models, cannot find appropriate applications in these realms. Probabilities, selective observations, and hunches will have to take its place.

We may still view religion, parallel to language and to art and mostly in close symbiosis with the two, as a long-lived hybrid between the cultural and the biological traditions. Another hybrid among anthropological *universalia* might illustrate the complexity of the issue: the case of the incest taboo, a social rule that immediately concerns procreation and often assumes religious dimensions. That the incest taboo is practically universal among human societies has long been recognized, not without amazement. It has been taken to be the very mark of culture.[75] It was another surprise when proofs accumulated that forms of incest avoidance are not confined to the human species but are common among most higher animals.[76] The biological advantage is clear in this case, since inbreeding has specific risks and dangers. But how did the biological recommendation enter human consciousness, to be transformed into spontaneous feelings as well as explicit verbalized rules of cultural institutions? This puzzling question has not been solved. Is it that random rules, adopted by chance, took root through their genetic success? But the effect only manifests itself through a long sequence of generations; it is hardly perceptible in individual experience. Norbert Bischof has devoted a painstaking study to this problem.[77] He ends up with a metaphor: social rules, if general and persistent, must somehow "fit the landscape."

It is the landscape, formed by age-old geological events, that makes water concentrate into rivers and flow in a preestablished course and sets limits even to the chaotic turbulences of weather.[78] How the architect perceives the landscape, or the landscape influences the architect, is still a mystery. Natural religion, that is, basic and common forms of addressing the supernatural, did not develop in a void but through adaptation to a specific "landscape," conditioned by the age-old evolution of human life. If there are certain predilections and attractions as well as fear and revulsion, feelings of needs shaped by biology, this complex may account for the stability of belief and concomitant behavior.

To use another metaphor: verbalized culture, transmitted by teaching and learning, may be called the "software" of humanity, easy to copy and to pass on regardless of its complexity. Still, the question is whether this software can be chosen and modified arbitrarily, or whether it remains bound to certain preconditions of the original programming, to patterns and effects left by the "hardware" that generated it.

The biological organization of the brain and other cybernetic systems of living beings existed long before verbalized culture; that it continues to influence our behavior and communication cannot be denied. Aboriginal programs of action, sequences, sentiments, expectations, notions, and values are inherited from the most distant past. Some of the most obvious are the search for food, fear, flight and aggression, and of course sex. Even meanings have their prehistory. It is notoriously difficult to construe semantics from pure logic, but quite easy to recognize certain reactions that have adaptive or communicative functions: a leopard, a snake, "fight or flight"—these are meanings which antedate language by far. The chicken knows the flying hawk before it has any experience of it; the cock knows the weasel;[79] certain monkeys have distinct signs for leopard, eagle, and snake.[80] The process of *semeiosis,* the use of signs and symbols, operates within the whole sphere of living organisms and was evidently invented long before the advent of man.[81]

This does not mean that genes prescribe culture—clearly, they do not. But it could be said that they give recommendations that become manifest in the repetition of like patterns, "the kinds of memories most easily recalled, the emotions they are most likely to evoke." The biological makeup forms preconditions or "attractors" to produce phenomena in a consistent fashion, even if these patterns are created and recreated afresh in each case. Scientific proof of such connections by means of statistics or experiment will remain impossible; what can be shown is the near-universality and persistence of patterns through place and time, and the existence of certain analogies or even homologies in structure and function in animal behavior.[82] This suggests that details and sequences in rituals, tales, works of art, and fantasies hark back to more original processes in the evolution of life; they become understandable not in isolation nor within their different cultural contexts, but in relation to this background.

The sociobiological question of the survival value or multiplication value of language, art, and religion remains open. It is probably important to realize that we are not dealing with a one-dimensional process, so that the answer cannot be just one formula. There is probably a cluster of factors in evolution and a cluster of functions served by new avenues of communication; functions may also be lost or altered. Nonetheless certain persistent and permanent patterns emerge and even seem to control interactions, since all these events occur within a unique landscape to which they are adapted. What we discern are the tracks of biology followed by cultural choice.

☟☜

To sum up: the thesis of sociobiology in the strong sense of "coevolution of genes and culture" cannot be verified in the case of religion, as such evolution antedates observable periods and remains too complex to establish unequivocal relations between the two. The absence of evidence is still not a license to separate culture from biology or religion from substructures formed within the evolution of life. Religion's hybrid character—between biology and culture—calls for an interdisciplinary meeting of methods: derivation should go together with interpretation. In this sense, an analysis of religious worlds in view of the underlying landscape may be attempted.

A Common World: Reduction and Validation

In human history language has been the decisive phenomenon, analogous to religion and related to it. Ever since the Greeks, language, *logos,* has been judged the crucial difference between us and other species: man is the "animal endowed with language," *zoon logikon.*[83] The course of evolution has been one of growing success in obtaining and processing information, in continuous feedback between the environment and living organisms.[84] The nervous system gave rise to the possibilities of learning, that is, of storing information and modifying programs in the course of the individual's life. "Software" of this kind, however, remains inseparable from the "hardware" and is destroyed with it. The effects of learning cannot persist; only the genes preserve information. The cycle of birth and death can be breached to some extent through sharing and passing on information. Incipient cultural tradition of this kind remained rudimentary, even if the distance from amoeba to ape was immense, until the momentous advent of language. Through language information can not only be acquired, processed, and stored individually, but fully transferred to others, to be processed and recalled in parallel efforts. Corresponding to the neural functions of sensation and of motion are two main forms of verbal interaction: to state the facts and to command action, which means sharing the sources of information on the one hand, and partaking in the results of information processing on the other. Through copying and exchange, programs and information have become largely independent from the hardware and from the accidents of individual death. Information survival asserts itself side by side with and even instead of genetic survival.

Language development means nothing less than the advent of a common mental world, allowing not only for common actions and common feelings but for common thoughts and plans, concepts and values. All humans henceforth are linked to an uninterrupted chain of tradition, taking over the mental worlds of their elders, working on them and passing them on.

Religion, defined at the level of communication, belongs to this mental world, and by virtue of its seriousness it claims preeminence. The problem of religion, in consequence, may be restated in the form of a question. How and why, within this common mental world shaped by language tradition, have certain realms been established for which no evidence exists, and for which we claim dominion over communication and action by virtue of seriousness? Is this a by-product, a degeneration, an "opium effect," or on the contrary some kind of *a priori* condition for a common world? If we adopt the Durkheimian concept of "collective representations," we might ask, why do people accept them, and why certain ones among them?

The suspicion has been voiced repeatedly that religion is mainly trickery and make-believe produced by those who profit from it. Forms of deceit abound already at prehuman stages.[85] All the greater is the possibility of verbal deception. Information can be withheld or distorted. The unseen in particular can be the object of manipulation. Among several species of monkeys, for example, an individual disturbed by an intruder may avoid confrontation by staring into a corner and voicing sounds of alarm, as if reporting "there is a monster in the corner."[86] But this would be a grossly insufficient foundation for the origin of religion. Even among monkeys the trick cannot be repeated very often without being recognized and losing all of its force.

The point is that the common world of language characteristically produces contents beyond any immediate evidence. Communication works via signs, and what they refer to must be guesswork at first, to be confirmed by repetition, by context, previous knowledge, or additional information and experience. Some signs will remain opaque and yet are stored in expectation of later clarification. As learning takes precedence over experience, a personal encounter with what has been learned and known in advance may or may not follow in the span of a lifetime. Language refers to objects far away as well as to the past and to the future, segments of reality inaccessible to verification.[87] Fiction, dreaming, and the workings of imagination evidently have some function for the individual, preparing or rehearsing human activities or helping with solving problems while avoiding direct confrontations. Thoughts or plans can be expressed or manipulated collectively through speech. Worlds beyond experience, or at least some misty provinces or blind spots, thus grow out of the process of linguistic communication. They may be reshaped by misunderstanding. This even happens within religious tradition, producing strange and fascinating items. Elysium, a name for a blissful spot in the beyond, seems to have emerged in such a way.[88] An accumulation of preformed, verbalized traditions will always transcend individual experience. Nobody has seen the phoenix, but all know about him.[89]

Such a process of accumulated verbal tradition can be anticipated by ritual, which refers through formulaic acts to nonpresent partners,[90] and is strongly reinforced by art. Ever since the Upper Paleolithic people have drawn pictures of well-known objects, bisons, horses, or mammoths, as well as of baffling, enigmatic icons that demand special interpretation. We are at a loss about how to understand the painting called "the sorcerer" of the Trois Frères cave, or those corpulent female idols which have been called Venus statuettes.[91] Do they reproduce reality, or do they refer to the supernatural, to some Great Goddess?[92] Most people today have seen pictures of angels, dragons, or the phoenix; it is by way of illustrations that we form our ideas about these creatures.

If a body of supernatural entities, communicable through language and pictures, comes to occupy a certain space in our common mental world, it is subject to the controlling functions of reduction and simplification. In the face of the constantly growing accumulation of data infiltrating personal experience, the common world must be simplified. Sheer addition of individual knowledge would soon surpass the capacity of any available system for recording it, even within a small group and within a few generations. Tradition consists of condensed, systematized information. Language continually operates in this way through two of its main functions, generalization and metaphor; these are strategies to keep the sign system finite. Logical functions too work to that end, through negation, class-inclusion, the constitution of patterns and analogies.

In *The Function of Religion* Niklas Luhmann stated that the main process of creating sense in the interactions of a system with its environment was "reduction of complexity," and he takes this to be the achievement of religion in particular.[93] By a process of reduction, religion provides orientation within a meaningful cosmos for those who feel helpless vis-à-vis infinite complexity. Certain religious systems go further than others in this function. One way to effect a radical reduction of complexity is to devise a dualistic system, positing two containers in which to place any new phenomenon or experience. Hierarchies and links of causality also effectively reduce complexity. And there is an avowed tendency in speculative religion to reduce reality to the most simple and general concepts: the One Cause, the Sole Being, the One.[94]

It is easy to make further suggestions about what makes religion "good to think" in a mental world.[95] Language itself, as a signifying system, seems to be in need of an "ultimate signifier," the absolute, god.[96] This may also serve the function of the algebraic x to solve the conflicting equations of life. Oppressive domination, for example, is easier to bear if the oppressor is dominated in turn by a god.[97] Likewise, an insecure and unjust distribution of goods is brought into balance by a transcendent gift system.[98] Affliction is made bearable by an ultimate if nonempirical answer to the grieving one's question, "why." To introduce the unseen is to interrupt the closed functional chain of events—which also means that religion is never fully integrated into any system of society but retains some character of "otherness."

Basic categories of being, of causality, and of goodness are reflected in the traditional predicates of gods or god as immortal or timeless, creator of the world, and the ultimate end of human destination. Even these *a priori* categories have been linked to biological evolution by the evolutionary theory of knowledge. They have been developed in the measure that they proved successful in managing an increasingly comprehensive objective world.[99] In realms beyond experience, these categories develop with uncommon ease, assisted by the mental device of self-reference to create an infinite series. The unattainable extreme, perfection, is found in the supernatural. In language, this will be expressed by the superlative: god is the first, the highest, the strongest, the absolute.

ဝင်္

In all such reflections about the conditions and functions of religious concepts within a mental world, validation remains the crucial problem. As Richard Gordon put it, how is it possible "to validate the existence of a purely imaginary world?"[100] The monkey trick of the monster in the corner cannot be repeated. There is disbelief as well as belief, distrust as well as trust, there is forgetfulness to match the acquisition of new information; there is manipulation and countermanipulation, concealment and deceit. Each person will end up with a very personal selection that forms her or his mental world. Is it possible to isolate the common and authoritative elements? Or are the possibilities of fantasy infinite? Yet gods are not just another chimaera.[101] How to substantiate the claims, postulates, and threats of religion?

Three main approaches are used to account for the uniquely realistic appearance of religious worlds. The reasons for acceptance, persistence, and preponderance of religion may be found either within the message transmitted, or in the circumstances of transmission, or in the special organization of the recipient. All these possibilities have been explored and discussed; they may well be combined.

The modern and sophisticated approach has been to look for reasons of stability within the message; this is the structuralist model.[102] It postulates that certain correspondences, equations, and reciprocities stabilize themselves in various and repeated forms of communication and thus give a powerful meaning to traditions which operate within a religious group. One might metaphorically speak of "resonances" accompanying the message—the way a radio or a similar electronic device sometimes creates its own piercing sounds. Reinforcement through resonance would especially apply to ritual, the concomitant means of religious communication. Should we look at religion as a form of resonance, of mental self-replications within a cultural system—replications which, functional or dysfunctional, arise and preserve themselves through their own structure to form part of culture?[103] This would mean abandoning attempts at making sense.

Within the process of religious transmission, a strictly biological hypothesis would assume that some form of "imprinting" happens. Biological imprinting is restricted to certain conditions, to special functions, times, and situations; in other words, it is totally dependent upon the "landscape" of a well-programmed species; it has unchangeable consequences. A newborn duckling, after leaving its egg, takes for its parent whatever creature makes the first contact; later experience cannot change this.

In humans too the brain is quite pliable in the earlier phases, and certain phenomena come at least close to imprinting. Childhood experiences play a decisive role for the development of the personality, including sexual maturity, political attitudes,[104] and religious propensities. Strong formative forces radiate from the mother and the father alike; "phenotypical cloning" is a catchword that has been coined in this context. No dependable automatism has been detected, however, comparable to that of the duckling. On the contrary, striking and drastic failures of pedagogic attempts to fix religious attitudes in children abound.

Finally, in examining receptivity to religious messages, it would be easy, probably too easy, to postulate that archetypal images of religious entities, of god or gods, are present in the human makeup and can be activated by appropriate stimuli with indelible results. This would be equivalent to "innate release mechanisms" as discussed in biology,[105] another form of predetermined programming, like that of imprinting. It means that fixed action patterns are activated through specific combinations of stimuli, without regard for individual accidents. This too resists verification.

The observable forms of religious transmission are learning processes effected through ritual and language. The most salient features in this process are repetition plus more or less harsh forms of intimidation. Repetition is a major factor in learning, and it is critical in ritual. There is no transmission of religion without ritual. A primary function of ritual is to initiate the young into the customs of their elders—the very epitome of cultural learning, which relies upon memory.[106] In the same spirit, it is for the sake of the whole community that "collective representations" are inculcated by ceremonies repeated at regular intervals.[107] Celebrations of festivals have become central manifestations of religion. People perform prescribed acts, learning that these have always been done in that way; in this context, they are also told their collective lore, their myths.[108] Two sign systems, ritual and language, come together to reinforce each other, to form the mental structures that determine the categories and the rules of life. The most effective elements are dance and song, in which repetitive rhythms and sounds combine to create the great collective experience.

A major force in this process is paternal authority. All higher animals are programmed to learn from their elders. In human society the role of the father has been especially magnified. An intense father-son relationship is the vehicle of many cultural traditions. Religions used to stress the importance of parents while presenting god or gods as superfather or mother, and parents did not fail to use that opportunity to enhance their own prestige.[109] When children saw how their parents deal with gods "in supreme seriousness on behalf of themselves and their offspring," wrote Plato, how could they venture to despise religion?[110] In such a two-way process, authority is stabilized through religion and religion through authority.

Some special forms of learning are made indelible "at a stroke," without repetition, usually in situations of utmost excitement. Every individual will have unforgettable memories of this kind, especially of a painful or humiliating character. Forms of "anxiety learning" have been studied in animals. Observers found special neuronal processing and memory for anxiety-arousing events;[111] the resulting behavior seems close to superstition.[112] Teaching by threat and maltreatment is customary in many civilizations without qualms. Exotic initiation ceremonies come to mind;[113] some European communities used to teach youngsters the place of boundary stones by boxing and flogging them at the spot.[114] One drastic way to create an unforgettable and unbreakable bond is to commit a common crime, using aggression to overcome anxiety.[115] A special thing to do in manipulating anxiety is to handle blood, which is required in many forms of sacrifice and purification. Terror does not develop rational abilities, but it leaves its marks. Thus we approach the "seriousness" of religion from the experience of fear.

There is no denying that anxiety is often evoked to validate religious messages, and that it has its repercussions upon the substance of religion. To transmit religion is to transmit fear.

"Fear, first of all, produced gods in the world," *primus in orbe deos fecit timor,* Statius wrote. While this is a criticism from his standpoint, which is that of ancient philosophical enlightenment,[116] it shares the self-interpretation of many religions. The main word to characterize gods and religion in Akkadian is *puluhtu,* fear. An Assyrian king, in all his arrogance, will proclaim himself the one "who strongly knows the fear of the gods and goddesses of heaven and earth."[117] For "the fear of gods creates kindness,"[118] or, as Solomon put it in one of his most quoted sayings, using the Hebrew variant of the same Semitic word: "The fear of god is the beginning of wisdom."[119] The equivalent Greek expression, *theoudes,* god-fearing, occurs as a mark of moral distinction in Homer. "The divine is fear for prudent mortals."[120] Another Greek word commonly associated with religious rites is *phrike,* hair-raising shudder. Moderns came back to the suggestion that awe was the basic religious feeling;[121] Rudolf Otto substituted a neo-Latin term, *mysterium tremendum,* shivering mystery.[122] Shudders of awe are central for the experience of the sacred. The very means of indelible transmission, threat and terror, are correlated with the contents of the religious part of the mental world: the prerogative of the sacred requires the fear of god.

Yet anxiety, fear, and terror are not just free-floating emotions brought on by psychological fantasy. They have clear biological functions in protecting life. Seriousness means giving priority to certain vitally important programs.[123] The utmost seriousness of religion is linked to the great overriding fear of death. The value of religion, manifest in the forms of religion's cultural transmission and in the insiders' confessions, is that it deals with the "ultimate concern" and thus fits the biological landscape. The drama of religion's interaction with the unseen by manipulating and displacing anxiety takes place with death as the backdrop. Man knows about death, and that death cannot be abolished, but this knowledge develops in a peculiar way. Personal death is a reality beyond imagination, an x, an unknown, inaccessible to experience; the experience of other people's deaths, however, prompts imaginative dealings with the unknown within the common mental world, with displacement, disclaimers, shifting substitutes, and continuing indelible shock, assuaged or rekindled in turn.

Anxiety was bound to multiply at the human level, the level of a conscious representation of the world both near and far, of past and future. We may wonder how herds of African zebras and gnus are able to graze in the presence of lions. The lions will attack at some point, but only at the moment of immediate danger does an animal take flight; the others save their energy and go on grazing, and before long so will the animal that escaped the predator this time—what else can they do? But humans, as they consciously seek to control their environment, storing recollections and anticipating the future, cannot forget the presence of lingering lions. They can try to attack and to kill the predators in turn; they may succeed in creating a peaceable environment: this is one reason why many primitive cultures enjoy the symbols of killing.[124] Yet man will fail in his attempts to remove all anxiety-arousing dangers from the world, especially as his violence meets with the violence of other men.[125] Death remains the constant.

To shield mental life from despair and depression, which are factually lethal, there must be counterforces, optimism, faith, or "opium." This may be the final necessity for sharing fictitious worlds which employ seriousness, nay terror, to counter worldly fears by fear in a hierarchy that reaches toward the absolute. "The highest fear is the fear of god," Aeschylus stated,[126] and he was not alone in offering this message. "The fear of god drives out the fear of men."[127] As religious reality claims precedence over mundane reality, frightful dealings with death and killing gain overwhelming importance in the form of funerary and sacrificial rituals.[128]

This apparently negative preoccupation of religion is just a foil for what is really at stake. A resounding voice in the self-interpretation of most religions, diverse as they may be in other respects, is the longing for life.[129] "Give us life, life, life" is the refrain of an African harvest ritual.[130] *Ahura,* key word of the Zoroastrian religion, means Lord of life. Egyptian gods carry the sign of *ankh,* life, in their hands. Greeks were keen to find the meaning of life, *zēn,* in the name of their ruling god *Zeus.* The Living God is a basic concept in the Old and even more in the New Testament.[131] "I am alive, and you will live," is Jesus' final message to his apostles.[132] Gods grant life, gods protect life, just as their wrath can destroy life. The impetus of biological survival appears internalized in the codes of religion. Following this impetus, there is the postulate of immortality or eternal life, the most powerful idea of many religions.[133] Even self-sacrifice is for the sake of eternal life. The negation of death presupposes the fact of death. The idea of the supernatural emerges within the landscape of nature. Religion's seriousness, so manifest in our feelings, reflects the hard rocks of the biological landscape, the dangers, limits, and the drive for the preservation of life. Religion keeps to the tracks of biology. Some extremists may happen to get off the tracks, but they will disappear unless they somehow make their way back.

Life's achievement is self-replication, self-regulation, and homeostasis. Hence the gods are the most persistent guarantors of order, the forceful regulators. Life needs seclusion for its own protection, building up cells to separate what is inside from the outside; the religious worldview usually adopts some privileged center to keep in touch with the divine despite chaotic or diabolical surroundings. If reality appears dangerous or downright hostile to life, religion calls for something beyond experience to restore the balance. Catastrophes do happen; but in the widespread myths of the flood the endings always tell of the survivors preparing to offer sacrifice.[134] Religion is basically optimistic.

2

❧

Escape and Offerings

Finger Sacrifice

A few years ago a colleague of mine was traveling in Africa by boat and ran into a storm that seemed to grow dangerous. Suddenly a fellow passenger, a politician of some rank in that country, began throwing dollar bills into the raging waters.[1] While we may share my colleague's astonishment, the very metaphor of "raging waters" shows how easily we let ourselves slip into personifying the natural forces.

Similar astonishment, and plain ridicule of such behavior can be found in some ancient sources, at least among the philosophers. Seneca, in his *Naturales Quaestiones,* writes:

> I do not hold myself back from revealing all the absurdities of our people. They say certain persons are experienced in observing clouds and capable of foretelling when there will be hail. . . . It's really impossible. At Kleonai there were official "hail-watchers" *(chalazophylakes),* watching for hail to come. If they said that hail was coming, what do you think the people did? Each person would sacrifice individually: one a lamb, the other a chicken; at once those clouds moved away to some other place, when they had savored some blood. You laugh? Listen to what will make you laugh even more. If a man had neither lamb nor chicken, he sacrificed what he could afford: he laid hands on himself—but don't think clouds are gluttonous

or cruel. He punched his finger with a very sharply pointed pen, and with this blood he performed his auspicious sacrifice; and the hail turned away from his piece of land as well as from places where they had been implored with greater sacrifices.[2]

Seneca adds that the hail-guardians were sued and punished if they failed to avert disaster from vineyards and cornfields.

The rationalist laughs at this response to panic because it shows no obvious link between means and ends, especially in the face of natural forces. The reaction of panic is to give up valuables, to kill one's own animals, to inflict wounds on oneself. Seneca does not hesitate to speak of sacred actions, sacrifice *(sacrificare)*. At Kleonai this was a well-established, institutionalized religious ritual. Some traditional context and background may be present even in the African example.

Toward the middle of the second century A.D., at the delightful site of the Asclepius sanctuary at Pergamon, a rich hypochondriac spent more than ten years of his life. His name was Aelius Aristeides.[3] He had been trained in oratory and became a very successful orator in his later life; his works have survived. Aelius Aristeides apparently had suffered some sort of psychosomatic breakdown when he was about to start his career. He left his work and retired to Pergamon to take endless cures with Asclepius, the god of healing. He firmly believed that the god himself would tell him, in dreams, how to proceed in order to save his life and to regain his health. Anxiously watching for revelations, he kept a diary about his experiences, wavering between petty indigestions, deep depression, and megalomania—"you are the best professor in the world," his dream once told him. When he felt better, he elaborated speeches in honor of Asclepius; these speeches are preserved.

One incident he recalls is of special interest. The god visited him in a dream and informed him he was to die within three days. This was determined, the god said, and signs and events of the following day indicated that the god did not speak in vain. Yet Asclepius was benign, so he showed Aristeides how it was possible to avoid necessity through ritual—a sacrificial ritual in which religion is seen to function as a defense against life-threatening catastrophe. This was the ritual prescribed: Aristeides would have to cross the river and to offer sacrifice on the other side in pits *(bothroi)* to unnamed gods; coming back, while crossing that river, he would have to throw small coins all around, not caring where they fell or who picked them up; finally, back in the sanctuary, he had to perform a full sacrifice at the Asclepius temple, which means slaughtering a sheep and inviting priests and friends for the feast; but in addition, he would have "to cut a piece of his body for the sake of saving the whole." A painful choice, no doubt. Upon second thought, however, the god proved to be even more benign. This procedure was too "laborious," he said, and he allowed Aristeides to dedicate the finger ring he was wearing instead. The sick man then presented his ring to Telesphoros, venerated at this sanctuary of Asklepios, in the guise of a child in a hood.[4]

Aristeides' account, preserved as a rhetorical text from the high point of Graeco-Roman culture, is at the same time a private and quite a primitive document of religious practice. It shows in an exemplary way how the performance of ritual grows out of anxiety and is designed to control it. We may assume that the personnel of the Asclepius sanctuary, priests and seers, were helpful in interpreting Aristeides' dreams and ensuring that the sacrifices kept to the track of proper ritual; private ideas are immediately engulfed by the streams of tradition.

The sequence of such rituals is easy to follow. First, the participant deals with the powers of death and the netherworld; then he crosses the boundary while throwing away money—remember the African example—and finally, he achieves integration with a group of celebrants at the god's sanctuary. The dedication of a valuable object, a practice common in all the sanctuaries in the ancient as well as in the modern world, can be interpreted as a substitute for one's own self, *pars pro toto*. Some part would have to be sacrificed to save the whole. We probably should not generalize and assume that the same idea was behind every finger ring and votive object commonly found in sanctuaries, but we must be sensitive to the supposition that some story of anxiety and hope is expressed by each of these objects dedicated to a god.[5] Aristeides expressly makes his dedication a substitute, a kind of ransom from the threat of death. The coins strewn around at the river evidently serve a similar function: a ransom in cash, a manageable loss in order to gain salvation.

The part of the body for which the god accepted the ring as substitute clearly would have been the finger itself. This puts Aristeides' private dream and pious action into a vast context of myth and ritual. Dreams too are culturally conditioned—though Asclepius' priests may actually have made direct suggestions. Finger sacrifice is recorded not only at Kleonai; it is a known practice in many parts of the world.

Near Megalopolis in Arcadia, Pausanias records, there was a sanctuary of the Furies, *Maniai,* with a small mound nearby called the Finger Memorial (Daktylou Mnema) exhibiting a finger made of stone; a place called Healings (Ake) was nearby. The story goes that Orestes, having killed his mother, was driven mad by the Furies just there, until he bit off one of his fingers. When he had done this, the black Furies turned white, Orestes regained his senses, and he performed two types of sacrifice at the spot to both the black Furies and the white ones. This ritual was probably still performed at the sanctuary during Pausanias' lifetime.[6] Pursuing demons are pacified by the act of severing a finger from the body; the partial loss is to save the whole man. This was the aetiology of a cult of *Maniai* in Arcadia of which further details are not known; possibly it was a healing cult, as the place name Ake indicates. The fury that befell Orestes can be seen as a kind of illness, cured by this special form of sacrifice. This brings Orestes even closer to Aristeides.

Finger sacrifice is also a common motif in folktale and fairy-tale, with variations including the fantastic, the grotesque, and the humorous. Take for example some medieval versions of the Cyclops story, the tale about the one-eyed ogre blinded by the cunning hero. The oldest text is a collection of tales entitled *Do-*

lopathus, by Iohannes de Alba Silva, written about 1200 A.D.[7]
The final and most thrilling episode of the story is the escape
from the blinded monster. In the *Odyssey* Polyphemus makes a
weak attempt to lure Odysseus by offering gifts. In the medieval
versions the ogre actually throws a finger ring, a golden ring in
our text, which the hero eagerly grasps; but as soon as he has
put the ring on his finger he is forced to scream—in other versions
it is the ring itself that screams—"here I am, here I am," *ecce
ego! ecce ego!* And it proves impossible to strip the ring off the
finger again. The hero thus has to make his final heroic decision:
he bites off his own finger and throws it toward the giant. Some
versions allow him a knife; at any rate he escapes, bleeding but
victorious. Salvation has to be bought by means of a small yet
serious and irreplaceable loss, unflinching separation from what
is treacherous and dangerous. "By the loss of a member I saved
the whole body from imminent death," just as Aristeides had
been told "to cut a piece of his body for the sake of saving the
whole." A sensible choice indeed.

What makes the motif of finger sacrifice more serious is that
it is actually practiced. As James George Frazer observed:[8] "In
Tonga on the Friendly Islands it was common practice to cut off
a finger or portion of one as a sacrifice to the gods for the recovery of a superior relative who was sick"; earlier, Captain
Cook reported the same thing: "They suppose that the Devil will
accept the little finger as a sort of sacrifice efficacious enough to
procure the recovery of their health." Likewise, "Hottentot
women and Bushwomen cut off a joint of a child's finger, especially if a previous child has died. The sacrifice of the finger joint
is supposed to save the second child's life. . . . Some South African tribes believe that to cut off the joint of a sick man's finger
is a cure." "Among the Blackfeet, in times of great public or
private necessity, a warrior cuts off a finger of his left hand and
offers it to the Morning Star at its rising." In India a woman who
"has borne some children, terrified lest that the angry deity
should deprive her of her infants, . . . goes to the temple, and as
an offering to appease his wrath, cuts off one or two fingers of

the right hand." Some would do so repeatedly, becoming more and more seriously handicapped; indeed, the colonial government of India tried to forbid the custom at the beginning of this century. An interesting variant is reported from the Fiji Islands: "a finger was sometimes cut off and presented to an offended superior to appease his wrath."[9]

Worldwide, it seems, in situations of distress and illness or even in anticipation of disaster, people would cut off a finger or part of a finger. The examples come from quite different civilizations, from America, Africa, India, Oceania; and ancient Greek tradition ties in as well. Emphases and elaborations vary according to the respective cultural conditions. Native Americans have the Morning Star, while in India there is the intermediary temple and its priests, of course, to give guidance and interpretation. In all cases, though, the action is not done spontaneously but according to some already established tradition. Yet the practice is surprisingly uniform, without direct cultural contacts: Aristeides would not have known about Orestes in Arcadia. The practice is simply felt to make sense. Salvation achieved in this way is judged to be worth the partial mutilation. What startles modern observers as superstition and nonsense is an experience of crisis successfully overcome for those practicing such forms of sacrifice or dedication.

In all probability we are dealing with a custom that is as widespread as it is ancient. In some of the famous Paleolithic caves there are handprints of people apparently trying to come in contact with the sacred or to leave the mark of their presence. In one cave some of these hands clearly are mutilated, and it has been assumed that some form of finger offering occurred even at this epoch. In other words, finger sacrifice is a Paleolithic ritual that has survived into the twentieth century, over more than 20,000 years. Another finding is from a late Neolithic site, Arpachiya in Iraq, where "five stone fingers and one human finger bone" have been found in a sanctuary.[10] This seems to attest the custom of self-mutilation in the fourth millennium B.C., while the clay objects show that gods were kind enough to accept substitutes even then, as Asclepius did with Aristeides. In India, after the prohibition of the rite by the British government, people would ceremonially cut off finger joints made of dough at the appropriate situations,[11] carrying on the ritual tradition by way of symbolism.

Biology, Fantasy, and Ritual

The "part for whole" sacrifice can be plainly rational in its calculation of loss and gain. Plenty of situations in human life require that similar alternatives be pondered, and decisions made accordingly. To leave one's purse to a hooligan rather than to run the risk of getting stabbed or shot is the regular advice in our civilization;[12] throwing part of the cargo from the ship in a storm was common practice.[13] Not too long ago men would cut off a finger to avoid getting drafted into the army, or try to get sent away from the battlefield through clandestine self-mutilation of nonvital parts. But the pattern also explodes beyond what is functional and rational as it moves into symbolism: instead of cargo, throwing dollar bills into the sea, presenting gifts to the tempest, or, as I have been told in one instance, throwing a handbag not to a robber, but to a barking dog.[14] The pattern is displaced as it loses contact with reality and turns into "ritual" in its exaggerated and demonstrative character. In this form it will follow prescribed examples or use expert advice; thus it will appear to be culturally learned behavior. But as it is generated afresh repeatedly, it evidently has a psychological impact, a therapeutic effect. Ritual of this kind may be called magical in the sense that it seeks to achieve a definite goal by some nonobvious chain of causality; but this merely introduces a convenient term instead of an explanation. At any rate, the nonobvious connection of cause and effect is widely acceptable, and it makes sense to those who practice it.

Partial mutilation has its analogues in the world of animals. Some spiders' legs break off easily and continue to move for a while; this is to distract the attention of simple-minded predator pursuers and give the spider a chance to retire to safety. Lizards' tails too easily break off and thus may remain in the grip of the pursuer, while the lizard itself escapes. Here mutilation is encoded in a special biological program, genetically fixed and followed in the construction of the skeleton, a program that works in this particular habitat with clear survival value. It can be rephrased precisely in the words of Aristeides: "to cut a piece of the body for the sake of saving the whole." Birds may experience "terror molt," which means that an individual, attacked by a predator, suddenly sheds its feathers and thus leaves the attacker with a mouthful of plumage while escaping in a "naked" state.[15] In the class of mammals, a fox caught with a paw in a trap will bite off its paw to escape. The smaller loss is outweighed by the very fact of survival.

Thus an age-old ritual pattern, spread over the world and expressed in tales, dreams, and religious cults of ancient civilizations, has its analogy in a biological program that is seen to work at various stages of evolution and with various animal species. The program is directly functional in the animal world, as it enhances the chance for survival by distracting the attention of predators. In human culture, it is a ubiquitous and persistent pattern both of behavior and of fantasy. The programs of behavior of man and animal are so close that they can be described with the same words, "partial sacrifice for the sake of survival in a situation of pursuit, of threat and anxiety,"—in short, the *pars pro toto,* "part for whole" principle. Religion and zoology are seen to join hands.

This is not to postulate a definite inherited program of behavior, encoded genetically and passed on in continuous evolution from more primitive to higher living beings and culminating in man. The examples from different species are not connected by a continuous chain of evolution; nothing like it has been reported about chimpanzee behavior or, more generally, about monkeys. We are dealing with analogies, not homologies. In fact, the programs that come into play are also different. The active self-mutilation of the fox is not the same as leaving a part that breaks off to the predator, as with spiders and lizards. Another much simpler and more general behavior of "abandoning" is to give up a source of food when disturbed by a stronger rival or a predator. And there is a formidable step from the biological program to the conscious and verbalized principle, the explicit calculus *pars pro toto* and the decision to be made about it, even if suggested by ritual and narrative tradition.

From the opposite side of the argument, it would be equally difficult to hold that these human rituals and fantasies owe their whole existence to some form of intracultural learning, to observation or empathy, or to sheer creative fantasy. The pattern's recurrence in time and space, our readiness for the response, and common understanding point to a biological "landscape" underlying experience. The human makeup includes biological programs dealing with anxiety and flight that are older than the human species, and these comprise or engender at least the rudiments of the ritual pattern, correlating threat, alarm, pursuit, flight, and the trick of abandoning what can be spared. Lumsden and Wilson made it a criterion for the "coevolution of genes and culture" to find "memoirs most easily recalled, emotions they are most likely to evoke";[16] this seems to be a model case of their findings.

It is well known and easy to recall, and even to rehearse in fantasy, how haunting and deeply disturbing the image of the pursuing predator still is, notwithstanding millennia of civilized life. Victims of psychosis often develop the anxiety of being pursued; for the healthy, a movie thriller will not do without scenes of pursuit and narrow escape. Demons, in myth and in art, usually take the form of predators.[17] To depict the terror of hell Christians pictured it as a huge devouring animal with yawning jaws, and *Jaws* still projects vicarious terror even today. Few contemporary people will have any terrifying experiences of that kind, but even the attack of a barking dog will normally produce a sudden physical shock far beyond the real danger: we "know" about the danger of a predator's attack even before any actual experience, as the chicken "knows" about the hawk.[18] Humans are more adaptable and less fixed in their repertoire than chickens, but primates and hominids, too, had predators for dangerous neighbors, and the appropriate reactions have been fixed in our biological makeup. The snake, the leopard, the wolf—the image of the pursuing predator is easily evoked by any kind of threatening danger, whether real or imaginary. No wonder it appears in religious ritual too.

A special sign arousing anxiety is the staring eye. This fearful reaction is most clearly based on a very old and general biological program. As nature invented the eye to search for food, prospective "food," alive and selfish, learned to beware of the eye. The fear of the eye is present in many animals, as a functional reaction to being hunted by sharp-eyed predators. In another variation, certain butterflies, among other species, display the staring eye on their wings to avert unpleasant pursuers, while the peacock uses the eyes of his tail just to catch attention. In human civilizations the fear of the evil eye is widespread; the concept is documented from the ancient Near East through classical antiquity and into contemporary practice.[19] The innate fear calls for countersymbolism: the power of the evil eye is broken by another eye, by a certain color, or by male aggressiveness, especially by phallic display, or finally by blinding. The Polyphemus tale introduces the ogre as the anthropomorphous predator. To blind him is to achieve the most brilliant success in overcoming anxiety.

The biological reality of pursuit by predators is easy to incorporate into religious tradition. A general Greek prayer is "that the foot of the pursuer be turned away."[20] Brahmanic myth in India tells about the origin of the normal and most common form of sacrifice, the libation of butter: when Agni, fire, had been created, he turned out to be an eater, roaming through the land and devouring whatever he met. Then Prajapati, the Lord of First Creation, produced butter to feed Agni; Agni thus was assuaged. Since then, pouring butter into the flames at the altar has been made into a sacred ritual.[21] Cult, by this understanding, means to avert danger by consenting to a tolerable loss, in this way manipulating the "eater." "To pour sacrifice makes life return," as Babylonian wisdom holds.[22] Greek ritual had a class of sacrifices called rites of aversion; *apotropaia*. Jane Harrison found apotropaic ritual an especially old and basic stratum of Greek religion.[23] The way of doing it is to throw or pour out to uncanny pursuers what is due to them; often a person is cautioned not to look back when leaving the scene of the sacrifice.[24] Evil demons are said to require these rituals, for which the corresponding Latin term is *averruncare*.[25] The Romans resorted to human sacrifice allegedly by order of the Sibylline oracles, when the scandalous unchastity of some vestal virgins offended the gods and presaged disaster. As Plutarch tells it, the oracles ordained "to send forth *(proesthai)* to certain strange and alien demons, in order to avert what was about to happen, two Greeks and two Celts, who were buried alive on the spot."[26] To avert evil by sending forth or rather throwing off *(proesthai)* or leaving the victims to these demons—it makes a pattern that could not be more explicit.

In a counterpart to ritual, there is a well-known story pattern, common in saga, folktale, and myth, of magical flight or magical escape.[27] It forms the thrilling conclusion of many a fairytale, including the Cyclops story. The magical flight usually takes this form: as the heroine or hero or both flee from the dominion of a witch, a sorcerer, an ogre, a dragon, or other unpleasant company, the powerful and swift adversary realizes they have escaped and takes up pursuit. There is just one way to stop him: the fleeing person must throw things behind that will grow into barriers to halt the pursuer at least for a while, until a decisive point is passed and safety is regained. Throw a comb, and it will grow into a forest or into a mountain range. This tale pattern can be found in the Indian *Veda* and in the Finnish *Kalevala* as well as in the Grimm collection of fairytales; nor is it absent from Greek mythology. In the *Kalevala,* Canto 43, Väinämöinen has got hold of a precious magical object and is escaping in his ship, pursued by the North Folk and their queen; as he sees them appear at the horizon, he throws a piece of flint over his left shoulder into the sea. This grows into a cliff where the pursuing ship is stranded, but the obstacle is only temporary. The pursuing queen turns into an eagle, and the fight goes on. Karl Meuli took the motif of the magical flight to be typical of shaman poetry,[28] fantastic stories surrounding the ecstatic performances of the Siberian charismatics who penetrate into the realm of spirits, meet all kinds of helpers and dangerous adversaries, and come back again unharmed, as magic is countered by magic. But the pattern has more general foundations.

The story pattern wanders off into pseudo-zoology in this yarn about catching tigers, told in antiquity. The Indians steal young tigers from the lair and rapidly retreat on horseback. But as soon as the adult tigers realize their loss, they take up the pursuit, and they are much faster than any horse. So the rider, as the tigers come near, abandons one of the stolen cubs, which the tigers carefully bring back to the den. Then they resume the pursuit, and as they reach the rider, again running with enormous speed, a second and then possibly a third cub has to be abandoned; if successful, the rider will keep one or two when he finally reaches the civilized region which tigers do not approach.[29] This picturesque zoological nonsense[30] exactly matches the pattern of the magical flight; there too the pursuer is stopped more than once, and there is a decisive frontier where the pursuer has to give up. Instead of demons or sorcerers, the tiger story has reinstalled the classical pursuer, the most formidable carnivore. An interesting detail is the precise point where the pursuer stops. In its territorial behavior each animal feels safest at the home base, and less and less secure with increasing distance; this results in a precarious balance of anxiety and aggression in the marginal region. In the world of the tale this turns into a clearly defined point, parallel to ritual behavior which establishes marks of territory, even on a prehuman level.[31]

In Greek mythology, the most elaborate and gruesome version of the magical flight is the story of the Argonauts. As Jason and Medea steal away from Kolchis with the Golden Fleece, King Aietes follows with his fleet. It is not possible to ward him off by force, but Medea knows how to stop him. She kills her brother Apsyrtos (*aps syrtòn,* meaning "to be swept off backward"), "cuts him to pieces, and throws these into the depths of the sea; while Aietes collected the limbs of his son, he was late for the pursuit; thus he turned back."[32] The story surely is very old. Such a tearing apart of a human body *(sparagmos)* is a magical ceremony, no doubt, and Medea is a sorceress. But the term "magic" does not explain much. Remembering the spider and the lizard, along with the tiger snatching of India, we find that fantasy and ritual follow the old and beaten tracks of the *pars pro toto* sacrifice, that biological trick for survival to distract the attention of the pursuer by abandoning, by throwing. The "part," in the Argonaut myth, is the small, the feeble, the replaceable member of the community, the younger brother. Any predator has his best chances with young and feeble quarry.

There is another variant with a strongly biological background which takes the step from the sublime to the ridiculous. One biological reflex which makes the individual leave something behind in a situation of alarm is involuntary defecation. The accident is commonly alluded to in coarse speech as the ultimate sign of cowardice; it did not escape Aristophanes.[33] In normal life we have built up enough precautions to avoid situations of extreme and uncontrolled panic—yet it happens with children, it may still happen in traffic accidents, it happened in war; already the Assyrian annals use the motif to defile the beaten enemy,[34] and the Greeks were not immune to it.[35] It is also a well-known chimpanzee behavior.[36] Language retains the primitive far beyond actual experience, adapted of course to the cultural context. It is the contrast to normal decency that creates this particular opportunity for verbal abuse.

Probably less known nowadays is a curious ritual from the nineteenth century. Thieves in Germany and Austria, perhaps generally in Europe, believed that they would be safe from pursuit and detection if they left their feces at the crime scene, and so they did.[37] The biological reaction of panic in a terrifying situation was turned into apotropaic magic; what may happen instinctively was done on purpose. The practice remains notable for the interplay of a biological program, superstitious yet conscious magic ritual, and rational control. Superstition arose as the act was reinterpreted to assume magical efficacy through nonobvious causality. In Greek religion, the goddess Hekate, who might be called the very impersonation of panic in the dark, is an "eater of excrements," *borborophorba*.[38]

Castration and Circumcision

Self-castration, a special form of self-mutilation, is a strange and repulsive chapter of ancient religions. The very term "castration" is connected in antiquity with another tale of pseudo-zoology. Beavers—*castor* in Latin—produce in special glands a fragrant secretion which was highly valued as a medicine. It was wrongly believed that the substance was produced in the testicles of the male beaver. Thus when the beaver is hunted and finds himself trapped beyond escape, "he bends down, and biting off his own testicles throws them to his hunters." In this, the ancient writer telling the story explains, he is "like a clever man who has fallen among robbers, he puts down whatever he carried with him for the sake of his own salvation, giving this as ransom."[39] The parallel to the human situation and behavior is explicit; partial sacrifice is again seen as ransom.

The story about the beaver was doubtless told in Latin, in which *castor* is reminiscent of *castus*, "pure and abstinent," hence *castrare*. In terms of animal behavior the story makes no sense. As biological beings, individuals, being survival machines for their selfish genes,[40] could not do worse than to sacrifice their potentially immortal procreative cells. In its distortion of biological fact the story gives itself away as a projection of typical human preoccupations and anxieties. Perhaps because in wars aggression is linked to masculinity, the asexual could count on better chances for survival. More important, in our conscious world self-preservation appears to be the *condicio sine qua non* of existence and hence the ultimate goal that can be envisaged rationally; the biological program of procreation, which makes the individual replaceable and hence superfluous, remains disturbing in this respect. This may be ultimately why sex is regarded with the strongest suspicion in many traditions of wisdom, of yoga and other forms of asceticism. The illusion is that by renouncing procreation men may stay clear of the maelstrom of life and death. A small loss seems possible, even advisable, to guarantee the salvation of the individual whole. This is one of those reversals by which the mental world tries to get off the tracks of biology, with short-lived results for the individual, but with persisting appeal to the species. Conscious and unconscious imagination remains fixed to the theme with all of its strong shock of ambivalence.

The alleged behavior of the beaver recurs in tales and rituals of castration. In sanctuaries from Babylonia to Asia Minor and Syria a Great Goddess was worshiped by eunuch priests; they were called *galloi* at Pessinus, the most influential center of this cult. This is not the place to investigate this phenomenon in all its aspects, nor to discuss the various theories which have been brought forward by modern interpreters to explain its origin.[41] The one cuneiform text that clearly refers to it explains that Ishtar, the Great Goddess, installed it "to spread awe among men."[42] It is difficult to decide which came first, the Great Goddess with her eunuch devotees or the institution of the royal harem with eunuch guards, purportedly invented by Queen Semiramis or Atossa[43] and in existence down to the beginning of this century at Istanbul and Beijing. Let us just have a glimpse at the religious side, for which Lucian, in his book on the Syrian Goddess, is the main source.

Lucian tells a foundation myth in a novelistic and satirical fashion.[44] Queen Stratonike of Syria was told in a dream to found a new temple of the goddess at Bambyke-Hierapolis. She went off accompanied by a young and handsome man, Kombabos, whom the king chose as his delegate. Kombabos foresaw the risk of serving as companion to a young and passionate queen. Suspicion would be unavoidable and could cost him his life. He therefore castrated himself and left his genitals, embalmed with honey and unguents, in a sealed box with the king. As he had expected, the lonely queen fell in love with him, and when he refused, the story of Joseph and Potiphar's wife was re-enacted in a new variant: slander that Kombabos had violated the queen, trial, and death sentence. In the end Kombabos asked the king to open the box and proved his innocence by his impotence.

The Kombabos story clearly is etiological in its details, especially with that sealed box—eunuchs really kept such boxes even in China.[45] The story may be quite old, since the name Kombabos seems to recall the old name of the Great Goddess Kubaba-Kybebe.[46] What is especially interesting is the psychological explanation it offers for the ritual of castration. It is the fear of the more potent sexual rival, the king with his power to kill, that drives the inferior partner to renounce his sex. In some monkey societies the younger low-ranking males suffer a sort of psychological castration as long as they remain in the family; in the course of time they grow bigger and stronger and finally get their chance.[47] The tale makes Kombabos act like the clever beaver, giving up what is of mortal danger for him in order to survive. According to Lucian, at Bambyke-Hierapolis castration would actually be done at the major festival, and the future *galloi* would "throw" the severed parts into the house from which they would receive their female clothing and adornment,[48] as the beaver threw his testicles toward his hunters.

No less strange is the story in an isolated passage from the Hebrew Bible which must be regarded as one of the foundation myths for circumcision. The text is usually attributed to the oldest layer of the Pentateuch, the Jahwist.[49] When Moses returns from Midian to Egypt together with his wife Zippora and their little son, they rest at night in the desert. "And Jahweh met him and wanted to kill him. Then Zippora took a flint and circumcised her son, touching Moses' private parts with the foreskin and said: A bridegroom of bloods you are for me. Then Jahweh let him go." The writer of the text already wondered at the story; he added an explanatory note, stating that this refers to circumcision.[50] The passage has remained enigmatic. How can the Lord appear in the guise of a killing monster of the nocturnal desert? But that is exactly how it happens. Suddenly, at night in the desert, one is struck by an irresistible fear of god, more powerful than a king and ready to kill. For ransom, man has to renounce his masculinity—in this case, the mother steps in to make the decision. At the same time, a double substitution takes place, child for man, and foreskin for penis. Sanguinary mutilation, both real and symbolic, is necessary to ward off the pursuer. Only a "bridegroom of bloods"—Moses in relation to Zippora—will survive. This is dealing with a super-father in the ways of Kombabos, mitigated by ritual substitution. It is the mother who wields the flint knife—as castration in the cult of the Mother Goddess was done with a flint knife. Doubts may remain whether this is the precise origin of circumcision, but apparently it is the oldest interpretation of circumcision we have.[51]

It is tempting to connect finger sacrifice with castration; the Freudian approach has become popular. Even before Freud, the finger monument of Orestes in Arcadia had been suspected of being actually a phallus.[52] And what will become, with a bit of Freudian and anatomical fantasy, of that finger with its eloquent ring in the medieval ogre story? Telesphoros, the child in the hood to whom Aristeides dedicated his finger ring, does in fact turn into a phallus in the hood in some ancient statuettes.[53] In a curious version of the Attis myth, Attis, dying from castration, will not be revived but neither will he decay, and as he lies dead, his small finger keeps moving.[54] Many myths also insist on the figure of the threatening female, Ishtar or Kybele, Zippora or the furies allied to Klytaimestra. It may be left to psychologists to establish to what extent the human psyche is apt to produce images and symbolism of this kind. The perspective adopted here suggests that there is a background even beyond the Freudian psyche, that there are pragmatic and not just Oedipal anxieties rooted in our biological makeup. There are real predators; awe wrought by ritual, meeting with the ambivalence of sexuality in the individual's experience, finds fertile ground to thrive in some appalling forms of religion.

Scapegoats

The *pars pro toto* principle, accepting the small loss in order to save the whole, is even more efficacious in group dynamics. "It is better that one man die than that the whole people should be destroyed," the high priest Kaiphas declares in the Gospel of John;[55] the evangelist is anxious to add that Kaiphas spoke "not on his own but acted as a prophet." This strange balance, salvation of all by the death of one, became one of the fundamental tenets of Christian theology. Yet Kaiphas' prophecy was in fact restating a much older principle, widely understood, accepted, and practiced.[56] It is presupposed already in the Babylonian epic of creation, *Enuma elish,* when sentence is pronounced on a guilty god: "He alone shall perish that mankind shall be fashioned."[57]

In some unfortunate situations it seems perfectly reasonable that one person or a few individuals should be given up in order to save the others. In wars generals make decisions to sacrifice a number of their own troops for superior strategic goals. A more picturesque instance is that of the sleigh pursued by wolves. As the horses grow tired, one person must be thrown to the wolves closing in on the sleigh—we are back to the world of carnivores pursuing their quarry. Comparable situations arise in times of catastrophe, fires, floods, or sinking boats, when helpers may lose their lives while saving others. Gratefully we honor their memory, and make sure to remain attached to the tales recalling those thrilling events. Ritual language prevails in this context: there are victims, there is sacrifice.

The *pars pro toto* calculus is highly rational and highly emotional at the same time. It repeats at the intellectual level what biology has long taught before. Yet it retains a mysterious ring and carries religious ramifications in its wake. The sacrifice of one for the sake of all, enduring a small, tolerable loss to confirm all life, is a motif dominating both fantastic tales and strange rituals. The pattern transcends what seems reasonable and functional and leaves a purely symbolic message; it can be termed magical or superstitious. The sequence of events feels right, makes sense to the participants, this triumph of the inherited pattern proves its autonomy.

Take the story of Jonah. The ship in the storm is a model situation of anxiety and despair. As the sailors begin to lose hope, they all agree with sudden unanimity that one man in the ship is culpable and has to be thrown into the sea. It is on the whole rational to throw part of the cargo into the sea to save the ship.[58] But it is the personalized Jonah version that made its way into the Bible and remains unforgettable. In addition, the tale introduces the huge swallowing monster, the fish to engulf Jonah; this was the character missing from the natural terror scene, and, with a fantastic reversal, it is to become Jonah's savior. Folklorists have collected many parallels to this obsessive tale.[59] In a special form the motif recurs in Virgil's *Aeneid* in which, to ensure a smooth voyage, one man must die in the sea at night; "one head will be given for many." Falling asleep through divine intervention, Palinurus the steersman is drowned.[60]

Among the stories about the Lacus Curtius at the Forum Romanum, one is especially memorable. At this spot, it was said, a yawning gap opened *(dehisse terram),* and the soothsayers announced that "the god exacted the bravest citizen." Then Curtius, by his own decision, rode on horseback into the abyss, and the gap was closed.[61] The yawning gap is a memorable projection of anxiety, linked to the image of devouring jaws. One person must be swallowed to save the rest. Later the deed is recorded in ritual, with gifts brought to the spot or coins thrown into the shallow pit that remained—something like those dollar bills thrown into the water in modern Africa. Anxiety is removed and normalcy secured by way of a specific payment.

Other rituals match other tales. A black lamb is slaughtered to stop a typhoon; storms are halted by drawing blood;[62] at Cyrene, "if a plague is coming against the country or the city, or famine, or dying . . . they sacrifice a red he-goat before the gates."[63] Legend has it that a child was buried to avert a plague in Austria in 1715, and in Swabia a bull was actually buried alive to stop a plague affecting cattle in 1796.[64] To ensure the effectiveness of a dam that checks the flood, a living being must be buried on the spot.[65]

The tolerable loss may nevertheless leave the survivors with a bad conscience. This can be countered by an alternative projection: the being chosen to perish was guilty, polluted, and detestable; the positive effect is enhanced by the negative criteria of selection. This is the famous and much discussed scapegoat pattern.[66] Alternatively, the victim may be marked by a touching ambivalence, despised and worshiped at the same time. This has been elaborated, most of all, in the Christian tradition.[67]

The scapegoat complex will not be discussed here at length.[68] Suffice it to recall the ritual for the Day of Atonement according to the Bible. A goat is selected "for Azazel," the sins of the people are placed on its head, and it is led away into the desert. It will probably fall a victim to predators there. One later source says the goat was hurled down a cliff.[69] An ivory plaque from Late Bronze Age Megiddo has often been adduced for illustration of this ritual. It shows an aggressive sphinx, a demon with a lion's body and a vulture's wings, grasping a goat: a demon depicted in the guise of a carnivore of the desert.[70]

Life for Life

Devouring demons who pursue men are prominent in the ancient oriental conceptions of disease, which can be countered by healing magic.[71] The normal practice is to offer an animal, with words such as: "Look, this goat is big and fat, take it and let the sick person go." These ideas and practices were influential in the classical world too. Ovid, in *Fasti*,[72] tells of demonic vampire birds flying around at night, called *striges* (witches are called by nearly the same name, *strigae*). The *striges* penetrate into the rooms where babies are asleep and suck their blood, leaving them to sicken and die. One wise, charismatic woman found a ritual to help the sick babies: take the inward parts of a piglet and say, "birds of night, spare the inward parts of the child. For the little one a little sacrifice is falling. Take heart for heart, intestines for intestines; we give this life-soul for the sake of a better life-soul." The entrails, cut to pieces, are to be spread under the open sky, and nobody is allowed to look back as they leave the scene. In the imaginative world evoked by myth and ritual, the pursuing predators that suck the blood of their victims have to be pacified by a substitution sacrifice, by killing another small animal. An action that would have a pragmatic function in dealing with real animals, to stop pursuing predators by feeding them, becomes a purely symbolic, magical procedure. But it also entails another transformation: instead of passive abandonment of a chosen victim, there is active killing. The victim-to-be saves himself by becoming a killer in turn. In a way this doubles the protection to be achieved, both assuaging and threatening the putative aggressor, in a practice that is most strongly felt to be efficacious.

Ovid's ominous words "soul for soul," *animam pro anima*,[73] are well known from more serious religious contexts, especially from votive inscriptions to Saturnus from North Africa.[74] In this context it is necessary to recall that substitution in sacrifice can be turned around, from animal for human back to human for animal. Saturnus-Kronos is the god with whom ancient tradition connects the Phoenician and especially Carthaginian sacrifices of children, sometimes called Moloch sacrifices after Leviticus.[75] Diodorus says they had been replaced by animal holocausts of the more normal form, but in a situation of disaster, such as during the siege by Agathocles, the Carthaginians resorted to human sacrifice again as the more efficacious means to secure salvation.[76] These were "ransom for avenging demons," Philo of Byblos said.[77] The Indian sacrifice of butter[78] and the Punic sacrifice of children are two extremes of the *pars pro toto* principle. The conviction that a threat to human life can only be averted by offering another human being is a form of logic that can arise everywhere. Thus Admetus accepted the death of his wife Alcestis in his stead; Aelius Aristeides dreamed about it;[79] Queen Amestris performed such killings; according to Herodotus, so did a king at Uppsala; and a seventeenth-century Hungarian duchess tried to prolong her life by slaughtering girls.[80] Caesar alleged that it was general custom in Gaul to resort to human sacrifice in cases of sickness, of battles, of dangers in general, "because they believe that unless for the life of a man the life of a man is given, the will of the immortal gods cannot be placated."[81] Reports on child sacrifice in India, to avert sickness or other imminent danger, still appear in our newspapers. In the Sumerian Inanna myth the "law of the netherworld" holds that a substitute must be given so that Inanna can rise from the dead; hence Dumuzi falls victim to the infernal *gallê* who persecute him. These fatal demons "do not accept offerings of eating and drinking, flour sprinkled for sacrifice, water poured out for libation." There is no offering to turn them away.[82] Even in such a context the edifying reversal into voluntary sacrifice is possible. Some Romans made vows they would die if the sick emperor recovered—and Caligula really enforced the fulfillment of such vows.[83] Rumor had it that Antinous' death was a magical sacrifice to prolong Hadrian's life.[84]

In the situation of the herd vis-à-vis the carnivore—the zebras attacked by lions—when one individual is killed, the others feel safe for a time. The instinctive program seems to command: take another one, not me. This ancient program is still at work in humans, still fleeing from devouring dangers and still making sacrifices to assuage and triumph over anxiety.[85] In this perspective sacrifice is a construct of sense that has proved almost universally effective throughout the history of civilization.

3

The Core of a Tale

"Caught up in Tales"

In Geschichten verstrickt (Caught up in Tales) is the title of a slim volume by Wilhelm Schapp, which appeared in 1953 and has made some impact at least in German philosophy.[1] His experience as a lawyer led Schapp to realize that what moves people, what they experience, recount, and recall, are stories. Each individual has a tale to tell which constitutes his or her problem, failure, or success. Personal knowledge about life usually takes the form of a tale, and that is how it is stored and communicated. Schapp's observation is of general philosophical interest. Ever since Aristotle, it had generally been assumed that knowledge takes the logical form of statements, predication on a subject. "The world is a totality of facts," Wittgenstein wrote.[2] We know, since we have learned it, that it *is* the case and it *is* true that the whale is a mammal and not a fish, that lightning is a phenomenon of electricity, and that St. Andrews is a city in Scotland. What we learn in tales is knowledge of a different kind: that a certain person has done this or that, and this is what came of it. Although it is difficult to explain how such personal knowledge can be generalized, it can still be said that tales are understandable; they call for empathy; they often dominate communication. The tale is the form through which complex experience becomes communicable.

The interest in tales has also animated studies of folklore, which have been flourishing at least since the beginning of the nineteenth century. They started from a revived interest in myth—in fact, from the very rediscovery of the concept of myth.[3] In the wake of the fairy tales collected by the Grimm brothers,[4] national mythologies were rediscovered or reconstructed in Europe and across the world. By 1913, when a *Mythology of All Races* was collected,[5] it was taken for granted that the tradition of a particular civilization, especially of preliterate societies, was mainly encoded in tales. While in a way this anticipated Schapp's findings, in contrast to his starting point, myths are not personal but generalized, the common possession of a group or tribe that helps to constitute its conscious group identity. Traditional tales are anything but homogeneous, however, and the problem of distinguishing, say, myth, saga, and fairy tale has proved to be too complex to yield to a general, transcultural solution.[6] This also makes a general definition of myth proper quite difficult, if not impossible.[7] Adding to the problems are the diachronical stability or changeability of tales and the interrelation of oral and written traditions.

It is obvious that many tales are quite similar to each other, appearing to be variations of general underlying patterns or types. The current index of *Märchentypen* by Aarne-Thompson enumerates about 1000 types of fairy tales,[8] but the number can be reduced by further generalization. At the same time, a tale is very easy to remember, at any rate if it is a good tale. Everyone could volunteer to tell a tale heard just once, if it has caught his imaginative attention. Contrast the effort needed to remember and to reproduce correctly just a few nonsense syllables, a 10-digit-number, or some words in a language we don't know. Yet this is what the simplest tape recorder or floppy disk will cheerfully do. What people do when they recount a tale evidently is quite different. It is not a sequence of sounds and words we remember and usually not a fixed text either—though children will sometimes exhibit exact memories. Storytellers expand, abbreviate, change words, and translate. A tale is not a series of words but a sequence of events and actions that make sense. While there are tools and props to help remember a text exactly, as in the Brahmanic tradition of Veda or in Islamic Quran schools, they

bring out, by contrast, how natural it is to recall a memorable tale. It has an obsessive impact combined with freedom of expression. A tale is a structure of sense.[9]

The Propp Sequence: The Quest

Much work has been done on the structure of tales in recent decades. One of the most successful, influential, and accessible studies is still Vladimir Propp's *Morphology of the Folktale*.[10] Propp wrote about Russian fairy tales, but the implications of his work go beyond his corpus.[11]

According to Propp, a tale is to be seen as a sequence of 31 functions (called "motifemes" by Alan Dundes). In the abbreviated and simplified version herewith, the tale starts with some damage, lack, or desire (8); the hero is told to go somewhere (9) and agrees to do so (10); he leaves home (11); he meets some being that puts him to a test (12); reacting to it (13), he receives some gift or magical aid (14); he gets to the place required (15) and meets an adversary with whom he has to interact (16); he is harmed in some way (17) but is victorious in the end (18); thus the initial damage or lack is put right (19). The hero begins his homeward journey (20); he is pursued (21) but saved (22); he comes back without being recognized (23); there is a wicked impostor (24), a test (25), and final success (26); the hero is recognized (27); the impostor is punished (28); the hero marries and becomes king (31).

Propp's thesis is that these functions or motifemes are the constant elements in tales; the number of functions is limited, and their sequence is fixed. They need not all turn up in a single narrative—the above selection omitted some of them—but every tale contains some combination of these functions, and parts of the sequence may also be repeated. Further formalization of Propp's approach, notably by Alan Dundes,[12] introduced higher levels of abstraction, which weaken the memorable and empirically accessible level.

Some critics of Propp's thesis question his exclusive reliance on his source, Afanas'ev's collection of Russian fairy tales, and Afanas'ev's original reliance on his main informant, a Russian peasant.[13] Conversely, other critics wonder if the author placed too much emphasis on the classical European tradition.[14] To counter such concerns, it is reassuring that Propp's analysis, whatever its foundations were, is applicable to a wide range of tales which neither Propp nor Afanas'ev, let alone the Russian peasant, had ever known or thought of.

In Greek mythology, which had not been included in Propp's study, the legend of Perseus had been treated as a model tale.[15] To get Medusa's head (9) Perseus sets out on a journey (11) to the edge of the world; he meets the *Graiai*, from whom he gets advice and magical aids (12, 14); then there is the confrontation with the Gorgon (16), the killing (18), the flight, and the pursuit by the Gorgon's sisters (21). Another famous set of tales in Greek mythology tells about the labors of Heracles. These, like the exploits of Perseus, are transmitted not by a classical poet but mainly by way of jejune summaries and allusions. These are popular tales, attested also by a rich iconographic tradition which confirms the popularity of the tales, beginning in the archaic epoch of Greece.[16] Heracles' labors conform to the pattern of Propp in multiple repetitions. To get the cattle of Geryoneus,[17] for example, Heracles, by command of Eurystheus (9), sets out on a long journey (11). He meets the Old Man of the Sea who gives him directions (12, 13); he meets Helios the Sun God from whom he obtains the magical object, the golden cup to cross Okeanos (14); upon arriving at the Red Island of Erytheia (15) he has a fight with the three-bodied "roaring" master of animals, Geryoneus (18), and seizes the herd of cattle (19). There is no direct pursuit on the return journey, but there are repeated adventures with impostors (24, 26), as the cattle get lost or stolen on the long way through Provence, Rome, and Sicily. The final marriage (31) occurs on Olympus after all the labors have been done.

Another model myth is the story of the Argonauts. Its definite literary form was shaped by the Hellenistic poet Apollonios of Rhodes; but centuries before, for the audience of the *Odyssey*, this was a song "dear to everyone."[18] Karl Meuli interpreted it on the model of a fairy tale, and it clearly agrees with Propp's pattern.[19] Pelias at Iolkos desires the golden fleece (8); Iason is told to get it (9). The collection of various helpers (12, 14) right at the start, the crew of the ship *Argo* in this case, is a special feature of this tale-type. Further helpers and adversaries show up on the ship's route until the voyagers reach their destination (15), Aia or Kolchis, where Medea, princess and witch, turns out to be the decisive helper who provides knowledge and magical means against the adversary, her father, King Aietes. Then follows the contest (18), the flight (20), the pursuit (21), and the magical aversion (22).[20] But the pattern seems to snap at the point of return and marriage, as it collides with another: Pelias' intrigues and death, Medea's crimes, and Iason's final failure. The goal of the enterprise, the golden fleece, loses its function; the quest tale recedes to become a preface to the tragedy of Medea. The *Odyssey* is atypical in many respects too.[21] But parts of it, single exploits of Odysseus such as the Circe or the Cyclops episodes, can still be analyzed as instances of Propp's pattern.

The earliest written tales are Sumerian, and here Propp's pattern triumphs. "Gilgamesh and Huwawa" has long been known as part of the Gilgamesh epic, but the older Sumerian version has been edited in its full form only recently.[22] It starts with the desire (8) of Lord Gilgamesh to go to the mountain to "put up his name." For this journey he collects helpers (14), foremost among whom is his servant Enkidu. There is also a curious group of seven with animal characteristics—lion, eagle, serpent—and superhuman abilities granted by the Sungod; other young men from his city come too. This early written text displays the duplication of motifs—or rather, gathering of competing variants—which underlines the necessity of this "function." Gilgamesh has to cross seven mountain ranges before he reaches the cedar tree (15) which he fells; the adversary Huwawa, the guardian of the mountain, attacks (16) and defeats Gilgamesh with a kind of superweapon, a beam of awe (17); but Gilgamesh recovers thanks to Enkidu. He then begins to trick Huwawa, offering him his sisters as concubines; finally Huwawa surrenders his wonder weapon, he is struck by force, and Enkidu cuts off his head (18). The head is brought to the god, Enki (20), who establishes a new distribution of powers. In this way the tale ends on a religious, aetiological note, but the narrative functions have shown up in the recognized sequence.

Another early and important Sumerian text is "Ninurta and the Asakku."[23] A kind of damage (8) has occurred because the demon Asakku, son of Heaven and Earth, installed himself on the mountain, had sex with the mountain, and engendered the rock demons who have rebelled against the gods. So valiant Ninurta goes out to fight them (9, 11). His helper is Sharur, his club, endowed with speech and intelligence (12, 14); the confrontation with Asakku (16) is difficult, but in the end Ninurta is victorious (18), annihilates the adversary, and organizes the country for cultivation. Ninurta has the role of a cultural hero, overcoming the demon of the mountain as Gilgamesh vanquished the demon of the woods.[24] The quest tale is about to turn into sheer combat tale, but it retains its character with the road to the unexplored region and the practical result of the action, whereby stones from the mountain's quarries become available for human use and timber for the temple in the city.

Even closer to the Propp pattern is the famous text of the "Descent of Inanna to the Netherworld."[25] In this tale, the first move of a quest seems to fail: Inanna, the goddess of fertility, gets lost in the Land of No Return (8). This would be a catastrophe to the world, but it releases a new sequence. Because of the loss, Enki creates heroic shaman-like figures (9) called *kurgaru* and *kalaturru*.[26] They set out for the netherworld (11), using magic to pass the door unnoticed like flies (15). When they meet the adversary, Ereshkigal, queen of the netherworld (16), instead of resorting to violence, they use their wits. They endear themselves to Ereshkigal and ask her for a gift: the disfigured corpse of In-

anna, which they sprinkle with the water of life (19). On the
return journey they are pursued (21) by a host of demons who
exact a substitution sacrifice.[27] Here myth meets with ritual in

the demand for offerings, but the situation of pursuit and magical
flight is still part of the Propp sequence.

The climax of the Gilgamesh epic is the greatest quest, the
quest for life. It is a grievous loss (8), the death of Enkidu, that
makes Gilgamesh abandon his home (11) and wander through
the steppe. How his idea to search for life comes about is lost in
a lacuna of the text. On his adventurous and fantastic way the
hero follows the way of the sun through the twin mountain,
beyond which he meets his helper (12), Siduri the alewife. She
tells him how to cross the water of death with Urshanabi the
ferryman so as to reach Utnapishtim, the hero of the flood, who
alone has escaped death (15). Utnapishtim proves a friendly
though talkative host, and after some tests that yield unpromis-
ing results, he gives Gilgamesh the crucial information about
how to appropriate the "plant of life" (19). Gilgamesh sets out
to return home, accompanied by Urshanabi who henceforth
quits his service. But at a fountain, when Gilgamesh falls asleep,
a snake comes and swallows the plant of life (24). The quest has
failed. Thereafter, snakes can cast off their old age by sloughing,
whereas man remains bound to death. Pessimistic wisdom over-
comes the inherent optimism of the tale.[28]

"The tale *(mythos)* is the soul of the drama," Aristotle wrote,[29]
"soul" being an organizing principle of nature. The Propp pattern acts as an organizing principle from the earliest tales that
have been recorded, through classical mythology and far beyond.
It would be easy indeed (and tedious) to trace the Propp orga-
nizations through romances, drama, and modern movies, science
fiction, and even computer games. A general and transcultural
form of organizing experience seems to be at work. It follows
that when we understand a tale, we can easily memorize it, reproduce it, even reconstruct it from incomplete records. Whether
by instinct or by routine, we seem to know what should happen
next. We like a tale to be retold. Repetitive and fascinating as it

is at the same time, it may be called the adventure *par excellence*, or just the quest.

From Biological Programs to Semantic Chains

One obvious hypothesis would be that the tale-telling program owes its existence to previous learning. As people, especially children, are told stories, a lot of stories of all sorts, they build up a storage system in the form of sequences and functions and thus gradually become better and faster in their understanding. This, however, should lead to the emergence of quite different forms of organizing experience, and hence different patterns of tales out of different civilizations. Yet the sequence of the quest is surprisingly persistent and nearly ubiquitous through more than four millennia. Is it legitimate to look beyond civilization for its basis or origin?

In 1979 I wrote confidently: "If we ask where such a structure of sense, such a program of actions, is derived from, the answer must evidently be: from the reality of life, nay, from biology. Every rat in search of food will incessantly run through all these 'functions'."[30] Studies of rat behavior show the compelling combination of energy and swift intelligence in this most successful animal species, as rats manage to solve their everyday problem, the provision of food. Even for our nearest relatives, the apes, the quest for food has remained the day's main occupation; nor can humans do without it. It is clear that the biological program necessary to fulfill the special needs of a highly organized being will contain a series of basic functions: pursuit of a need (8); leaving home (11); finding the place required (15); meeting competitive, often dangerous adversaries (16); success (18), meaning realization of desire (19); but return to the home base (20) may be difficult in case of pursuit (21); the outcome is the individual's salvation (22). As it turns out, practically the whole of the Propp sequence is prefigured in this series of biological necessities. The main strand of Propp's sequence can be summarized in one word: the quest, which may entail many dangers, including combat.

The biological equivalent of the quest is the search for food, which includes the struggle against others who are in quest for the same resources, and the possibility of tricks, fight, and flight.

As I wrote in another context:

> Actions are represented by the verb, and the verbal root, the "zero form" of the verb, in most languages—including English, German, French, Latin, Greek, Semitic, and Turkish—is the imperative; and communication by imperatives is more primitive, and more basic, than communication by statements. The deepest deep structure of a tale would, then, be a series of imperatives: "get," that is, "go out, ask, find out, fight for it, take and run."[31]

Surprising confirmation of this point has emerged from a field which many will judge intermediate between biological functions and human actions: chimpanzee language. Among the apes that have been taught sign language, the most successful was a female, Washoe. The extent to which this is "real" language is hotly debated, but this is not the decisive issue here. It suffices that humans and chimpanzees can communicate through this medium, even if the apes' interest is limited; it continues to concentrate on food. Roger S. Fouts records the following conversation with Washoe.[32] "*George:* What you want? *Washoe:* Orange, orange. *George:* No more orange, what you want? *Washoe:* Orange. *George* (getting angry): No more orange, what you want? *Washoe:* You go car gimme orange. Hurry."

This is obviously a sequence for getting food. The chimpanzee is intelligent enough not only to realize and express the desire but to organize the necessary sequence of actions. She had not been riding in a car recently, we are told, but she knows that one gets oranges by driving to the supermarket. The Propp sequence is present in an incipient stage, and it makes sense. There is a need (8); the hero is told to go (9) and to use the appropriate magical means (14); then need will be fulfilled (19). Washoe has her goal and she makes her plan, articulating it in a chain of commands/events. It is safe to say that the chimpanzee is able to correlate the series of necessary actions in her brain: she organizes her thoughts by mentally preparing motion before starting real action; and having been taught sign language, she can express this program in language, in a sequence of imperatives.

This is strikingly similar to protolanguage as observed in the case of an abandoned and hence retarded child. The most distinct utterance recorded from this child was "applesauce buy store."[33] Again, what is expressed is not just desire, but knowledge about the means to fulfill it, and that expression is put in a speech sequence, with a verb at the center to be understood as imperative.

I do not claim that Washoe has told a tale; but we may be in a position to localize here, as it were, the missing link that makes the transition from biology to language, from program of action to verbalized account.[34] An important program, such as the quest for food, can be prefigured mentally as a sequence of actions and is most easily verbalized as a sequence of imperatives. The sequence involves analysis of the general urge into goals and means and their pragmatic interaction. The organizing principle of a tale, the soul of the plot, is found to operate at the level of biology. The tale is created as a necessary sequence of "motifemes," and it has the pragmatic function of solving a problem. In other words, the quest is established as the means for problem-solving, and it is represented and communicated through the tale.

This is not to claim explanation of the origin and function of language as such, or even explanation of the whole of the Propp sequence. It is not my purpose to ascribe animal biology to man, but to recognize what is specific in human civilization when it is viewed against its nearest background; to place man-created monuments within the biological landscape which still prescribes their original design.

Looking back, or rather looking ahead toward the developed Propp sequence, one strange but characteristic detail is the incident of meeting the giver or helper (12 to 14) who provides the magical means to make the quest a success.[35] This flight of fantasy in fairy tales also appears in myths, with the *Graiai* on Perseus' way to Medusa, or with Hermes presenting the plant *moly* to Odysseus to help him overcome Circe.[36] It seems to be a far cry from fantasy to biology. Still, what makes the difference between failure and success in each quest is that at some decisive moment the various attempts and possibilities get organized into one definite, feasible plan, to be executed without delay. We may call this the moment of inspiration, the *aha-Erlebnis*. "A god put it into his mind," the Homeric formula would say; it is the moment when Athena meets disoriented Odysseus and makes him recognize Ithaca.[37] When chimpanzees solve problems by thinking, they clearly have their *aha-Erlebnis* too. Tales are a human prerogative, no doubt, but the moment of inspired decision is keeping to the tracks of biological reality, no less than a hair-raising shudder.

Another strange characteristic of the quest tale is the asymmetry of going and returning. The way back often is different from the way taken before the decisive encounter. The normal geometry of space seems to disintegrate. In defiance of geography, the Argonauts have to take a totally different route to return to Iolkos; nor can Odysseus retrace his steps. In fact this asymmetry also reflects the experience of biological reality, for problems and perspectives rapidly change with the moment of success. The rat that got the cookie has to run fastest to escape the others and to reach a safe place. This is the end of a successful quest.

The transition from pragmatic imperatives to nonpragmatic tales is not hard to imagine. It is obvious that women and men like to use language in ways that are not directly linked to information. Humans are talkative; we can hardly stand to be together without saying a word.[38] We can visualize our ancestors sitting around the fire in the evening, rehearsing the sequences of imperatives that occurred in the important activities of the day. In talking about them the imperatives change their meaning, and a tale is born. It has the sequence of motifemes as encoded in the program. This is why it is understood by all and makes sense. During the evolution of mankind, for hundreds of thousands of years the most important form of the quest has been hunting.[39] The first examples of tales within the quest pattern may well have been hunting tales, with combat tales following closely. In time tales assumed their basic functions, to rehearse some important "out of gear" moves in the mental world and thus to uphold the common world of a cultural society.

Curiously enough, the Indoeuropean language had one special category of verb inflection, a most simple category called "injunctive" that was used both for the imperative and for the tale.[40] It is fully preserved in the Vedic language; relics exist in Greek. In his book entitled *Der Injunktiv,* Heinz Hoffmann describes that second function as "beschreibende Erwähnung," which means mentioning what is basically known, in contrast to conveying information. Of course even Indoeuropean, spoken perhaps in the fourth millennium B.C., is already far from the earliest human language. It nevertheless illustrates the possibilities of transition from imperative to tale in the context of the quest.

The Shaman's Tale

One theory makes of the special ritual of shamanism the guiding principle, if not the origin, of storytelling. The shaman, in a state of ecstatic performance, acts out a quest of supernatural dimensions; he can ascend to heaven or go down to the netherworld; he meets with spirits, demons, and gods. His purpose is to retrieve the souls of sick people that are held prisoner in the beyond, or to release for the hunt animals held back by an offended master or mistress of animals. The classic reports of shamanism come from Siberia and from the Eskimos. By using mimicry, symbols, and normal speech the shaman makes the sequence of his adventures clear to those present at the séance—who, by the way, know about the normal program of the exploit anyway. The sequence can easily be reproduced by telling or rather, retelling the story. Thus shaman poetry is presumed to play a role, perhaps

The Core of a Tale

even a basic role, in the development of preliterate narrative, and hence in the growth of literature.[41]

Quite a few instances of the quest tale seem to recall a shamanistic pattern. The quest of the Argonauts to get the golden fleece from the land of the Sun, or to "bring back the soul of Phrixos," with a hero named Iason or *Ieson,* whose name can be understood as "healer," are all shamanistic elements.[42] In the Sumerian story, Inanna's retrieval from the netherworld is clearly a shamanistic exploit.[43] *Asinnu,* the hero's designation in the Akkadian version, refers to a peculiar class of people in real life. These are social outsiders of uncertain sexual identity who play special instruments and are needed for certain rituals. They seem to be debased shamans. Similarly, Gilgamesh travels the way of the sun to the beyond, as does Heracles on his way to Geryoneus; Odysseus reaches Circe, daughter of the Sun God, at the dancing place of Dawn; Odysseus also goes down directly to the netherworld. All these are shamanistic feats, all these heroes could be described as shamans. One characteristic of shamans' tales is that they are told in the first person. The performance enacts the immediate experience of "I go, I see," which is reenacted in the story of "I went, and I saw." With Odysseus, the device has become literary artifice, but its shamanistic background looms large.

Shamanism ritualizes the fantastic, giving shape to realms of the unknown. The shaman concentrates on the realistic action program of the quest, how to get what is needed. The action includes leaving home, assembling helpers, arriving at the essential spot, making deals with an adversary—usually a god or master—which may involve supplication, laborious service, trick, or force. Then it is necessary to find the way back through dangerous realms, and to evade pursuing demons.

Shamanism and tale-telling appear to have the same intimate relationship as that between tales and imperatives. It is not surprising that a tale is turned into a play, following the impulse of the program and acting out the events in sequence. In this perspective the myth-and-ritual complex must have quite distant roots.[44] One form of consistent elaboration is the shamanistic séance; another, in a different cultural environment, is the theater—which remained under the guidance of myth in ancient Greece.

Shamanistic experience surely is specifically human, implying, as trance does, the supremacy of the world of meaning as against actual pragmatic interaction. Yet the imagination necessarily elaborates on natural programs as these developed in biological evolution. In other words, shamanism is a special development of the general program of the quest, with characteristic refinement or surplus that has its repercussions on preliterate narrative.

In many respects this is close to dreams, another field parallel to narrative fantasy. Some thinkers, notably Carl Gustav Jung and his school, perceive dreams and mythology as being in close contact. It should not be overlooked, however, that dreaming predates the advent of man. All higher animals seem to have dreams, though of course they lack verbalization. Dreams appear to reproduce action and visualization patterns, and this brings them close to plays and tales. Dreams may add to the repertoire and mood of human narrative, as shamanism does, without having to be the origin of mythology.

The Initiation Tale: The Maiden's Tragedy

The quest narrative is outstanding but not unique. There are other types of tales, such as wanderings, genealogies, miraculous birth and death, revenge, and deception.[45] One favorite fairy tale, documented in about 1,500 variants worldwide, is *Amor and Psyche* or "the animal bridegroom."[46] The text, as it appears in the *Metamorphoses* of Apuleius, has often been called the one surviving fairy tale of antiquity, although the characters involved bring it close to allegory: Soul, Psyche, meeting Love, Amor (corresponding to the Greek *psyche* we would expect *eros*) and giving birth to Pleasure, Voluptas. Psyche, the beautiful daughter of a king, is expelled from her father's house by command of an oracle and abandoned on a cliff near a precipice. Winds carry her down to a wonderful valley with a mysterious house, where she is tended by invisible servants; at night, a male visitor whom she is forbidden to see—Amor himself—makes her his wife. Happy life continues until Psyche, upon the instigation of her sisters, is overcome by curiosity to see her husband; by the light of her lamp she beholds Amor but scalds him with a drop of oil; he disappears. While searching for her lost husband, Psyche is caught by Venus, her mother-in-law, who maltreats the younger woman severely and puts her to various tests; finally Psyche is accepted among the gods and officially married to Amor, to whom she bears Voluptas.

In a brilliant and polemical study of 1977, Detlev Fehling proposed that all the known variants of this story are dependent upon the literary text of Apuleius, making an argument against romantic ideas about folk tradition that persists through the ages, untinged by literature. The romantic view has come under attack from other scholars, too.[47] It must be accepted that the literary tradition and the folk tradition have interacted, and folk tradition became containable only through writing. Nevertheless, Fehling's thesis leaves us with the problem of where Apuleius got his tale from; that he simply invented his story is hardly an answer. It is quite difficult to invent a tale; even a new creation will inevitably merge with the stream of tales heard before, and thus become a variant of what has already been around.

Parallels older than Apuleius are not lacking; if not fairy tales, then relevant myths. Closest to Amor and Psyche are some Orphic versions of the myth of Kore-Persephone.[48] Here is, to begin with, the enchanted house to which Kore the Maiden has been confined by her mother, Demeter, for protection. It stands at the fringe of the earth close to Okeanos; it has special servants, including the Sirens to make music, just as Psyche's house is filled with music. While Kore is working at the loom, Zeus, in the form of a snake, penetrates the house and impregnates his own daughter. After this Kore, enticed by her sisters Athena, Artemis, and Aphrodite, leaves the house to collect flowers in the meadow,

whence she is abducted by Hades to become queen of the netherworld. There she gives birth to chthonic Dionysus, son of Zeus.
The Orphic poems survive only in fragments which are difficult
to date but are most likely earlier than Apuleius (the extant po-
etic elaborations by Claudian and Nonnos were done much
later).

The stories within this category exhibit the same basic structure and clearly parallel motifs. *Kore* means "maiden"; the pattern has been called the Maiden's Tragedy.[49] It has been said to
provide a "model for the surface level of the narrative structure
of the female fairy tale."[50] The pattern clearly is different from
the Proppian sequence, the heroic quest. It is tempting to call it
typically feminine, in contrast to the male adventure sequence,
though there is nothing in nature to forbid female quests; indeed,
a quest is included in the second part of Psyche's adventures.

The Maiden's Tragedy can be analyzed by the methodology
used by Propp, to make up a sequence of functions or motifemes.
There are at least five of these in immutable order: (1) A sudden
break in a young girl's life, when some outside force makes her
leave home, separating her from childhood, parents, and family
life; (2) a period of seclusion, often elaborated as an idyllic
though abnormal stage of life, in a house or temple, or instead
of being enclosed in a house, she may be roaming through the
wilderness out of reach of normal human settlements; (3) the
catastrophe that upsets the idyll, normally caused by the intru-
sion of a male, in most cases a special male, a demon, hero, or
god who violates the girl and leaves her pregnant; this results
(4) in a period of tribulation, suffering, and punishments, wanderings or imprisonment, until (5) she is rescued and there is a happy
ending after all. The ending is directly or indirectly related to the
birth of children, most often a son; in Greek mythology the child
is usually an important tribal hero or eponym. In fact the tale
often serves as an introduction to the heroic quest of the son; in
this sense the pattern has been called "the birth of the hero."[51]

Some examples from Greek mythology are Danae, mother of
Perseus;[52] Auge, mother of Telephos;[53] Io, mother of Epaphos,

The Core of a Tale

the forefather of the Danaoi;[54] Kallisto, mother of Arkas, the eponym of the Arcadians;[55] Melanippe, mother of Boiotos and Aiolos; Antiope, mother of the Boeotian Dioscures, Amphion and Zethos.[56] All these stories have the same basic plot, structure, and happenings.

Although the pattern seems to be especially prominent in Greek mythology, it is not confined to it. It exists, for instance, in Maya civilization.[57] The earliest example is implicit in the legend of King Sargon, the first Great King of Mesopotamia: "Pregnant with me became my mother, a High Priestess; in secret she gave birth to me. She put me in a basket of rushes. . . ."[58] No more about the woman, nothing about the father. But the priestess giving birth in secret implies the period of seclusion and the breaking of the taboo, followed by the auspicious new beginning. The tragedy of the young woman who has to expose her son was repeated often.[59] The stories of Moses and of Romulus and Remus, born to the Vestal Virgin Rhea Silvia, are particularly close to the Sargon legend.[60] Did the legend spread from historical Sargon through more than 2000 years to characterize the new king?

The pattern reappears in well-known fairy tales. In "Rapunzel," for example, the girl is secluded in a tower, but the prince intrudes nonetheless. Discovery of the secret union results in separation and tribulation, but there must be a happy ending. The French author of this tale claimed she had freely invented it.[61] In reality, she must have drawn, consciously or subconsciously, upon the many tales of virgins secluded in a tower, and simply rearranged well-known motifemes. The pattern is even clearer in "Snow White," from the Grimm collection.[62] The heroine, expelled from home on account of her beauty and destined to die by command of her stepmother, arrives at the house of the dwarfs, where she leads an idyllic yet—according to German morality—virtuous and industrious life among these hard-working miners. The idyll ends when she is made to swallow a poisoned apple, which leaves her in a death-like sleep, lying in a coffin of glass. Finally, of course, the prince arrives to awaken her with his kiss. A more realistic and ribald version is told in a popular German song, attested since the sixteenth century.[63] This tells of a horseman who had an affair with a maiden and disappeared; when the girl became pregnant, her mother made her lie down on a bier as if dead; the preparations for the funeral brought the rider back to do decent mourning, but behold, the girl rose from the dead and marriage became unavoidable.

It is obvious that the sequence of the maiden tale closely follows the natural, biological life cycle of women in transition from childhood to adulthood. By nature, there are three dramatic events that work this change: menarche, intercourse, and pregnancy. The parallels in the tale pattern are seclusion, sexual encounter, and childbirth. This is no coincidence; the biological foundation of culture, however much it is verbalized in the tradition of the tale, could hardly be more obvious.

The connection is, of course, most evident at the sexual encounter that separates the two stages of transition: the bed of Amor and Psyche, or Zeus and Danae, Heracles and Auge. Greek mythology is explicit as to sex, while fairy tales as edited in the nineteenth century are opaque on that subject. "Rapunzel" is comparatively frank, but Snow White's swallowing the apple is more circumstantial. That pregnancy should appear as a period of tribulation is nothing but realistic. It is equally clear that the final salvation has to do with the birth of a child. There may be some overlapping of time at the level of the tale: in the Theban myth of Antiope, for example, the vexed mother is finally rescued by her grown-up sons. It is true that menarche is never explicitly mentioned in myth or fairy tale. Menstruation is unspeakable, *arrheton,* and women themselves avoid mentioning it, leaving males with only vague knowledge about it. But the fact that Auge is washing clothes when she is attacked by Heracles may be a relevant pointer.[64] Instead of talking about pubescence, the tales dwell on the provocative beauty of the maiden as cause of her expulsion, without explaining the necessity of it. Yet the biological reason underlying this motif is obvious. Sexual maturity breaks up the family structure, or its analogues in higher animals, the mother-child relation. The ties that bind the individual to the older generation must be dissolved for the sake of autonomy.[65] The tales bring in motifs of female jealousy or of patriarchal anguish, as the elders try to resist their own replacement, but the oracle's necessity must prevail.

These findings merely mark the beginning of the really intricate problems. How are we to account for the interaction of nature and culture in this type of tale? How does the biological program of individual development, a very old and natural program indeed, penetrate language and get transformed into the narrative chain of these traditional tales? The biological program functions without words and without much conscious reflection.

It is here that ritual comes in. Worldwide, rituals are performed to mark and to act out the natural stages of female development. Although they take different cultural forms,[66] they generally bear close resemblance to the tale pattern which has been in focus here. Female puberty initiation has become a model case of the close connection of myth and ritual, ever since Jane Harrison's book of 1890, *Mythology and Monuments of Ancient Athens*.[67] The story in Apuleius is, after all, about the meeting of soul and sexual love; *kore* just means "maiden." The Isis mysteries and the great painting in the Villa of Mysteries at Pompeii have also been drawn into the context of initiation toward marriage.[68] The pattern of tales as well as rituals conforms to the famous structure of rites of passage as elaborated by van Gennep:[69] separation, liminal period on the periphery, and reintegration; at the same time, the tale pattern closely follows nature. Female initiation rituals may start from the first menstruation— which often means separation or seclusion—and go on to the birth of the first son, which marks the definite status acquired.[70] Initiation rituals follow biology, and the narrative structure of the female fairy tale keeps to the same tracks.

Yet some hiatus remains. Initiation rituals are anything but natural. It is a mistake to make the assumption that nature transforms itself into ritual, and ritual in turn is followed by language. Rituals are complicated, ambivalent, and not seldom opaque even to those who practice them. We cannot project into some vague prehistoric period the ideal of a natural yet well-ordered life, with wise Zarastros leading every Tamino and Pamina toward the desired end. Elaborate initiation rituals are not natural, ubiquitous, or continuous. Far from being simple transpositions from nature into culture, they rather contradict nature in certain cases.[71] It makes more sense to see them as cultural attempts to make the "facts of life" manageable and predictable; to perform an act of artificial social creation, as if to veil biology. In performing such rituals people act as if the adolescent, male or female, could not simply grow adult on his or her own, but must be made a man or woman by society. Ritual activity follows the clues of nature, but works on them with the force of conscious tradition elaborated through unnatural, cultural choice; with exaggeration, repetitiveness, and other complications. Because the force of cultural tradition is so strong, the pattern here is less universal than the uniformity that had been found regarding the quest.

Ancient Athens had two main religious institutions connected with girls' initiations: the service of *arrhephoroi* for Athena at the Akropolis,[72] and the cult of Artemis at Brauron by girls called "bears," *arkteia*.[73] At first glance these seem to correspond to the two possibilities of seclusion during initiation, in the house within the sanctuary, and at the periphery, at the seashore. In the case of the *arrhephoroi*, while we do find a very close parallelism of myth and ritual, the connection with initiation is questionable. With the *arkteia* we come as close as possible to female puberty initiation, but we have difficulties finding the expected myth; instead of it we are confronted with different mythical patterns that seek explanation in terms of divine wrath and expiatory sacrifice.[74] Even the myth of Iphigeneia is connected to Brauron.[75]

About myths, it is striking that the same myth can refer either to initiation or to sacrifice, to natural maturing as well as to the most unnatural violence.[76] In the Bible Jephtha, the Judge of Israel, is forced to sacrifice his daughter because of a vow made before his victory in war.[77] The daughter willingly complies, but asks as a favor to be allowed to wander about in the mountains with her girlfriends before her death, weeping for her never-to-be-lost virginity; and this, says the Bible, has become a custom in Israel. Every year, for four days, girls go to the mountains to dance and to sing of the daughter of Jephtha, who never knew a man. The custom clearly has initiatory motifs and functions. The girls leave their families and spend some time *en marge* in a strange and possibly idyllic environment, playing the tambourines, dancing, and mourning. The ritual is reflected in a tale about death by sacrifice. Thus the mythical heroine is presented in stark contrast to what normal girls will experience. For another reversal, we may point to the girls' ritual lament at Troizen as described by Euripides in his *Hippolytos*. They mourn and shear a lock of hair for Hippolytos, the beautiful youth who died by the wrath of Aphrodite without ever knowing a woman.[78] Death, sexuality, and birth are close to each other in the world of nature; sacrificial ritual and myth make of death a barrier, as if to block that transition.

Gloomy associations with death and sacrifice abound in other variants of the maiden's tragedy. What happens to Kore-Persephone is, by common understanding, death. A strange yet characteristic ambivalence surrounds the optimistic, natural sequence leading to marriage and birth, and an unnatural variant that leads to sacrifice. Iphigeneia, of "powerful birth" in her name but sacrificed as a virgin to the virgin goddess, appears as the epitome of this ambivalence. And the death of the virgin is not merely symbolic. The gloomy garments offered to Artemis at Brauron are relics of young women who had in fact died. At Rome, the vestal virgins are selected by the *pontifex maximus* to live a secluded life for thirty years, tending the perpetual fire at the hearth of the Vesta temple; if the fire gets extinguished by accident, they are flogged; if any of them is found to have intercourse with a male, she is buried alive.[79] This is uncannily close to the sequence of seclusion, sexual crisis, and punishment. It is not impossible to derive even this peculiar Roman institution from original initiation rituals.[80]

Even in the less somber initiation myths we should be alert to unnatural social factors and motifs. The tribulations typically following the sexual encounter usually come from real families, a vindictive father, a stepmother, a mother-in-law; these are tensions characteristic of the family in many civilizations. The search for the lost husband, on the other hand, in nineteenth-century versions of *Amor and Psyche* or the "animal bridegroom," appears to be more of a bourgeois concern.

The prominence of the pattern in Greek mythology, in tales mainly reshaped and retold by men, may give rise to further suspicions. The prominence of the sexual encounter may be especially gratifying to males, and the virgin's seclusion all the more inviting for those who dare to break the taboo, with Zeus leading the ranks. Seclusion has consigned the virgin to passivity; as a consequence, the sexual act approaches rape.[81] Another, hidden aspect might be the masking of a closely parallel homosexual pattern for boys. We get the abduction, the homosexual idyll, and the return to normal male society for struggle and combat, until the married status may be attained by the fully adult. A foremost example is the story of Pelops as told by Pindar—Pelops is abducted by Poseidon and brought back later to win the horse race for Hippodameia.[82] We know how closely this corresponds to ritualized homosexuality in Crete.[83] Kaineus, raped as a girl by Poseidon and then transformed into an unbeatable warrior, is an earlier attested myth on similar lines.[84] This gives a special, cultural tinge to the more basic pattern. If stories of the maiden type were regularly told by Greek males, they may well have reflected their own development, recast through proximity and distance into things that happen to females.

Although the parallelism of tale structure and biological ontogenesis is undeniable, and ritual interacts with both, the form of transition envisaged for the quest type is not applicable in this case. The program for "getting" could be expressed in imperatives which enter the level of communication at a primitive stage

The Core of a Tale

(remember the chimpanzee). The tale was seen to develop in protolanguage from an established basis. The ensuing pattern, apart from its shamanistic adaptation, was apt to develop into the typical male initiation myth whereby the hero has to perform the quest before taking up full social responsibility. The initiatory elements in the stories of Perseus, of the Argonauts, of Heracles, and of Odysseus need hardly be stressed. The Perseus myth was in fact connected with an Argive initiation ritual.[85] Vladimir Propp himself at a later point tried to trace back his morphology of tales to the initiation pattern.[86]

The maiden's tragedy seems to be the female counterpart, but it is not fully equivalent: imperatives will not make sense in this case. The underlying biological program is more primitive, more remote from consciousness. This makes the distance between nature and tale much greater than with the straightforward adventure series. The tale does not spring directly from such origins. The "female fairy tale" is a cultural creation that purports to retrace the steps of nature with the consciousness inherent in a tale.

Who is telling these tales? If we choose Apuleius as a guide once more, we find an old woman retelling the story of Amor and Psyche to a young girl, in a situation of suspense, in the robbers' house; the tale is to console her, and to prepare her for what to expect. "Old wives' tales" became proverbial already in antiquity;[87] they are by no means negligible tradition-bearers in shaping a child's mental world. Women know about the sequence of menstruation, intercourse, and birth, they can instruct the young, both in a serious and in a playful way. This provides a verbalized sort of script to accompany natural change, handed down in oral tradition, to facilitate the understanding of memorable developments while hiding part of them. This produced the narrative structure of the female fairy tale. No doubt it could be retold by males. The tales could even help bridge the gap between the sexes and promote understanding by shared imagination, as both sexes share the common basis of life.

☯

Creation of the Sacred

An epilogue is due. For many decades, the modern trend in literature has been to get rid of the tale, and the same trend dominates the more sophisticated movies. Comics keep traditional elements, but explode them in a continuous fireworks of immediate effects. Old-fashioned fairy tales recede, though they may still be used in psychiatric institutions for their therapeutic value. There is no use deploring this development in a changing world, which makes us live with highly sophisticated gadgets in lonely compartments of individual existence. The slogan "stop making sense" is a fitting companion to the demise of the tale.

4

⚭

Hierarchy

The Awareness of Rank

Religion, said the German theologian Friedrich Schleiermacher at the beginning of the nineteenth century, is "the feeling of sheer dependence on God."[1] One term of this famous and influential definition was inspired by Goethe, whose Faust declared that in religion "feeling is everything." It is not the Romantic aspect of feeling, however, that will be in focus here, but the acknowledgment of "sheer dependence," the acceptance of inferior rank vis-à-vis a flow of power emanating from the superior. This contradicts the ideal of independence that has been cherished for an equally long time in philosophical, humanistic, or heroic morality, the construct of the autonomous and self-responsible personality. "Autonomy" had been restated in Kantian philosophy as the precondition of moral decisions; the French Revolution of 1789 put *liberté* ahead of *égalité* and *fraternité*. Schleiermacher, addressing "the cultural despisers" of religion, was reacting to this school of thought.[2] His definition proved to be widely acceptable to theologians, the practicing clergy, and the general educated public. People could share the feeling of religious dependence and thus allow religion to occupy a place of honor in their mental world without subscribing to confessional dogmatism or taking sides in theological controversies.

Yet Schleiermacher's definition, challenging the rational eighteenth-century views, itself builds on a much older foundation. Religion is generally accepted as a system of rank, implying dependence, subordination and submission to unseen superiors. The awareness of rank and dependence in religion is particularly clear in all the ancient religions. God means power, rule, and honors due. Already in Sumerian a god may be invoked as "my king." In Akkadian, a common word for "lord" is *belu;* in particular this is the title of Marduk, the most important god of Babylon; its West Semitic equivalent is *baal,* the title of local gods in Syria and Palestine. A god may also be called Lord of Lords and King of Kings, just as the monarch himself.[3] In Hebrew, Jahweh is king, of course;[4] his name, related to the root of the word "life," was replaced by *adon,* translated as *kyrios* into Greek, which became *dominus* in Latin, Lord in English, *der Herr* in German. "My Lord and my God": this is the proclamation of Thomas converted from disbelief to belief.[5] An Indoeuropean word for a powerful lord, *potis,* appears in the name of Mycenaean-Greek Poseidon[6] and in the title of Mycenaean and later goddesses, *potnia.*[7] The title of the Mycenaean king was *wanax,* which remained the epithet of gods long after Mycenaean power crumbled. In addition to Zeus anax, some goddesses of ancient pedigree used the title *wanassa* as a proper name, for instance, Aphrodite at Paphos and Artemis at Perge.[8] The later Greek words for lord and ruler made their way into religious contexts as well—*despotes* and *despoina, basileus,* even *tyrannos.*[9] It is power that defines the gods; they are the "stronger ones," *kreittones.* Zeus is not only father—an Indoeuropean concept—but has the greatest *kratos,* strength.[10] The idea of an almighty god, *pankrates,* emerges already in Aeschylus, though current polytheism envisaged a family of gods rather than absolute monarchy.[11] Archaic society is based on honor, and "gods too rejoice when they are honored by men."[12]

It is surprising that the expressions of power and lordship are much less obtrusive in the language of Roman religion. *Dominus* got its prominence only with Christianity, translated from *kyrios.* Was it the ban on the word *rex* that became a linguistic barrier, or was it the system of clearly defined sectors of *potestas—praetor, consul, dictator*—that forbade metaphor?[13] The important gods are called *pater*. Still, Iuno *regina* was worshiped at the Aventine Hill, introduced from Veii, and Jupiter *imperator* at Praeneste,[14] while Mithraists were allowed to call Mithras *rex*.[15] From Achaemenid Persia, even the word *satrapes,* "guardian of the king's power," spread as designation of a god.[16]

Traditional forms of domination nevertheless always include some mutual obligation. The Lord, honored by submission, grants protection and ensures security.[17] This is naturally implied if the god is invoked as father.[18] It is no less characteristic of the concept of Islam, a word that means "surrender to the will of god."[19] A variation on the notion of the superior who grants protection is shepherd or pastor, a metaphor widely used for both kings and gods.[20] Hence dependence can be accepted with relief and gratitude. Dominance also limits fighting among inferiors; according to Georg Simmel, the "elimination of antagonism" is one characteristic of religion.[21] Dominance makes possible forms of solidarity not easily encountered elsewhere, at the cost of accepting dependence on what is beyond our reach.

It is tempting to associate the ideology of rule and dependence in religion with the evolution of the first high cultures that installed kingship as the central social organization.[22] But clearly it is much more widespread. Moderns will be more prone to translate dependence and submission into psychological terms, in the wake of Sigmund Freud.[23] According to one school, god or gods represent the father figure, as the child's experience of helpless dependence on the powerful father has been interiorized in the acceptance of an almighty god; conversely, feminists introduce or reintroduce a great goddess instead, recalling the child's even more intimate dependence upon the mother. Still, if we accept an evolutionary view of anthropology, as Freud himself did, it is necessary to broaden the perspective and to account for the role of authority in both society and the structure of the psyche by going back to earlier stages in the evolution of life.

A highly developed awareness of authority within a complex

system of rank is well established in all primate societies.[24] While the intellectual capacities of monkeys and apes have scored higher than expected in experiments, it seems that most of these capacities go into the incessant social games concerning inferiority and superiority that are played within the group. In the "attention structure" within primate groups, "the attention of subordinates is always on those above them in the hierarchy."[25] Frans de Waal's *Chimpanzee Politics*, based on long periods of observation in the zoo of Amsterdam, contains startling revelations.[26] The chimps not only know each other personally, not only realize who is superior and who is inferior, but they use long-term strategies of exchanging social favors and forming alliances to get some advantage or promotion of status in the end, or even to overturn the top individual.

Note that high rank is immediately and generally visualized by humans in a vertical dimension, rather than as a horizontal sequence or some centripetal arrangement. There is no logic to this; what dominates the imagination is the reminiscence of the prehuman habitat. Gerhard Baudy has made reference to the trees in which many primates live, trees that provide both food and safety, escape from predators, and also the place to play the games of rank from branch to branch.[27] It is from the tree that the vertical image derives. If the most successful primates are for the most part found moving bipedally along asphalt streets today, this does not mean that humans have renounced those games of lower or higher rank while continuing to "exalt" the "higher" ideals. In religious veneration the image of the tree still looms large; it grows to cosmic dimensions in myths about the "world tree."[28] But it can be outdone by the mountain which no doubt is more exalted,[29] and the mountain in turn is superseded by heaven;[30] at all events, gods are high, preferably the highest.[31] The awareness and feelings of inferiority and superiority on the vertical axis are part of our biological inheritance.

"Whatever is powerful, is taken for a god."[32] Dominance and submission in the religious sphere require that the "attention structure" be redirected toward a nonobvious but final and absolute orientation.[33] It is characteristic of a mental world, encoded in language, that it becomes independent from time and place. In the case of primates the social system normally remains linked to physical proximity and is visible in space: those who belong together keep together, in families and in groups. For humans, personal ties and relations of rank can persist without togetherness for a long time and across remarkable distances. Order becomes stabilized without continuous interaction; not only do we acknowledge "mine" and "yours," but also the property and interests of a third person not present at the moment. Such stability finds its ultimate guarantee in the unseen authority of the highest power. We can describe it as the extreme consequence of inherited tendencies.[34] Although appeals in the name of the highest power may be challenged again and again, they do not fail to find their response; they fall into place within the old landscape.

Whether enthusiastically accepted by *homines religiosi* or criticized by the advocates of emancipation, dependence is a form of "making sense." It is a truism that we are unavoidably dependent upon a variety of circumstances both known and unknown, whether personal, political, economic, or environmental. Germs and radiation and cancer cells possibly developing in our bodies are but instances of the innumerable factors that cause concern and are quite impossible to control. Religion makes all this secondary by turning the attention structure toward one basic authority, thereby achieving a most effective "reduction of complexity" and creating sense out of chaos.[35] A sane world is structured by authority which determines what is high and low. Since Sumerian times gods, men, animals, and plants have been neatly arranged in superimposed registers, descending from top to bottom.[36] An early Byzantine writer put it this way: "In the universe we find beings who rule exclusively, i.e. the divine; others who both rule and are ruled, i.e. the humans, ruled by the divine but ruling the animals; and others who are ruled exclusively, i.e. the animals, bereft of reason."[37] Man's position is described and legitimized in the sequence of ruling functions, defined by higher and lower rank.

Hierarchy is a term introduced by the most influential work of Christian Neoplatonism, Pseudo-Dionysius Areopagita, in the fifth century A.D. The philosopher examines New Testament texts that speak of the stages of powers surrounding god—"thrones, lordships, leaderships, powers"—and develops them into a consistent system.[38] Neoplatonism sees the totality of beings dominated by a great golden chain of authority proceeding from a single principle, the One.[39] It has often been remarked that Neoplatonic-Christian *hierarchia* is represented in architecture by the building that has set the model for Greek Orthodox church building and later even for the Moslem mosque: the cupola of Hagia Sophia at Constantinople-Istanbul.

Rituals of Submission

If, according to Schleiermacher, religion occupies the realm of feeling, it is evident that practical religion is less introverted than that, and more demonstrative. Such feelings as exist are acted out, reinforced, and even generated anew through common action. In other words, dependence and submission in religion appear, first of all, in ritual. Encountering the divine, "we shape ourselves to all kinds of representation of modesty."[40] Rituals of submission, strikingly prominent in religious activities, are or were common forms of behavior in other contexts and are not specifically religious in themselves.[41] Hence they are widely understood. Not confined to one particular civilization, these rituals are found around the globe, and several of them are demonstrably prehuman. A comparative survey of ritual submission in primates, in human secular interactions, and in religious practice reflects the basic unity of the world we live in.

The obvious aim and function of demonstrative submission, especially in prehuman societies, is to avoid or to stop aggression and the ensuing pain, damage, or even destruction. The simplest means to impose one's will and to make threats is merely to be big—remember nature's trick of hair-raising.[42] In order to stop aggression, by contrast, one has to be small and humble, *humilis,* which originally meant "close to the soil." To create this impression, one has to bow, to kneel down, to cower to the ground, to crawl—in short, not to puff oneself up.[43] Humans have invented hats and varieties of clothing to enhance their contours; submission entails taking off these accessories. It is of special importance to avoid staring: the staring eye is an evil eye and sets off an inherited program of alarm.[44] The signals of smallness applied to reduce aggression are reinforced by childlike behavior; animals are normally programmed not to attack their own children. Human adults commonly revert to weeping, but it is also possible to try smiling. Another means to ward off aggression is to make and keep personal contact: to touch the stronger one if he allows it, to stroke his chin without being bitten, to extend at least an open hand, all of which are signs of dependence.[45]

We commonly understand these gestures and forms of behavior. Most of them may be observed among chimpanzees and gorillas. While they do not weep, they express themselves in a range of moans. In the movie *Gorillas in the Mist,* which deals with the work of Dian Fossey among gorillas in central Africa, the way to avoid damage by a charging silverback was to cower to the ground, touching it with one's head, and above all to avoid staring. Assyrian reliefs show envoys to the king of Assyria assuming a strikingly similar position; the Akkadian expression was "to wipe one's nose" on the ground.[46] In the wake of Assyrians and Babylonians the Persian king insisted that visitors performed *proskynesis,* touching the ground with their forehead.[47] Later, sultans did not hesitate to follow suit. European monarchs, somewhat more civilized, still required everyone to bend his knee to do homage. The minimum act of submission is to bow one's head while taking off one's hat, which is still widely used and taken for granted as a gesture of politeness.

More dramatic and more formal were the rules of surrender in warfare. The defeated, or even their envoys, would approach their victorious adversaries in ragged clothes or half naked, bent down, with their hair undone; they would weep and throw themselves at the feet of the victors. Ancient historians, including Caesar, indulge in scenes of this kind.[48] Homer describes the special practice of the *hiketes,* a warrior pleading for his life even on the battlefield. As the word indicates—it means "he who reaches"—the success of the plea depended on coming so close to the adversary that he could be touched. Even the leaders of the enemies "in the turmoil of battle . . . grasped my hands, for the sake of their lives," Assurbanipal recounts. Odysseus, in the midst of battle, "took the helmet from his head, the shield from his shoulders, threw the spear from his hands, and . . . kissed the knees of the enemy king."[49] In a graphic scene from the *Iliad,* young Lycaon runs to touch the knees of Achilles, while Achilles' spear, which had already been thrown, hits the ground behind his back. Touching the knees sends a message to the powerful one to relax and sit down, instead of remaining ready to attack.[50] In another gesture Priam, pleading for the release of Hector's corpse, "extended his hands toward the mouth" of Achilles in supplication; he also kissed Achilles' hands.[51] Kissing hands has remained a sign of deferent greeting in parts of Europe, especially those within reach of the imperial court of Vienna, and also within the Catholic Church; it combines bending down with making contact. More modern styles of democratic behavior have made most of these forms disappear from our experience. There may still be some families left in which wife and children fall to their knees before a dominant father. But archaic ways are preserved or resuscitated in extreme situations. A modern press photograph in *Time* magazine, taken at the time of the war between India and Pakistan, still shows the gesture of touching the superior's knee in exactly the way we see it in ancient illustrations and texts.[52]

It almost goes without saying that all these forms of submissive ritual also appear in religious contexts. The most general act of veneration clearly is to bend, to bow. "To bend down" is the term for veneration of gods in Hebrew as in Akkadian.[53] Abraham "throws himself down on his face" in the presence of Jahweh.[54] Moslems touch the ground with their foreheads when praying to Allah. The vocabulary used in Greek is the same in both religious and civil use, "to grasp the knees," "to place a kiss," "to reach" *(gounazesthai, proskynein, hiketeuein).* There has been some controversy about whether kneeling down for prayer was common in Greece; it did occur at least in certain cases.[55] In extreme anguish some worshipers will prostrate themselves at the image or altar.[56] There is no ambiguity about Latin *supplex, supplicatio,* bending one's knees; even an Assyrian king knelt down for prayer.[57] Christianity was even more emphatic about bending one's knees before god—Eusebius calls this "our common form of worship"—at least until Protestants decided to oppose Catholic ritual.[58] The universality of behavior does not preclude the cultivation of special forms to distinguish individual groups or denominations.[59]

Further tokens of humiliation may accompany the encounter with god or gods. In antiquity, loose hair, outstretched hands, and free-flowing tears were expected of people taking part in processions to entreat the gods for mercy in moments of crisis. Tears are also commonly mentioned in Hebrew psalms and later in Christian forms of prayer and repentance; they already mark Sumerian and Akkadian prayer.[60] To extend the arms with the palms up is the usual posture for prayer in oriental and Hebrew as in Greek and Roman worship;[61] Christian custom, however, turned against such open pleading and directed that prayer be performed with folded hands.[62] Note that bowing one's head also prevents one from staring. In the model scene of prayer in the New Testament, the publican does "not raise his eyes toward heaven"; he "beats his chest" while saying "have mercy on me, the sinner."[63] *Propitius sis mihi peccatori* has become a liturgical formula in Christian service, and it follows much older rules. When Inanna returns from the netherworld with an infernal retinue, all those who throw themselves at the feet of the goddess or sit humbly in the dust are spared; but Dumuzi, still "sitting on the high seat," is destroyed.[64] To be humble before the gods is a lesson taught long before Christianity.[65]

Students of religion have attempted to make a clear distinction between veneration and submission. Yet they may be trying to differentiate two things that are at least quite close to each other. Most ancient religions did not hesitate to postulate the fear of gods. In Akkadian fear or even terror, *puluhtu,* is the basic concept associated with gods; in Solomon's Proverbs, "the fear of god is the beginning of wisdom"; for Aeschylus, the fear of Zeus is the "highest fear."[66]

Humiliation can take drastic forms. Some rituals anticipate a dreaded outcome and counter it by conscious and controlled action: a person that is pursued by demons will kill a substitute victim.[67] In a similar way, in rituals of submission certain forms of debasement may be executed before they are requested. Thus in fear of the evil eye, of jealousy of the gods and ensuing disaster, Greeks would spit on their own garments; this is "to honor Adrasteia," the goddess who has "inescapable" in her name.[68] By this token of defilement the penitent hopes to escape the inescapable. This category encompasses acts like rending one's clothes, making oneself filthy, even wallowing in the mud. "The Syrians, if they have eaten fish in failure of self-control, swell up at their feet and their stomach. Then they take a sackcloth and sit down in the street, in the dirt, and pacify the goddess by humbling themselves so much."[69] "In the mud hole your servant lies," intones a Babylonian penitentiary psalm.[70] A more violent form of self-abasement is self-wounding, which occurs in various ancient cults and has also been observed in other societies.[71] Evidence for self-flagellation has recently turned up in a Cretan sanctuary at Kato Symi.[72] Processions of flagellants were a feature of the late medieval epoch in Europe, appealing to the mercy of God amidst the spreading pestilence. In some places such rituals of penitence persist to the present day. The human capacity for reorienting or even abusing such forms of ritual is striking: the *galli* and similar *fanatici,* castrated priests of Semitic and Anatolian goddesses, of Dea Syria, Mater Magna, or Bellona, made a public show of self-wounding and self-flagellation to elicit gifts from the onlookers. They claimed they were in the grip of divine

Hierarchy

possession when they performed their superhuman sacrifices.[73] In cases like this, humiliation is an instrument of selection.

Humiliation could take another form, that of sexual submission, which means that men accept female roles. This seems to apply to the *fanatici* just mentioned, eunuchs who presented themselves for homosexual encounters.[74] Requirements of celibacy and transvestism exist in other contexts: Heracles' priest at Kos was dressed as a woman, and one myth held that Heracles had once fled and hidden in woman's clothes, an extreme reversal of his normal role.[75] The Eleusinian hierophant had to undergo a kind of chemical castration by drinking hemlock.[76] In early Sumerian ritual priests sometimes appear naked—statuettes of such priests survive—in contrast to the Jewish and Christian traditions, which do not allow priests to show the slightest indication of nakedness or sex.[77] We must acknowledge the highly ambivalent status of sex in all human societies, with all sorts of disclaimers, secrecy, and repression, and the concomitant possibility of outrageous reversals.[78] The reaction to the *galli* could be both awe and contempt; normal religion claimed solemnity. Conversely, religious practice could seek to ensure continuous good relations with a male god by offering him a concubine or even a legitimate, permanent wife. This was ceremoniously done for Amun in Egyptian Thebes and in the Bronze Age in Syria, as a recently discovered text has shown in great detail.[79] An offering like this attempts to replace submission by familiarity.

The Strategy of Praise

The other pole in a construct of humiliation is the exaltation of the divine. This is most commonly expressed in iconography, which, in turn, reflects ritual. Once again there are striking parallels in the codes of representation for rulers and for gods. Divine statues are raised up and carried in procession, but at Persepolis it is the king's throne that is lifted up and carried by his people.[80] The goddess or god, like the king, has an elevated throne with a footstool: Isaiah saw "the Lord sitting on a high, sublime throne."[81] A wall painting from Minoan Thera depicts the seat of the goddess on top of a stepped pedestal.[82] Bronze Age gods dwell on mountaintops, and the final exaltation is heaven.

The Great Goddess in the Near East and in archaic Greece is distinguished by a tall headpiece called *polos*.[83] Other gods wear crowns to increase their height, or a pyramid of horns as in Mesopotamia. Temples are developed into towers, a striking feature of sacred architecture in Mesopotamia as in Mesoamerica. Worship means exalting the superiors to whom we bend in veneration; and the higher they are raised the less we are forced to bow down ourselves.

This has given rise to an ingenious language game. It achieves something that would be impossible in ritual action, that is, to do the work of exaltation without toil and even to unite submission with exaltation. It is the invention of praise.

Praise may have a special basis in preverbal behavior, what we call cheers, which means identifying with one side in a combat and encouraging the champion by vocal display. Greeks used the ritual cry *ieie paian* in the cult of Apollo in that sense;[84] and while few Christians understand what *halleluja* and *hosanna* mean, it makes powerful music.[85] Rhetorically developed forms of verbalized praise are frequent in many civilizations. Since the earliest times it must have been a challenge for noble, stylized poetry to give praise to both rulers and gods. In a way the work of the poet is a double trick. The performer expressly acknowledges the difference of rank, looking up from the depths to the splendor at the heights, but by force of his verbal competence he not only rises to a superior level in imagination but succeeds in reversing the attention structure: it is the superior who is made to pay heed to the inferior's song or speech of praise. Praise is the recognized form of making noise in the presence of superiors; in a well-structured form, it tends to become music. Praise ascends to the heights like incense. Thus the tension between high and low is both stressed and relaxed, as the lower one establishes his place within a system he accepts emphatically. Praise is rarely informative but rather tautological—*laudamus te, benedicimus te, adoramus te, glorificamus te . . . propter magnam gloriam tuam*—but it lifts the heart in a resounding experience of community. Note the vertical dimension of *gloria in excelsis* where glorification means exaltation.[86] Exaltation even transcends logic: "Zeus is the universe—and what is still higher than this."[87]

This is not the place to enter into a detailed analysis of the genre of hymns, which has been a common and recognized form of religious poetry in the Near East and the Mediterranean from antiquity into the present.[88] The expected parallels in metaphors, whether praising the ruler or praising a god, especially in the older forms, appear in Sumerian and Egyptian texts. A visible model for praising the one on high is the sun, rising in splendor all over the earth; hence the sun is a favorite metaphor of praise in different languages.[89] Terror, however, remains mixed with exaltation. The higher being is also able to kill or to grant life. Incessant praise will move him to exercise his benevolent powers and discourage his hostility. May he be "good-humored," *hilaos,* as Greek hymns put it.

Praising the king will bring direct emoluments to artful performers; sanctuaries likewise invite and remunerate hymnic praise. Apollo of Klaros, through his oracle, routinely commanded delegations of singers, *hymnodoi,* to come to his site and to perform there.[90] In this way the god organized his own festival. Praise serves to stabilize the system of rank and power: the king is declared and, in a way, made to guarantee safety and good life, while the god upholds the world. Religion operates to stabilize the accepted order, praising its highest starting point.

Music is the most frequent accompaniment to praise. Song is the musical form that combines uncommon sound with distinct clarity, and with a resonance that casts a spell upon the listeners. The spiritual world they share finds perhaps its most forceful expression in music, and the repetition in song provides further reinforcement of this commonality. Songs of praise are thus one of the most powerful means of expression, of attraction, and of propaganda in many forms of religion.

The world of the gods also admits hierarchies: "The gods of heaven bow to you, the gods of the Earth bow to you, whatever you say, the gods fall down before you," is a climax of praise for an exalted Hittite god.[91] Even the praise of monotheistic Jahweh is not destitute of similar effects, as heavens tell the glory of the eternal God.[92] The hierarchic structure of praise replicates itself and embraces all the more forcefully the human worshipers far below, allowing them to feel secure in their own position through voicing their hymns of praise.

Two-Tiered Power

To take submission as the main characteristic of religion is definitely one-sided. The other side, often disclaimed or deplored in the Christian tradition but still permanent and obtrusive even there, is the rise to power and the exercise of power in the name of religion and through religion.

In the ancient world the alliance of religion and power is frankly proclaimed. Sargon II, the Assyrian king, boasts how he united people of diverse languages in his capital and put Assyrian overseers above them, "to teach them how to fear god and the king."[93] As a consequence, enlightened skeptics in antiquity held that religion had been invented for the interest of those who hold power, of the rulers and the state. Polybius found that religion—or rather, superstition *(deisidaimonia)*—"held together" the Roman republic; religious ritual, he said, had been elaborated into a kind of theater that dominated private as well as public life.[94] He suggests that this was done "for the multitude . . . full of unlawful desires, irrational anger and violent rage," which must be kept in order "by nonobvious fears." Aristotle makes similar remarks.[95] That thesis can be traced back at least to the sophists in the fifth century B.C., and evidently there was much in reality to support it.

Long before the rise of Mediterranean city states, oriental despots had been wont to claim the special protection of their respective gods. The Pharaoh was a son of god; everywhere it was the gods who granted victory, and indeed the gods themselves were believed to hold power as a consequence of their own mythical victories. Myths told how a god had violently overcome his adversary—a dragon or Tiamat the Sea in Mesopotamia or Typhon the impersonation of drought in Egypt—and thus established order in the cosmos. Whenever a ruler subdued his enemies by force and cruelty, he was repeating what the gods had done.[96]

Power was handed down by the god, directly if symbolically. The relief on the famous Hammurapi stele shows the Sun God Shamash handing the royal insignia to Hammurapi, and the introduction to Hammurapi's *Laws* proclaims that when the supreme gods Anu and Enlil determined the supremacy of Marduk and his city Babylon, they also "named me to promote the welfare of the people, me, Hammurapi, the devout, god-fearing prince, to cause justice to prevail in the land, to destroy the wicked and the evil . . . and to light up the land" (I: 1–41).[97] We sympathize with the king's ideals of justice that lights up the land, but putting them into effect nevertheless presupposes that power must be used "to destroy the wicked and the evil." Who decides whom to destroy? A direct line connects Hammurapi to Darius, king of Persia, who says in his great proclamation preserved at Behistun: "According to the will of Ahuramazda I am king; Ahuramazda presented the kingship to me."[98] Nor did Darius hesitate to destroy the false and the wicked and the adherents of "falsehood," *drug*. Moderns even suspect him of playing the foulest of tricks: killing the legitimate king, Bardiya-Smerdis, and branding him as an impostor and *magos*. His god was with him. That iconographical tradition continued, displayed in the Sassanian reliefs with Ahuramazda investing the kings.[99]

The ancient Greeks had no "great king, king of kings, king of the lands." But even on a more modest scale a "sceptre-bearing king" would claim to have received his power and authority from Zeus; his *kydos* as Homer puts it. A king is simply first among peers.[100] The tyrant Pisistratus came closest to the Oriental model, claiming that the goddess Athena in person installed his rule at Athens. Whether the masquerade described by Herodotus (of a girl dressed up as Athena leading Pisistratus back to Athens) is historical in this form will remain controversial. But some form of Pisistratean propaganda about Athena's special protection of the tyrant must have been its source, although democratic and rational citizens found the relationship less than convincing.[101] Alexander the Great fell back on the Egyptian model; he claimed to have been sired by a god, Zeus himself or rather Zeus Ammon; the Diadochs were hence obliged to follow his lead in various ways.[102] Later, when the Roman world turned Christian, the Christian god was claimed to be the source of victory and power; hence the ruler became installed "by the grace of god," *dei gratia*. This formula remained attached to the title of every decent monarch in Europe.[103] The mosaic at Palermo, which has Christ presenting the crown of Sicily to King Roger, is equivalent to the message of the Hammurapi stele, even without a direct iconographic line of tradition.[104] "As all people which are under Roman rule do military service to you, emperors and principals of the world, you yourself do service to the all-mighty God and to the sacred Faith," St. Ambrose wrote to Emperor Valentinian.[105] Neither Hammurapi nor Darius, nor a Sassanid king nor Constantine relied on prayer alone to establish their kingships; but it was from religion, from the authority and power of the god that they sought legitimization. The gods stand behind those who exercise worldly power; conversely, the monarch is "the head, immersed in prayer."[106]

Submission and sovereignty inhabit the same hierarchic structure. Dependence on unseen powers mirrors the real power structure, but it is taken to be its model and to provide its legitimization. It is a two-tiered sovereignty that stabilizes itself through this structure; god is to ruler as ruler is to subjects.[107] This lends theoretical support to the ruler, who ceases to be alone at the top of the pyramid as a target of potential aggression. In reality, while power games are played out in a continuous dialectic of aggression and anxiety, in the stabilized power structures of the human mental world this duality has become neatly dissociated, producing fear of god or gods along with constant readiness to attack and destroy lower humans, buffered by the good conscience provided by piety.

Sumerian King Gudea built a house, a temple for "his king," the god; in this way the actual king exalted the unseen to the status of superking.[108] When Jahweh, through his prophet, promises that King David's throne shall be set up to last forever, King David, offering his thanks, emphatically proclaims himself the "slave" of his Lord—which does not alter but rather validates the fact that he and his offspring will continue to be kings over all the others.[109] A Hebrew psalm is repeatedly quoted in the New Testament: "Jahweh spoke to my lord: Sit down at my right hand, until I set your enemies a footstool for your feet."[110] As "my lord" is exalted by Jahweh, than whom none is higher, even he who is singing this praise will find himself in an exalted position.

The double tier of power may be acted out through dramatic reversals. At the New Year festival in Babylon, the king is led to the Temple of Marduk. The priest takes away the king's scepter, circlet, and sword and places them "before the god"; then he strikes the king's cheek, accompanies him to the presence of the god, drags him by the ears, and makes him bow down to the ground. The king must say "I did not sin." Then the priest consoles him: "Have no fear . . . the god will exalt your kingship . . . he will destroy your enemy, fell your adversary." The king regains his insignia, but is struck on the cheek once more. If tears flow, the god is friendly; if no tears appear, the god is angry, and "the enemy will rise up and bring about his downfall."[111] The signals of submission, of bowing to the ground, receiving slaps, and shedding tears are essential means to win the favor of the superior, the god of Babylon, for the king of Babylon; the god's favor means destruction of the enemy, for within this world of strife which no king can escape, the enemy will either rise to bring the king's downfall or will be destroyed. In the Book of Daniel King Nebukadnezar of Babylon, by the word of god, is expelled from his city and even from human society. He has to feed on grass like the cattle and to spend nights under the dew of heaven, until he acknowledges the highest god whose power is eternal; then Nebukadnezar is reinstated to even greater kingship than before. Abjection and submission to the highest power can confirm the ruler's earthly power.[112]

We must go down to go up. From another part of the ancient world, the Rome of Augustus, Horace gave this message its classic formulation: "Because you keep yourself subordinate to the gods, you rule the empire," *dis te minorem quod geris imperas*.[113] He was addressing Rome, the power that had conquered the world, the power that was accused of recklessly sacking and devastating the *oikumene*. But it was not through self-righteous insolence, said the Augustan poet, but through bowing to the gods that the Romans acquired and kept their empire. Look at the temples which they dedicated to celebrate every victory—temples to be restored by Augustus. Already Polybius had noticed the great theater *(tragodia)* of religion at Rome. Every magistrate had both *imperium* and *auspicia,* the power to command and the privilege to get informed about the will of the gods; officials would do nothing without seeking the gods' consent. The mighty one submits to the mightier one and can thus exercise his power in a legitimate fashion, with good conscience, and with success.

Outside the shadow cast by monarchic power the two-tiered structure seems less oppressive. The idea of civic equality is based on the postulate that power should operate in a circle of equivalence: to be ruled and to rule in turn.[114] The religious two-tier theater of power still tends to manifest itself in the normal family structure. As the parents honor god, they educate their children: "Honor first god, secondly, your parents."[115] In the Christian monastic orders obedience is the major obligation, both to the monastic officials and to god. "Obey those who lead you," the Epistle to the Hebrews says, "give in to them; for they work intensively for your souls, because they will be held responsible."[116] It can be observed in practically all forms of religious humility that the person who bows to gods makes others follow his example, and in this way may secure a leading role for himself.

One of the basic functions of language communication is to give orders.[117] The essence of power among humans is to issue commands that are obeyed. Within a hierarchical system opportunities to give orders multiply, as verbalized commands can be passed on in a chain of dependence: A tells B what C shall do, and B is eager to tell C. Intelligent primates know, in their system of rank, that it is an advantage to be close to a high-ranking individual because his or her prestige will extend to those who keep up the connection; it is possible to use a partner as a "social tool."[118] But it is only through language that a full and widespread system of command can be established. The will of the superior becomes transferable in its verbalized form. This in turn creates the role of the messenger of power, someone who passes on commands that are not his own, telling others what to do. He administers the power of the stronger one without running the full risk of responsibility.

As the chain of power grows in extension and ramifications, systems of dependence arise that leave the individual unable to penetrate to the main source of power, either physically or intellectually. Think of Kafka's tales, *The Process* and *The Castle*. Even in less complicated systems some unseen superior may gain authority and give commands without ever showing himself. The nonobvious source has the obvious advantage of being unassailable; nothing much can be gained from fighting envoys. The pseudo-Aristotelian treatise, *On the World*, describes how the king of Persia remained invisible to everyone in his palace, closed in by gateways, doors, and curtains, but still communicated with all of his realm through his informants, administrators, and fighters; this, the author says, is just an imperfect model for imagining god, the invisible king of the universe.[119]

With the system of two-tiered power, royal orders and actions can take the shape of divine ordinances. An illustration is a text of Samsuiluna, king of Babylon about 1700 B.C. The highest god, Enlil, spoke to his son and his daughter, Zababa and Ishtar, and they in turn "exultantly" communicated the message to the king: "Samsuiluna, seed of gods, Enlil has made great your destiny; we are going to be at your side; we are killing your enemies; . . . but you shall build the wall of Kish higher than whatever there was before." The king obeys, starts a war, wins a victory, and builds the temple for Zababa and Ishtar at Kish.[120] We are not told just how the king received the divine command, whether by dream or by oracle; in a later period messages from the gods are sent from their sanctuaries to the king of Assyria, while charismatic prophets and priests act as intermediaries.[121] The chain of promise and command is clear, starting from the highest god and transmitted to the ruler, with minor gods serving as messengers and the king acting accordingly. The real event, the war that destroyed cities and brought booty to Babylon, is framed by order and obeisance.

We need not dwell here on the role of angels as messengers in the Jewish and Christian religions.[122] It is more important to note that founders of religion repeatedly chose to present themselves as envoys of their god. Jesus relied on "the father who has sent me,"[123] as John the Baptist had already referred to "him who sent me to baptize people."[124] Jesus sent out his apostles in turn to act as envoys of the second degree: "As my father has sent me, I am sending you."[125] Mani, the founder of Manicheism, wrote to King Shapur of Persia:

God's envoys do not cease bringing forth, from aeon to aeon, wisdom and works. Their advent happened to be at one age in the person of the envoy who was the Buddha, sent to the regions of India; in another age in the person of Zarathustra, sent to the land of Persia; again at another age in the person of Jesus, sent to the Western lands; then this revelation . . . presented itself in this age, which is the last, in the person of myself, Mani, the envoy of the true god, sent to the land of Babylon.[126]

Allah directly dictated to Mohammed the text of the Quran, using the prophet as his mouthpiece in the propagation of Islam.

Although the revelation has become literate, the role of the messenger remains. The basic formula of Islam proclaims Mohammed to be "the messenger of Allah."[127]

This system is much less elaborate in the Greek world, but the commands of gods transmitted through their envoys are ubiquitous there too. Hesiod's Zeus has 30,000 invisible guardians who roam around the earth controlling the deeds of mortal men.[128] Later on, *daimones* were credited with the role of messengers.[129] Normal religious practice includes oracles, dreams, visions, and voices, all of which take the form of commands; in addition, there are interpreters who speak in the name of the god, through special knowledge and technique or through trance and ecstasy. They proclaim the will of the god; the fundamental role of language could not be clearer in this apparently irrational sphere. "Thus spoke Apollo," the seer will solemnly pronounce. He takes his authority from Apollo, who in turn is the mouthpiece of Zeus.[130] The evidence of poetry is augmented by countless votive inscriptions that claim that an offering to the gods has been made "at their command," *kat' epitagén, keleustheís, iussu deorum.* In the Hebrew Bible the term for prophet is *nabi'*, "he who speaks out." "There was the word of Jahweh to Jonah, son of Amittai: go to Nineveh . . . and preach,"[131] and Jonah tells the people of Nineveh what to do, and—quite unexpectedly—they obey. Nathan says to David: "Thus speaks Jahweh."[132] Again, in this chain of command the prophet-messenger is the intermediary. Aristophanes parodies this in comedy when he has the seer say what Bakis said the Nymphs said—the chain appears more and more problematic with each additional link.[133] At Rome, in 102 B.C., a certain Battakes, priest of the Great Mother of the Gods from Pessinus, stepped forth announcing "that he was here on account of the command of the goddess," and by this authority he gave order to the Roman authorities that public purification ceremonies be performed. One official, unimpressed, had the priest driven off the Forum—and died three days later.[134]

Men are cunning by nature and prone to disobey; this is the constant complaint of prophets. Ritual may invite imitation, and this may be true even of rituals of submission if they make the others feel and accept the presence of superior powers,[135] but individual needs and desires often cause men to disregard threats and claims of invisible actors. The question of how such other-worldly messages and commands can be made compelling brings back the fundamental problem of how to validate the nonobvious.[136] Systems for making the unseen authorities speak, forms of divination, and claims to direct experience by ecstatics, shamans, and mystics may or may not succeed.[137] These charismatics are not hypocrites. Some of them experience an irresistible constraint to deliver their message at all cost and are often ready to die for their cause. "The Lord has sent me ... forced by necessity, willing or unwilling," a Montanist prophetess proclaimed.[138] The messengers themselves are links in a chain: *pherei pheronta*. In the words of an ancient Greek proverbial saying, while the bearer of the load bears down on others, the load is heavy on himself.[139]

5

Guilt and Causality

Religious Therapy and the Search for Guilt

Greek literature begins with Homer's *Iliad,* and the *Iliad* begins with the story of a plague. Chryses, a priest, goes to the camp of the Achaeans to ransom his captive daughter, Chryseis. Rejected and insulted by Agamemnon, he turns to Apollo, his god, and prays that the Achaeans be punished—as priest *(areter)* he has the power to wield the *ara,* a word that covers prayer, benediction, and curse. The god then sends the plague, which provokes the quarrel of Agamemnon and Achilles. We need not follow the skillful development of the plot of the *Iliad,* the wrath of Achilles and its consequences. It is not the narrative art of Homer that will be in focus here but the chain of events that the poet used to trigger the plot. It starts with the common life experience of illness and a pattern of expectations and manipulations to control it.

If we leave aside the omniscient narrator and try to imagine how the events appeared to the common man in the camp of the Achaeans, the main and most notable event would be the plague. People dying, pyres burning—it was an experience of catastrophe all too common in life and all the more terrible because there was no recognized form of medical treatment. Still, one has to do something about it. Achilles, who takes the initiative, immediately decides (and expects the others to agree) that the calamity must have a cause, and that the cause is the anger of one particular god, Apollo; he is the god of healing as well as of pestilence. Apollo evidently is angry, very angry with the Achaeans. So Achilles proposes to "ask a seer or a priest or even an interpreter of dreams . . . Why has Phoibos Apollo become so angry?"[1] Kalchas the seer rises to tell the assembly what the poet has already told his audience: the god is angry because Agamemnon has insulted his priest. Hence double satisfaction is called for: Chryseis must be given back to her father, and a ritual must be performed both at Chryse, the home of the priest, where a hecatomb is to be sacrificed, and in the camp of the Achaeans. Here a ceremony of purification, *apolymainesthai*, has to take place before the sacrifice (313), and a special ritual song (the *paian*) is to be sung during one whole day, accompanied by dance. This is the first time we encounter a religious ritual in Greek poetry that involves divination, purification, animal sacrifice, prayer, and dance.

We are dealing here with a sequence of events which by far transcends Homeric poetry; it even transcends Greek civilization and may practically be called universal. Four characteristic steps mark the process. First comes the experience of evil, disaster, or catastrophe which is threatening and anxiety-arousing; this immediately provokes the questions why? why now? why to us?[2] This calls for the second step, the intervention of a special mediator who claims superhuman knowledge: a seer, priest, or interpreter of dreams. Third is the diagnosis. The cause of evil must be defined and localized, normally through establishing guilt, identifying what wrong was committed and by whom, and whether recently or long ago. To know the cause is to find the way to salvation. Fourth are the appropriate acts of atonement, measures both ritual and practical to escape from evil and to find salvation. These usually include religious ceremonies but do not exclude rational proceedings. Therefore, give back the daughter—and also sing the *paian*.[3]

A closely parallel story from the Bible is set in the time of the Philistines.[4] This sort of literary genre, the saga or quasi-historiography, comes closer to reality than does the heroic epic—which of course does not guarantee the details of the tale to be historical fact. The Philistines of Ashdod have defeated Israel and taken away the Holy Ark, which they bring, as booty and dedication, into their Temple of Dagan. Thereupon "the hand of the Lord became heavy on the people of Ashdod, he wrought catastrophe among them and afflicted them with pestilence, both Ashdod and its surroundings." Here is pestilence again, with the omniscient narrator telling us in advance about the cause, and the Philistines feeling this is the hand of god, as Achilles had immediately recognized the wrath of Apollo. What must they do? The first and simple measures fail. They send the ark to another town and to a third one, but pestilence follows them; the lamentations of the cities rise to heaven. So the Philistines assemble "the priests, seers, and conjurers"—this is the text of the Septuagint; in Hebrew only "priests" and "soothsayers" are mentioned.[5] The Philistines ask: what shall we do with the ark of Jahweh? The answer is: you must give it back to the Israelites, and in addition you must present golden offerings to Jahweh, in the shape of five buttock-tumors in memory of the pestilence, and also five golden mice.[6] The connection, not uncommon, of pestilence and mice is interesting (rats were not yet around at the time); the buttocks, realistic in relation to bubonic plague, are at the same time derisory of Philistines. The Philistines comply, and the pestilence comes to a stop. The parallels with the beginning of the *Iliad* need hardly be stressed. Both stories relate the same kind of disaster, the same proceedings to find out the cause, a similar finding, and similar means of atonement—only there is no interest in Philistine dancing or feasting in the biblical text. In fact Homeric Greeks and Philistines are not far separated in time or space. The Philistines are among those "peoples of the sea" who roamed the Aegean about 1200 B.C. They settled in southern Palestine, leaving for archaeologists a form of barbaric Mycenaean pottery, and one hypothesis is that they were in fact Greeks.[7] Since they did not write, we shall never know.

I am not pursuing here suggestions of common heritage or literary borrowing. We are looking at the general validity of a pattern. An earlier example from Bronze Age Anatolia is the text called the Plague Prayers of Mursilis, king of the Hittites about 1340 B.C.[8] A plague afflicts the land of Hatti. The text preserved mentions what we would call the natural cause, infection through contact with foreigners ("prisoners carried the plague into the Hatti land"). But such knowledge does not help. Instead, the king "made the anger of the gods the subject of an oracle." Just as Achilles recognizes the wrath of Apollo, Mursilis acknowledges the anger of the gods, and both take the same measure: they consult an oracle or seer. Mursilis, a king living in a literary civilization, had turned to the ancient records. The results were indecisive, and they needed to be confirmed by the oracle. He learns of two causes of guilt, two transgressions that have occurred. Sacrifices to the River Euphrates have been forgotten— in the *Iliad* too, Achilles suspects that Apollo is angry because of neglected votive offerings or hecatombs—and a treaty has been violated by Mursilis' father, Suppiluliuma. So the king tries to make atonement: "the reasons for the plague that were established . . . these have I removed. I have made ample restitution . . . offerings for those oaths I have made to the Hattian storm-god. . . . The offerings to the River Euphrates I promise to make."[9] Here is the series of events: the catastrophe, the common supposition that this is due to the wrath of a god, the mediation by the oracle, the statement of religious and moral guilt, and the atonement through religious ceremonies. This pattern seems to be fully established in the Bronze Age.

But we need not keep to the past nor to literature. A few years ago, in a little village called Kirjat Malachi, close to Tel Aviv, six people had died within a few weeks.[10] The inhabitants, appalled by this coincidence, turned to a famous rabbi in Jerusalem. He declared that the cause must be a sin committed in the place, whereupon the inhabitants remembered that recently a striptease show had been held in a communal building of the village. They decided to do penitence by observing a day of fasting and sacrifice. The newspaper reporter found this funny, and we may join in the laughter because we know that germs or viruses spread disease, not a striptease show. But this event exhibits exactly the same sequence as in ancient times: disease and death, the divine mediator, declaration of guilt in breaking a religious-moral taboo, and ritual performance to make amends.

In classical literature the most sublime instance is provided by the beginning of Sophocles' *Oedipus Rex*. Some global form of disease, *nosos,* is infesting Thebes. Plants are withering, women and animals are miscarrying, people are dying. Oedipus the wise ruler does what needs to be done: he sends his envoy to Delphi to ask what causes the evil.[11] The answer points to a crime committed long ago, the slaying of King Laios. Oedipus takes the measures required, both on the ritual and the rational level. He pronounces his curse and starts the inquiry, which will lead to himself. It is true that the art of Sophocles nearly makes us forget the beginning at the end. We do not ask whether the plague has run its course, and Oedipus is not sent immediately into exile.[12] Sophocles may have invented the whole introductory sequence. The pattern was readily available, as it had been to Homer. It is a pattern of practice that easily develops into a story.

After Heracles killed Iphitos, he fell ill and asked the oracle at Delphi how to recover his health. He got involved in a quarrel with Apollo about the Delphic tripod, but finally had to give in to Apollo's command that he be sold into slavery for three years.[13] After undergoing this form of disgrace, Heracles regained his health and status.

Virgil, in his *Georgics,* tells how Aristaeus lost his bees to a sudden pest. Following his mother's advice, he turned to the sea-demon Proteus to inquire about the cause of the bees' sickness. It was revealed that Aristaeus had been guilty, through sexual assault, of the death of Eurydice. The wrath of the nymphs had to be assuaged through lavish cattle sacrifice, which is also the magical ritual of *bugonia* that brings bees.[14]

The pattern is not confined to mythology alone. A decisive event in the history of the second century A.D. was the great plague that spread from the East during the war against Parthia in 167 A.D. As the doctors gave up—Galen left Rome—the cities

106

turned to oracles; various oracular responses from the period are extant, which refer to the wrath of the gods and give instructions for cult rituals that should help.[15]

A further example from contemporary Africa was witnessed by Vittorio Lanternari.[16] When a little child got sick, the mother turned to one of the prophetic healers. This wise woman did not even look at the sick child first but started to query the mother about the family situation and half-forgotten conflicts with relatives. She found out that the mother had not performed a sacred libation rite in honor of the guardian spirits which had been due the previous year, and for some years an uncle had neglected his duties toward his sister and her offspring, for whom he was responsible. So the wise woman required the mother to go to that uncle, to reestablish good relations, and to perform the neglected ritual at once. Only then, at a second meeting, the prophet inspected the sick child and administered a treatment which restored his health within a few days. Disease is not confined to a special state of physiology in one individual but is seen as a bad state of the whole social field encompassing mother and child, their relatives, and their rituals. We might protest that the one is taken as a pretext to interfere in the other, but on second thought we might admit that a child's sickness can be related to a tense family situation. We should at any rate recognize that this is a way of establishing a world of sense in which evil can be pushed away and health can be found.

It would be easy to accumulate further parallels, from Eskimos to Africa and from Oceania to America, for the treatment of disease according to this procedure. Let us add one story in Livy which seems like a parody of the pattern.[17] When, in 331 B.C., a deadly disease spread in Rome, a slave girl said that certain matrons were concocting poison, whereupon they were made to drink their own potions and all died. In consequence, 170 more women were executed—"the event was considered a prodigy." Then, according to ancient custom, a "dictator for fixing a nail" was appointed, and he performed this strange and simple ritual. Even if the cause of evil seemed clear and patent in this case—though doubts remained, as Livy indicates—things could be fixed only through ceremonial dealings with the supernatural.

Present Sufferings

So far we have been dealing with cases of disease. Disease may be the most common occasion to trigger the mechanism. In fact disease is most intimately linked to religion in most civilizations.[18] If asked why they keep to their strange and sometimes bizarre religious ceremonies, so-called primitives will usually reply that they would fall sick if they didn't. Sickness is known to follow transgression; it becomes all the more oppressive if divine warnings are not heeded.[19]

Still, disease is not the only thing that starts the sequence. Recall the situation of the Greek fleet at Aulis, graphically described in Aeschylus' *Agamemnon:* day after day strong north winds blew, ships were damaged, people despaired—until the seer, Kalchas, proposed "another means against the storm, a sharper one, declaring Artemis" as the cause.[20] The fault has been Agamemnon's; he has to sacrifice Iphigeneia.

The disaster of adverse winds also appears in the *Odyssey.*[21] Menelaos finds himself trapped with his crew at the island of Pharos and asks why this should be so. To get the appropriate mediator turns out to be tricky in this case, as Menelaos has to capture Proteus, the Master of the Seals, with the help of Proteus' daughter, Eidothea. Proteus indeed knows what the fault has been—not surprisingly, it was a failure to make sacrifices. Menelaos has to return to Egypt and to perform what he had forgotten to do. The mechanism is used by Homer lightheartedly to introduce the delightful tale about Proteus and his seals—it was so natural to let his imagination follow the pattern.

More dramatic is the story of Jonah, the prophet who tries to flee from Jahweh and instead of going to Nineveh, sails westwards from Jaffa. A terrible storm rises, and the sailors are in despair. Disaster must have a cause, some fault committed by

Creation of the Sacred

one person. Something has to be done by way of divine mediation, but as seers are not available, "Let us draw lots to see on
whose account this disaster is happening to us."[22] The measure
is effective, and the culpable man is identified. Jonah confesses
his sin and agrees to be thrown into the sea as a willing sacrifice,
and apparently the others are saved.

In a less dramatic vein, an unpretentious lead tablet from the
oracle of Dodona records the question: "Does god send the winter (or storm) on account of the pollution of a certain person?"[23]
This documents an official consultation of the oracle in the
fourth century B.C. We are free to speculate with some uneasiness
whether a "yes" answer resulted in some form of scapegoating
in the inquirer's community. Winds and winter at any rate hold
the threat of infertility and famine. When once a great famine
came over the land of the Lydians, "they turned to the seers."
The holy men declared that the gods were demanding the king's
atonement for the death of Daskylos; thus the king went into
exile and offered compensation to the son of the victim.[24]

There are other experiences of catastrophe. Sargon II, king of
Assyria and forceful conqueror, was finally slain in battle, and
his corpse could not be found for burial. This made his son and
successor, Sennacherib, who called himself the "circumspect,"
ponder the ways of the gods.[25] "Pondering in my heart over the
deeds of the gods, I thought about the death of Sargon my father,
who was slain in enemy country and was not interred in his
house, and I said to myself: let me investigate by means of ha-
ruspicy the sin of Sargon." It was clear to him that the catastrophe must have had its cause in a sin, and he proceeded with the
investigation. Sennacherib assembled the diviners in "three or
four" separate groups, so that they could not communicate, and
asked his question. He suspected that perhaps Sargon had put
the gods of Assyria above the gods of Babylon. And behold, this
is the very answer the seers unanimously produced. Hence Sennacherib prayed to the gods and felt relieved. To "straighten the
rites and ordinances of Assyria and Babylonia," he made a beautiful statue for Marduk in Babylon, as he had made one for Assur,

and he bequeathed this advice to his son: never make any decision without the diviners. He also stated that it was the scribes of Assur who had prevented him from giving Marduk the honors due. Some politics is involved here: the relations between Babylon, the old center, and Assur/Nineveh, the center of Assyria, had always been strained. Sennacherib's solution recognized equal rights, at least at the theological level. There was also rivalry between the "scribes" of Nineveh and the "diviners" unanimously siding with Babylon. The balance was achieved by reinforcing the religious party as against the administration. The king exercised rational control by separating the seers into three or four groups to test their veracity.

The worst disaster is defeat in war. When Carthage was under siege by Agathocles, the Carthaginians, feeling the wrath of the gods, explored various forms of supplication; they recalled forgotten sacrifices due at Tyre in former times and started again to perform the horrible child sacrifices they had formerly offered to Kronos. This is the report of Diodorus. Priests or seers are not mentioned, but they cannot have been absent in the search and decision-making.[26]

Two more examples come from Greek history. When the disastrous earthquake destroyed Sparta in 464 B.C., an explanation was at hand: "At one time the Lacedaemonians had removed certain helots who had sought asylum at the sanctuary of Poseidon (at Tainaron), leading them away and killing them. For this reason, they believe, the great earthquake has happened at Sparta." These are the words of Thucydides.[27] We may assume that seers pointed out the transgression and urged sacrifices to Poseidon, the "Savior from Downfall" *(asphaleios)*.

When the whole city of Helike slipped into the Corinthian Gulf in 373 B.C., a parallel exegesis was given. Ionians from Mykale had wanted some items from Poseidon's sanctuary at Helike, *aphidrysis,* for their own cult of Poseidon Helikonios, but the Achaeans had denied them their pious petition. And behold, in the following winter the catastrophe occurred: Poseidon revealed his wrath. A contemporary author tells this story, apparently from the point of view of the priests and seers of the Panionion sanctuary at Mykale.[28]

Pausanias has an older story about failure and success at the Olympian games. The Achaeans wondered why for a long time none of their athletes had won a victory at the Olympian games. Turning to the Delphic oracle, they learned that long ago a certain Oibotas, Olympic victor in 688 B.C., had not been honored properly by his compatriots, so he laid on a curse that none of the Achaeans should win in the future. Henceforth the Achaeans installed special honors for Oibotas at his tomb and set up a statue of him at Olympia, and immediately afterwards, in 496, they enjoyed a victory; "and there remains until my day the custom that those of the Achaeans who are to compete at Olympia do sacrifice to Oibotas; and if they win, they put a wreath on the statue of Oibotas at Olympia."[29]

At once more general and more private is the story about a certain Paraibios in Apollonius Rhodius. The man felt that he was living a luckless life *(akerdes bios),* and he turned to the seer Phineus to ask if there was a special reason for that. Phineus found an offense committed one generation back: Paraibios' father had felled a tree in the mountains and harmed the hamadryad living in that tree. So Paraibios was told to erect an altar to the nymph and to offer the kind of sacrifices that bring relief, *lopheia hiera.* "Thus he finally escaped from the evil sent from the gods."[30]

An even more private variant is told in the myth of Melampus the seer.[31] A certain Phylakos asks why his son Iphiklos cannot beget children; apparently he is impotent. Melampus the birdwatcher finds out from a conversation of birds that long ago Phylakos, while castrating his rams, had scared his little son with the bloody knife. He had then left the knife in a sacred tree, and the bark had grown over it. Melampus manages to retrieve that knife, covered by rust, and for ten days he mixes some of that rust in a concoction he gives to Iphiklos to drink. In this way the son's generative power is restored. This may well be the first— we can say classical—case of Freudian psychoanalysis: discovering the hidden trauma from the patient's youth, which of course has to do with the father and castration phobia, and curing it by gradual familiarization with the frightening object of old. The treatment looks medical rather than religious in this case, but only the diviner can direct it. The sequence is the same: disaster, the seer, the hidden cause, and the corresponding cure. Has psychoanalysis become so acceptable and effective in our century just because it is moving on old and beaten tracks? In this case, as in the modern version, the fault revealed by the medicine man is not the patient's but the parents'; they have to pay for it.[32]

The question is about "the cause of the present evil," as Herodotus puts it.[33] In a fragment of Euripides this is phrased with special vigor. The dead are conjured up "for those who wish to know in advance about sufferings. From where did they spring? Which is the root of evil? Which of the blessed gods must one placate by sufficient sacrifice to find an end of sufferings?"[34] Knowledge beyond ordinary human reach is needed to find the source of evil and to indicate the appropriate sacrifices. Or, as Plato has it in the *Phaedrus:* "when diseases and the greatest sufferings manifest themselves in certain families on account of some ancient wrath, madness-arousing and prophesying found deliverance for those who needed it, taking refuge in prayers and worship of the gods."[35] In this context Plato puts the stress on madness as the form of mediation, but he neatly sums up the suffering, divination, discovery of old guilt and wrath, and the remedy.

The pattern easily develops into a tale. The very question "why?" calls for a tale. When people are faced with strange behavior, they say, "tell me, why are you doing this?"[36] Sense is created by finding a way to speak coherently about events. One result may be the typical cautionary tale. The tale, however, is likely to invert the sequence experienced in practical life: it starts with the original fault or mistake, whether an infraction of taboo, a violation of law, order, or morality, or just some rash and imprudent action; it explains how, in consequence, evil mani-

112

fested itself; it goes on to describe how it was finally overcome by the appropriate means.[37] Tales allow variations that include catastrophe in the end, but in practical life we cling optimistically to the possibility of overcoming disaster.

The Foundation of Cults

Two aspects of the pattern will especially attract the attention of historians of religion: the foundation of cults, resulting from this fictive but powerful "causality," and the role of mediators in the proceedings.

"Disaster brought religion back to mind"—*adversae res admonuerunt religionum*.[38] As the pattern in focus here is practically universal, it can be seen to work as one of the foundations of religious practice and institutions. A Jewish legend tells how the last king of Babylon, Nabonid, came to acknowledge the true god. Having suffered from an ulcer for seven years, he received an explanation for his ailment from a Jewish seer: he had worshiped false gods. He confessed his error, turned in prayer to the highest god, and was healed.[39] In this way Judaism was confirmed.

Pagan religious rituals and institutions are even more likely to emerge out of disaster and be decisively reinforced by it as the disastrous event is interpreted and cured by reference to religious guilt, with the help of mediators who subsequently become active on behalf of the cults. Guilt is commonly attributed to the breaking of religious taboos, neglect of sacrifices,[40] or violation of sacred rules, which are dramatically inculcated in this way.[41]

In Greek mythology, the standard etiology of a cult or festival is the following: a plague or famine (*loimos* or *limos*) spreads in the land because murder has been committed or a taboo has been broken; the oracle is then consulted, and it gives an order to perform rituals that are repeated ever since. The Karneia, for example, the characteristic festival of the Dorians, was founded when the Heraclids, returning to the Peloponnese, accidentally killed a diviner named Karnos. Although details of the story differ, the pattern remains fixed.[42] More circumstantial is the story told by Theophrastus about the Buphonia, a festival at Athens. A farmer had "murdered" his plow ox, and a plague ensued in consequence. Hence the oracle commanded that the "crime" be repeated every year in a strange and complicated ceremony.[43] Homer introduces the *paian* in connection with pestilence; a historical account claims that Thaletas brought the *paian* to Sparta because of an epidemic, of course.[44] In Rome the temple of Ceres Liber Libera and the temple of Apollo were founded on the occasion of an epidemic.[45] We have already looked at Virgil's complicated story about guilt and propitiatory sacrifice that accounts for the magical ritual of *bugonia*.[46] The cult of Asclepius was introduced to Athens in 420, in consequence of the great plague. The cause of the plague was generally found in the violation of the taboo of the Pelargian Wall, although Thucydides has his own ideas as to this chain of causality.[47]

Ritual remedies can include temple building. Herodotus tells that Lydian King Alyattes, during his siege of Miletus, inadvertently caused a temple of Athena Assesia to burn. He fell ill, and when the illness would not disappear, he asked Delphi about the cause. The oracle recalled the burning of that temple, which he had to rebuild. Indeed, he constructed two of them at Miletus, monuments of divine wrath and grace, with the warning attached to them by the story of Alyattes.[48] Livy records similar stories about the origins of Roman cults and festivals. Already the companions of Odysseus, when breaking the taboo of Helios' cattle on the island, thought they would undo that offense by building a rich temple to the Sun God after their return; in this case, they failed.[49]

Taking account of the foreknowledge of gods, the narrative sequence may change and put the god's initiative at the beginning. Queen Stratonike, for instance, had a dream commanding her to build the Temple of the Syrian Goddess at Hierapolis. She neglected to do this and—predictably—fell seriously ill. She then made up her mind to tell her husband, and the two of them secured the construction of the temple.[50]

Experience of the kind is not limited to kings and queens. A touching epigram from a Cretan cave tells us that Salvius Menas, together with his wife, used to honor Hermes there regularly by sacrifice. When she died he gave up the practice, but after much suffering he has learned finally that one must honor divinity. So he brings back offerings and intends to care for that sanctuary permanently.[51] In a similar vein, many of the so-called penitential inscriptions from certain sanctuaries in Asia Minor have such stories to tell.[52] They usually record that the dedicator had fallen ill, that he recognized his offense, which may have been moral (some form of cheating or an illicit sex act) or ritual (cutting sacred wood), and that he repented, acknowledging the greatness of the god who cured him by his grace. The stele is a testimony of his gratitude.

The same sequence was operative at other fringes of the Greek world. Herodotus has a story like that about the Etruscans. After the battle of Alalia, about 540 B.C., the Phocaeans who had fled from the Phoenicians were stoned to death by Etruscans close to Caere. Afterwards, "everyone or everything that passed the place where the murdered Phocaeans were lying became twisted and crippled and lame as if by stroke, men, sheep and donkeys." Then, by order of the Delphic oracle, a festival was inaugurated—a heroic cult with athletic contests and horse races, exhibiting by contrast the perfect bodies of animals and men.[53] Most probably the festival took place on the spot, at Caere. The etiology attached was typical for Greeks, but not for Greeks alone. The "female illness" of certain Scythians was traced, according to Herodotus, to guilt incurred by plundering the sanctuary of Aphrodite at Askalon; the modern view would consider this a form of shamanism.[54] In a more recent example, at Oberammergau in Bavaria the Passion Play is still performed today because of a vow made during a pestilence in 1634. The festival has become a tourist attraction—but in this case we know the *aition* to be true.

A more remote example is known from direct observation.[55] The Nzima of Ghana have a polytheistic system, and each god has a special group of worshipers directed by a priest who performs ecstatic dances. Each god can "select" a new worshiper, and this is how it happens. When a person has a serious illness, suffers the death of some relatives, or gets enigmatic dreams and visions, he turns for help to some old diviner. The mediator then says, in a menacing tone: "If you do not comply with the will of the god who calls you, you will experience still worse misfortune, or even die." The diviner finds out the name and identity of the god or spirit who has "called" the new initiand. He becomes integrated into that group and in this way seeks to recover and to find relief in a comprehensive way.

The Mediators: Risks and Opportunities

The role of the mediators deserves special attention: the seers, the oracles, the shamans, the medicine men, the rabbis—in short, persons who "know more" and hence may help against all kinds of present evil, make good whatever has gone wrong.[56] They are greatly needed because in practical experience the evil cause is hidden, evident as it may appear in the cautionary tale composed afterward. Even if a sin is the cause of the difficulty, it may be unknown to the perpetrator.[57]

This is the great opportunity for those who mediate with the unseen; the moment of decisive influence and even power. It is at the same time not without risk, as the mediator may meet with aggression due to unpleasant revelations. "Seer of evil," Agamemnon bursts out against Kalchas, and Oedipus is even harsher against Teiresias. But their greatest risk is that they may fail. There may be a rivalry of competing mediators with fatal consequences; the Book of Daniel toys with the execution of all the inferior seers, the Chaldaeans outdone by Daniel.[58] Sennacherib split the diviners into groups, and only their unanimous declaration was considered valid; what would have happened if they had disagreed?[59] Herodotus has an account of how the Scythians proceed if the king gets sick.[60] They call three diviners, who inevitably declare that somebody has committed perjury "by the hearth of the king" and thus has caused the king's disease. If an accused man claims his innocence, six more diviners are summoned, and this multiplication may be repeated until a majority vote has identified the real culprit, whereupon the minority diviners are burned to death.

The more immediate problem of the diviner is profane disbelief. Even so-called primitives are not ignorant of cunning, of tricks and deception. With reference to Greece, Herodotus is positive that the Pythia of Delphi could be bribed, and he offers case histories to document it.[61] King Oedipus, identified as the murderer of Laios by Teiresias, immediately suspects a conspiracy of high treason by Kreon, who may have manipulated the seer.[62] Aristophanes in his comedies constantly ridicules the seers with their oracle books; they are clearly seeking their own profit. And isn't it typical that Kalchas, in the *Iliad,* determines that the offense committed was the maltreatment of a priest?

The most impudent manipulation is perpetrated in the tale of Ino and Phrixos, staged in a lost tragedy of Euripides. The crops fail, and the oracle commands that Phrixos must be sacrificed, but it was his stepmother, Ino, who had made the women roast the grain before sowing so that nothing could grow, and it was she who had bribed the oracle to bring about the death of her stepson.[63] The whole development, from catastrophe to sacrifice, is manipulated. Euripides may have invented this version of the Phrixos myth; it presupposes the inveterate machinery of scapegoating, of searching for the culprit, and turns it to cynical misuse.

In another part of the world Eskimo shamans are sent to consult Sedna, the Mistress of Animals, if the men do not catch enough seals. The shaman usually finds out that Sedna is angry and has become polluted because "the women" have broken their taboos, so these women must immediately step forward to confess their sins; only then will Sedna become clean and kindly again and provide success in hunting.[64] Isn't it a good trick, to stabilize the patriarchal system through special taboos made for women?

That religion is mainly *Priestertrug,* manipulations by priests for their own benefit, has been repeatedly voiced since the Enlightenment. Yet in spite of suspicions both ancient and modern, in spite of the unimpeachable existence of cunning and trickery among humans, the hypothesis of pure deception does not explain anything. The "present sufferings" are obvious, and often the salvation attained is no less impressive. It is not only the case that charismatics of one or another kind are needed and that many of them are successful in the eyes of their clients, even in the twentieth century. They do provide a frame of interpretation for women and men confronted with evil, usually by conforming to a chain of tradition, ritual, knowledge, and belief, which are widely shared and accepted beyond individual mistrust and deception. The mediators create sense to counteract what seems unacceptable: sheer coincidence.

The mediators generally use signs to establish their findings. Many kinds of signs are employed by seers; apart from intuition, dreams, and shamanistic trance, signs may be offered by chance or produced by certain manipulations.[65] It is important that not even the mediator be able to manipulate or predict the result. Thus a message must be conveyed in some sort of special language or, in the metaphor of more advanced civilizations, a "writing" that can be read. The mediator's achievement is to make sense of it, to integrate the details into a comprehensive view of the situation and the persons, the past and the future; this may have the force of compelling truth, and it is often called the will of the god. This is in fact what we are constantly doing in our mental constructs, integrating innumerable confused signals into one mental whole. This mental world breaks down in situations of crisis. It is for the charismatic to restore it.

Explanatory Models: Fetters, Wrath, Pollution

Various interpretations and corresponding strategies are operative in reactions to disaster. One of the simplest ways of describing the experience of distress is the impression of being bound, fettered, caught in a trap. "My life has escaped like a bird from a fowler's trap: the fetter is broken, and so we escaped," the psalm says, giving thanks to Jahweh.[66] The corresponding Greek term is *lysis*, "release." Pelasgians ask Delphi for *lysis* of the present evils.[67] Klytaimestra, alarmed by a threatening dream, sends her daughter to Agamemnon's tomb "to offer means of her release *(lytéria)* from the murder."[68] One might even "release killing by killing."[69] Greek purification priests offer *lysioi teletai*, rituals to release individuals from the bonds of evil, especially in the name of Dionysus who himself assumes the epithet *Lysios*. "Tell Persephone that Bakchios himself has released you" is the text of a gold plate from Thessaly, addressing the initiate who has just died.[70] Here *lysis* is claimed to be effective in the beyond; but the same *teletai* were also good for the living, freeing them from "manifest sufferings," as Plato has it in his *Phaedrus*.[71] In the situation of being fettered by adverse winds, *lysis* may be found through sacrifice. Note that one of the oldest documents of German literature is a spell about "fettering" and "unfettering."[72]

The experience of being fettered by evil can be attributed to supernatural agents. This is the hypothesis of aggression out of the dark, of "black magic." Any kind of disturbance could be surmised to have been caused by an outside agent, by somebody knotting bonds of evil. This is especially common in Mesopotamia, where extensive books of incantations and rituals were compiled to "set free" the victim of such machinations.[73] "Everything evil, which has no name, which has taken hold of me, which has pursued me, which is bound to my body, to my flesh, to my sinews, which does not get loose"—this must be released by countermagic, clearly corresponding to *lysioi teletai* in Greek.[74] In Greece, however, there is plenty of evidence that evil machinations of the kind were not just surmised but intentionally and circumstantially performed; that people, with the help of appropriate specialists, strove to fetter and thus to disable their adversaries, or even prospective partners for sexual encounter. This is called "binding," or *katadesis* in Greek, *defixio* in Latin.[75]

The familiar pattern works in a Christian as well as in a pagan milieu. When a boy was afflicted by unbearable pain in his hands and feet, Saint Kyros and Saint Ioannes intervened with the strange advice that he should make fishermen go fishing at the seashore. They retrieved a box with a puppet resembling the boy which had nails through his hands and feet; as soon as the nails of the voodoo doll were torn out, the boy's ailments stopped.[76] Libanius, the eminent fourth-century rhetorician, was suddenly handicapped in mind and body until the carcass of a mutilated chameleon was discovered in his classroom, proof that magic had been worked against him; he felt better after that.[77] We note the progression from present evil through diagnosis to the discovery of the cause and final release. Here the magical interpretation avoids the realization of self-incurred guilt and projects the cause to malign aggression coming from without, even if the cure the innocent victim has to undergo may be circumstantial, unpleasant, and costly.

The model of binding and release, by contrast, adopts a matter-of-fact view without much concern about ultimate causation. The fetters are felt, and one must get rid of them. In fact, the experience of being bound or trapped and striving to get free again is basically a biological experience, the need to escape a really dangerous situation, with corresponding anxiety but also various programs to counteract it; this is much older than humanity. Struggling to get free if ensnared by holds or fetters of any kind, making frantic moves to get away or to find out where the binding and the pain come from—efforts which may finally prove successful—is a situation familiar to most animals. Apes can try to pull out a thorn that has pierced the flesh, recognizing the tiny object that causes pain. Humans in panic are also still likely to make frantic and disoriented moves to get out of the traps of disaster. But their mental resources give them more chances to gain cognition and try to localize the cause of present evil. They dispose of a mental world with an immense choice of possibilities and a host of configurations that can be fitted to make sense. Anxiety, excitement, and fear of aggression persist, however, and time is running short. This will make individuals eager for nonobvious as well as for evident solutions, hopefully accepting any *lysis* from the impasse. Mediators in their traditional roles present themselves to help; and they will teach the psalm of gratitude.

A third model for dealing with the cause of evil is even more personalized: it is that of the wrath of a superior being who is punishing his subjects. We may call it the hypothesis of justified aggression. The concept of gods behaving in this way must have been established long before our documentation begins, but all kinds of spirits, ancestors, and demons may be credited with similar activities. Remember the graphic scene at the beginning of the *Iliad:* down comes Apollo, "angry in his heart." "Why has he become so angry?" Achilles asks. The seer will establish the cause and the means to deal with it, and in the end Apollo will rejoice in his *paian.* The Philistines feel the hand of the Lord. Mursilis inquires about "the anger of the gods" and turns to them in prayer. "Toward which god did we commit transgression, that we are suffering this?" Greeks will ask in distress.[78] Even while angry, the superior may still wish to communicate; a just punishment does not break communication, on the contrary, it reestablishes communication. There must be a reason for wrath that can be expressed and understood in common language, and the extent of the consequences may be negotiable. Even in the face of infinitely more powerful beings, enraged and threatening, one may use speech, say a prayer, together with all the well-known rituals of submission and debasement.[79] These follow upon the recognition of evil and include supplication, wallowing in the mud, self-castigation, self-inflicted wounds.[80] The victim may be tempted by vicarious sacrifice: "Through the killing of the sacrificial victims, the feelings of wrath and offense of the gods are mitigated."[81] But it is also possible that the gods may smile upon us, especially when music gladdens their hearts. In Greek belief, rituals are constantly claimed to restore good humor to gods, *hilaskesthai;* in Akkadian, the expression is "bringing to rest the heart" of the angry god.[82] Alternatively, the concept of universal and unchangeable divine justice may be invoked. In this perspective, all the sufferings of humans are explained as divine punishment. The Hebrew prophets found the hand of Jahweh in all the catastrophes of history. Other religions would introduce transmigration of souls to substantiate the thesis of relentless retribution at the individual level.[83]

Within the realm of language, an effective demonstration of submission is the confession of sins; it means that the punisher and the punished agree on a common formula. Mursilis is quite explicit in his plague prayers: "If a servant has incurred a guilt, but confesses his guilt to his lord . . . his lord's soul is pacified, and his lord will not punish that servant."[84] The confession of sins is required in many healing cults, especially in Asia Minor, but also in Egypt, with the cult of Isis.[85] There are penitential psalms in the Hebrew Bible, as with the Babylonians. Confession of sins is also reported, among others, of Native Americans in case of illness.[86] Mursilis and modern aborigines join hands. These culture patterns prescribe appropriate behavior toward those in rank and prominence, helping to express superiority and inferiority and to uphold status even through crisis.

The practice of confession is, however, conspicuously absent from classical Greece, at least at the official level; only Aristophanes has some passing references to it, such as: "We have done wrong. Please forgive us."[87] Apparently the style of Greek society was averse to the form of humiliation expressed by confession. In the context of a political system run by self-responsible citizens without king or overlord, the belief system led to a certain pride of endurance ("the unwise cannot bear this, but the nobles *(agathoi)* can"[88]) or to tragic insight beyond all hope, as exemplified by the end of King Oedipus in Sophocles. Not surprisingly, the very general, intercultural program of behavior we have been discussing so far does have specific differentiations, with alternative options in single civilizations.

The idea that held sway within ancient Greek civilization, archaic and classical, was the concept of pollution and purification, *miasma, agos, katharmos.* This again is not peculiar only to the

Greeks. The fear of pollution and rituals of purification play an enormous role in other forms of religion, too, especially in so-called primitive religion.[89] At the beginning of this century taboo became a fashionable word.

It is clear that the alertness concerning pollution and purification, universal as it appears to be, has biological roots. To keep oneself clean is a basic necessity for all higher animals, as dirt disturbs the normal functions of the body and has to be removed, though unfortunately it tends to come back and build up. What is functional even in humans—to wipe and to wash one's body, to fumigate with sulphur to destroy pests—long ago became ritual, with all the characteristics of ritual in being demonstrative, exaggerated, and repetitious, as well as elaborated by specialists in an artificial way according to particular traditions.

The evidence from the Greek world has been assessed in Robert Parker's *Miasma*.[90] At the beginning of this century scholars used to express their astonishment at the primitive superstition inherent in the idea of a contagious pollution; today we are more inclined to examine the social and psychological processes and appreciate their subtleties. To find pollution is to give meaning to an uncomfortable status quo and to arrange for its elimination. The contagious aspect of pollution is the necessary corollary of the effort to achieve the separation of what has been mixed up. As Martin West summarizes Parker: "To predicate pollution is formally to declare a state of abnormality so that it can be tackled by the appropriate ritual measures."[91]

This formulation recalls the sequence with which we are now acquainted. A state of uneasiness or even disaster is made explicit and manageable by the diagnosis of guilt or pollution; to discover and pronounce this is the work of a special mediator—in Greek he is called purifier, *kathartes,* but he may well be identical with the seer, Melampus providing the mythical, Epimenides the historical example. Melampus, besides acting as Iphitos' psychotherapist, purified the daughters of Proitos who had become mad as a consequence of transgression; Epimenides purified the city of Athens, troubled by the killing of Kylon's adherents who had sought asylum with Athena.[92] The treatment was, of course, through ritual. This purification took place about 600 B.C., but the concept and practice of getting rid of filth, *apolymainesthai*, appear already in the scene from the *Iliad* with which this chapter started. A parallel historical example is the case of Pausanias. When this member of the royal house of Sparta, victor in the Persian war but convicted of high treason, had died miserably of starvation in the precinct of Athena Chalkioikos, a state of uneasiness, nay anxiety, persisted at Sparta. Plutarch says that ghosts made an appearance there, and that the "conjurers of the dead" *(psychagogoi)* from Phigalia were called to provide help. Thucydides only mentions that the Delphic oracle was consulted. Speaking through it Apollo declared that there was pollution *(agos)*, and that "two bodies" had to be given to Athena "instead of the one," meaning Pausanias, forcibly dragged from the sanctuary as he was dying. Hence two statues were erected.[93] Once more we have present sufferings, transcendent diagnosis, and measures taken on the supernatural and on the public levels, namely, conjuring up the dead and setting up statues.

For the function and meaning of such proceedings, the experience of a modern ethnologist, Maja Nadig, is of considerable interest. In an Indian village in Mexico disease is commonly traced to *mal aire,* or bad air. This diagnosis is made by a wise woman who also knows about practical or ritual treatments which are in fact quite similar to ancient Greek *katharseis.* The ethnographer found that, in the context of village life, this was a strategy "to designate and to treat social tensions in a super-individual way, as recognized by that special culture . . . there is social consensus that disease is worked through aggressions, and there is a cultural pattern both to designate these connections and to make them less explosive as the originator of aggression is left in the dark."[94] Disease is presumed to have a personal cause, but the concept of *mal aire* is used both to localize and to disguise the offender.

This analysis gives a good reason to rethink a certain assumption that has long dominated studies of Greek intellectual history,

124

namely, that the concepts of pollution and guilt represent two stages in the evolution of the human mind; of these, the fear of pollution is supposedly more primitive and hence should be earlier in the development of civilization, whereas the concept of guilt is more modern and reflects the awakening of self-consciousness. Guilt is related to personalized ethics, whereas pollution somehow harks back to the Stone Age. Kurt Latte published a rich and confused article in 1920, "Schuld und Sühne in der griechischen Religion," in which he tried to describe how the Greeks arrived at a rational concept of personal guilt only at a ripe and late age, having started from impersonal and primitive "taboo."[95] In a more general and suggestive way, an important chapter of E. R. Dodds' book, *The Greeks and the Irrational,* is entitled "From Shame Culture to Guilt Culture," an indication of the author's belief in the development toward a more personal consciousness.[96] Dodds' title has had a great impact on subsequent scholarship; it has also met with profound criticism from students of anthropology and moral philosophy.[97]

Most probably, the "history of the mind" is neither linear nor clearcut in its progress. Alternatives may coexist or take turns in an irregular way. From what we have found so far, we must conclude that the pattern of causality, of guilt established by transcendent diagnosis in situations of disaster, is universal and aboriginal and typical of the human mind and human behavior in general; it has its avatar in the behavior of an animal pursued by a predator or caught in a trap. In this sense the predication and experience of guilt cannot be a special and late achievement. Another almost universal trait is the tendency to concentrate guilt on one individual, with the consequence of scapegoating.[98] Special juridical elaborations, with clear distinctions as to free will and responsibility, are of course products of advanced and enlightened civilizations. But in most of the examples discussed here the declaration of guilt was no more rational, the causality no more obvious, than a statement of indistinct pollution would be. No rational causality describes what happened to Agamemnon or to Jonah, to the Philistines or to the people of Kirjat

Malachi; these stories express rather the tendency to find connections at all cost, to concentrate on one person or action in order to have a fixed point from which to tackle a catastrophic situation. The procedure is nearly the same with the pronouncement of pollution. In both forms causality is stated, starting with an intervention in the midst of trouble and in the presence of evil, the cause of which has to be discovered. There is no time for leisurely reflection when something must be done. The two interpretations, pollution or guilt, are seen to guide similar practices.

This leads to the conclusion that the two models of causation are parallel in their occasion and function, since they are mixed in "action"—recall the *Iliad*—if not in "origin." Pollution tends to arouse feelings of uneasiness, as against the panic of feeling trapped. But one interpretation can well take the place of the other; to make them exchangeable can even be the first step of a cure. What matters is to establish a structure of cause and possible relief. The appeal may be to the personalized sphere (to voice repentance and make it up to your superior will please him) or to the imagery of defilement (to hold still for a while and submit to unpleasant yet necessary treatment will help you regain your previous status in the world). A difference exists at the level of verbalization. If the concepts of guilt, wrath, and punishment demand a tale, the declaration of pollution calls for silence. There is no use discussing dirt; it simply must be removed in a practical way.

The choice between the alternative models of guilt or pollution or even a third, malign aggression, depends on recognized forms of interaction within the society or social group, which may range from quite aggressive to polite and refined. Here we come back to a typology of civilizations. If face-saving and shame are most important, the construct of pollution can be a means of saving important individuals from degradation and still making them responsible in an indirect way. It can happen to anybody that he steps in mud, and he will silently take appropriate measures to restore cleanliness. If a murderer, in consequence of his act, has to go into exile, this still constitutes a grievous sort of punishment; other forms of purification can be quite unpleasant too. A real beating may be termed *katharmos:* "beat the hell out of him."[99] Though it may not be called punishment, it is still a form of acknowledging consequences. Even a god may be declared unclean and made to go through a process of purification, as myth has it with regard to Apollo, the god of purifications.[100] But never could a Greek god "confess his sins."[101] If purification became important after Homer, in the archaic age, this was not due to growth of superstition but to the greater requirements of noble conduct and personal responsibility. The concept of pollution thus turns out to be a face-saving strategy, and anything but primitive. Later, still along the same lines, the healing cult of Asclepius became widely popular. The characteristic of Asclepius was to be "mild and friendly," *epios.* He never diagnosed either guilt or pollution and did not stir up causes. For him it was the result that mattered, the successful cure, which still resulted in Asclepius worship offered by the grateful.

It is striking how the rival interpretations coexist or clash even today. Confronted with an untractable evil such as AIDS, many tend to find the scientific explanation insufficient and resort to alternative hypotheses: aggression—some secret organization concocting viruses—or guilt, for which the disease is the punishment, with unlawful sex looming large under this aspect. The public ends up with polite and noncommittal recommendations of cleanliness.

ळ

In short, I postulate a dynamic program that operates in different civilizations and epochs, from so-called primitives to high cultures, a program dealing with the causality of evil. It appeals to unseen powers through what has been called transcendent diagnosis, and it tends to establish and to reiterate religious ritual in order to restore the previous situation of normalcy. It turns out to be one of the main factors in enforcing religious practice.

This program, universal as it may be, is not primitive. It is rather an excessive elaboration of the principle of causality which Kant has termed the transcendental foundation of possible experience—and which most modern science is gradually leaving behind.[102] By establishing connections of fault, consequence, and remedy, it creates a context of sense and premises a meaningful cosmos in which people can live in health and at ease; it is in fact the postulate and the acceptance of a surplus of meaning in the world, sharply contrasting with the reductions made by empirical science. It is not an achievement of pure reason nor of disinterested speculation, but it takes its initial impetus from the snares of disaster from which one struggles to get free, looking for the root of evil, or desiring at least to find some answer to the question "why?" The invention of guilt is one explanation in this context, as is the statement of nonobvious pollution. The rituals devised or reused at such occasions may appear inappropriate and superstitious in our eyes. But even they "make sense." A Greek *paian* or a Ghanaian dance group alike contribute the active elaboration, enhanced activity, and hence joy and satisfaction in an experience of necessity and sense. Danger is overcome by constructing or reconstructing a world of meaning. However fictitious, it often proves effective.

For Martin Nilsson, religion was "man's protest against the meaninglessness of events."[103] People are quite inclined to accept their own guilt, a readiness which makes the course of events understandable and offers a way to handle or refashion one's own fate, in contrast to the oppressive burden of chance and necessity. Hence irrational associations and expectations, especially in matters of health and disease, persist to the present time. Modern science, which is fascinated by chaos beyond causality while worlds of meaning are fractioned and pulverized within our multicultural mass society, will not easily prevail. People prefer to cling to the surplus of causality and sense, and there is no lack of mediators to explore the hidden connections.

6

ঙ৩

The Reciprocity of Giving

Le don *in Perspective*

Perhaps the earliest Greek votive inscription extant is incised on a bronze statuette of Apollo, now in the Museum of Fine Arts in Boston; it is dated about 700 B.C. and reads: "Mantiklos has dedicated me to the far-shooting god with the silver bow, from the tenth of his profit; you, Phoibos, give pleasing return."[1] This plainly states that the relation between a god and his pious worshiper is an exchange of gifts. "Mantiklos" means "famous as a seer" and may be the trade name of a practicing diviner. This man offers a rare and precious object of art to his god, setting it up *(anetheke)* in some sanctuary, and he asks for an "exchange" *(amoiba),* the god's countergift; the transaction also requires a pleasing atmosphere, a smile *(charis)* of mutual understanding.

In the *Odyssey* Athena disguises herself as Mentes to visit Telemachus at Ithaca. She introduces herself as a "guest-friend *(xenos)* from father's time." Telemachus receives her with due respect and offers a gift, *doron,* which will be a "treasure stored in the house" *(keimelion);* the donation is put off, though, until the friend's next visit. "Choose a very nice one," Mentes says, "it will be worth a recompense for you."[2] Just as Mantiklos asks for an *amoiba,* Telemachus is encouraged to expect a "return" when offering his gift. It will be worth a recompense: the word *axion* implies the image of the scales, of a balance that accompanies gift exchange.

The inscription of Mantiklos and the text of the *Odyssey* may be nearly contemporary. It is through gift and countergift that relations of friendship are established and maintained, whether among men—aristocrats, at any rate—or between man and god. The same terminology and ideology regulate the two sets of relations, through the exchange *(amoiba)* of gifts *(dora)* with a standard of equivalence *(axion)*. The essential feature of a gift, the relevance of its worth, is the expectation of the reciprocity that constitutes social relations, friendly and obligatory alike. The rules of society and of religion are taken to be homologous.

The phenomenon of giving, the principle of reciprocity and its importance for social systems, has been brought to scholarly attention by a celebrated work of Marcel Mauss, *Essai sur le don*, first published in 1924.[3] It is the coincidence of moral, social, and economic interaction and the paradoxical link of freedom and obligation that constitute the special interest of this phenomenon. Gift-giving regulates the standards of justice, the practice of partnership, and the circulation of goods. In modern perspective the economic aspect may well have become preponderant, while gift exchange has been relegated to the basis of archaic and primitive economies. But at the same time it is the foremost expression of rank and status and thus accompanies social interactions of all kinds. Its basis is an unexceptionable expectation or even obligation of return. Every gift demands a countergift.[4]

Gift exchange appears to be one of the *universalia* of human civilizations. "To give" is one of the basic verbs in most languages; the dative is established in Indoeuropean noun declension. Empirical studies have been devoted to the principle of gifts and its manifestation in so-called primitive societies.[5] The principle of reciprocity is recognized in every case. There are of course forms of violent acquisition of goods which may be equally frequent or even more common, not to say honorable, in the same societies: robbery, piracy, cattle-stealing, wars waged for plunder, and trickery of all sorts. But the phenomena are distinct. It is giving that controls a system of rank and honor and thus guarantees stability in the inner circle. Giving is neither disinterestedness nor pure self-interest.[6] It rather creates some precarious balance between the two.

The phenomenon of giving has long made its impact on studies of ancient civilizations, from the Bronze Age to archaic Greece. Moses Finley, in his book on the *Odyssey*, has an important chapter on the role of gifts in Homer; Nicolas Coldstream wrote an essay on the archaeological evidence for "Gift Exchange in the Eighth Century B.C."[7] Even in the Bronze Age, there is no treaty without exchange of gifts.[8] In the midst of a Homeric battle, when Glaukos and Diomedes recognize they are guest-friends, they have to exchange gifts, and they change armor.[9] Gift-giving is much older and more widespread than any attempts to control bribery: "The Gift a man gives provides space for him and escorts him to the Great one."[10] It is interesting to read in the "Letter of a Princess to the Prefect of Ugarit" that the sender, in need of silver, tells the correspondent: "Send me much of it, and not little"—no quantity, no price; regulation will be through continued exchange.[11] "Give a very nice one—you will get your return," Athena told Telemachus. Trade is still in the form of honorable gift exchange. The system pervades poetry as well as reality.

The invention of the free market, of money, and of putting a price on the merchandise brings changes to the system. Whereas giving creates a bond between the persons who give and those who receive, money exchange is impersonal. Still, "exchange" remains the basic process, goods for money, or money for goods, on the basis of choice, of partnership, and, ideally, of bilateral profit. Even if state-controlled contributions are paid by taxes, the expectation remains that the citizen will get a return for what he is giving, be it privileges, prestige, or just personal safety. Even the prestigious gift has remained, sometimes called "sponsoring" in a more modern vein; it is a form of ceremonial waste not without the expectation of the "pleasant returns."

Pierre Bourdieu has elaborated a "theory of practice" in which

The Reciprocity of Giving

social interactions in general are transfers of assets, so that giving gifts becomes an investment, an accumulation of symbolic capital which will be used again at a later time.[12] Taking a study of Cabyl society in Morocco as his starting point, he shows that capitalism operates even in primitive systems of interaction. The universality of giving remains basic for rank as well as for economy, and this is how social systems function.[13]

If reciprocity of giving is one of the *universalia* of anthropology, it is worth examining the anthropological characteristics implied. Giving presupposes evolution of the hand that makes it free for "manipulation," something that distinguishes man from apes; it presupposes the intellectual achievement of constituting an object which is detachable from the personal sphere, to be given away at ease and without pain; it also recognizes not just an adversary but a partner of equal status, whose thoughts and interests can be represented through empathy. And it implies awareness of the time dimension: credit projects into the future the return of past obligations, with an invariant standard of value. In these processes more distinctly intellectual activities are seen to develop, namely counting, calculating, measuring, and weighing. Some concept of equality and of measure, the *axion* in Homer's expression, must underlie the process of exchange. No wonder the principle of reciprocity has been found highly satisfactory in the construction of mental worlds.

It is common to find extensions of the principle of reciprocity which are not logically necessary, indeed are irrational in certain aspects, and which still remain highly satisfactory to the human mind. The principle is applicable to quite different spheres and works to make them manageable, foreseeable, and acceptable.

The gift aspect dominates sex and marriage. Sexuality is one of the oldest programs of biology, certainly not invented just for humans but indispensable for them and highly valued in individual experience. It has often been termed irrational because it refuses to conform to conscious planning; gift exchange is one means to impose rationality on sexuality. From the patriarchal point of view, the female becomes the "object" for exchange. A bride is "given" to her suitor by her father—this is called *ekdi-donai* in Greek, *in matrimonium dare* in Latin. Through an exchange of women families and tribes establish their mutual ties of friendship. Between families marriage largely becomes a contract concerning property rights: either the bridegroom has to give a price in exchange for the bride, or he expects to receive a sizeable dowry together with the bride; sometimes both. Details vary in different societies; in Homer even the terminology seems to oscillate between both systems.[14] But giving there must be; love stories recede against well-regulated transactions of goods. Even the most intimate relation between male and female requires gifts, as the female is "giving" her virginity and claims remuneration; *anakalypteria* are the gifts due after the bridal night.[15] But exchange of valuables is also the basis of the worldwide phenomenon of prostitution. In Greek the prostitute is called simply the object of trade, *porne*.[16]

Another application of the principle of reciprocity pervades the sphere of punitive justice.[17] Punishment is accepted as just if it is subsumed under the concept of reciprocal giving, of retribution. Retribution can be seen as a simple inversion of action: the culprit is to suffer what he has done.[18] Even this understanding of correspondence presupposes a distant, "objective" view. But there are limits to the *lex talionis*.[19] The ideology of reciprocal exchange, of giving, is much more widely applicable. In Greek, to be punished is termed "to give justice" *(diken didonai);* but it can also be said that the culprit gets or receives his due after having "given" offense; these are still current expressions in English as in German.[20] The twofold possibility of metaphor points to the artificiality of this verbalization when it is applied to overt aggression and brutality. The epitome of rationality is easily at hand: "measure for measure" and counting numbers— blows, for instance, or days of imprisonment.[21] In Homer's *Odyssey,* when Odysseus' comrades have eaten the cows of Helios at the island of Thrinakia, the god asks for a "fitting return," by which he does not mean remuneration for the slain cattle—in fact Odysseus' comrades promise to provide it—but that the culprits must be put to death.[22]

Yet universal and aboriginal as the principle of reciprocity may be, it is not innate; it has to be learned afresh by every individual, it has not changed our genes through cultural evolution. In the depth of his heart *homo sapiens sapiens* will always dream of a paradise where all good things are available for free, without retribution of any kind; in a more rationalistic mood humans will try to find some art or trick to avoid reciprocal obligations, as Strepsiades figures out in Aristophanes' *Clouds*. Higher education, he says, should teach him how *not* to pay his debts, not to give back returns which, from his point of view, are anything but pleasant.[23]

There are just faint analogies to giving among animals. The most obvious example, parents feeding their young, ought to be set aside. This is instinctive behavior mostly bound to the dyad of mother and child, sometimes taking the father in company. Animal young beg for food, relying on the propensity of their elders to feed them. This may be the ultimate origin of *charis,* the mutual smile of closeness and understanding. But the permissive attitude toward children usually contrasts with the expected behavior of adults who are "taken seriously." There may be cooperation in hunting. The dog fetches what it has helped to hunt, but will give it up yielding to superior authority. Some practice of "offering gifts" is found in the context of courting and mating at different levels of zoology, especially with insects or birds. This is a means to an end, to arouse interest and to diminish anxiety. No principle of reciprocity derives from it. There is some food sharing among hunting chimpanzees,[24] as well as incipient forms of intentional revenge among them.[25] Systems of gift exchange go far beyond these and can be said to constitute a universal human achievement.

Giving in Religion

In religious dealings, gift exchange is simply ubiquitous.[26] This seems to be another true universal of religious history as of anthropology. The formula of Mantiklos, the gift accompanied by the demand of "pleasing return," is found repeatedly in archaic Greek inscriptions, such as votive tablets from Corinth and a stone basis from Smyrna.[27] It also appears in Homer: "give pleasing return to all Pylians for the grand hecatomb," Mentor-Athena prays to Poseidon. Equally, the singer-poet prays to his god: "give graciously delightful life in exchange for my song."[28]

No wonder the first and apparently most obvious definition of "piety," in Plato's *Euthyphro*, is "sacrifice and prayer," which in turn means "to ask and to give," so that religion becomes a "craft of trade" *(emporike techne)*. In his criticism Plato asks: how can we really give to the gods?[29] But in his *Symposium* Plato has Diotima explain that the "traffic" between men and gods, executed by "demons," consists in prayers and sacrifices from one side and commands and returns for sacrifices *(amoibe thusiōn)* from the other.[30] Since commands of the gods normally concern sacrifice, *amoibe thusiōn* could well serve as a general way of describing religious interaction as a "sacrificial exchange system." Even before Plato, the Hippocratic author of *Peri aeron* agrees with Euripides that gods enjoy being honored by men and hence "give back their favors for this."[31]

The idea of mutual gifts exchanged between gods and men has quite an old pedigree. One of the clearest examples of Indoeuropean poetry that can be reconstructed from Greek and Sanskrit says that the gods are "givers of good things," *doteres eaon* in Homeric Greek.[32] With this wording Homer is accepting and passing on an idea that has come to him through a tradition of, say, 2000 years. In Mycenaean, the proper name Theodora means "gift of god."[33] The Persian King Darius proclaims that Ahuramazda, creator of heaven and earth, "gives everything good to people"—and "kingship to Darius."[34] Democritus concurs that "the gods give to humans all good things, in olden days as well as now," while the bad things that happen are due to men's "blindness and want of sense."[35] This is not to say that the idea of divine gifts is an Indoeuropean-Greek creation or prerogative. The Hebrew Bible stresses again and again that Jahweh

The Reciprocity of Giving

is the giver of all good things, giving food to all living beings, and giving progeny in particular. A similar formula of the New Testament has formed its own tradition of another 2000 years to the present day. "Every perfect endowment and every good gift comes from above," James writes in his letter, "coming down from the father of lights," from god.[36]

Of course the gifts from above, the good gifts from a god or gods, are just one side of the trade. They are to be answered by the gifts of men to gods in turn. This is our form of thanks or "grace," *charites*, as the Greeks said.[37] In the formulation of the pagan Sallustios, "since we have everything from the gods, and it is just to return firstlings of things given to the givers, we give firstlings of goods through monuments, of the body by hair, of life by sacrifice."[38] "Thou shalt not come to me with empty hands," Jahweh commands; all peoples are obliged to bring gifts to Jahweh.[39] In a West Semitic text, the god Hadad "gives pastures and waterings for men of all cities, gives a share of sacrifice to the gods his brothers" (the cycle of gifts goes on even among the gods themselves).[40] Mantiklos has brought his tithe to the god. Socrates takes sacrifices to be the gifts of men to gods, accompanied by prayers asking for exchange.[41] Return is obligatory from both sides. In the *Iliad*, Zeus feels he should help Hector, because "he has burned many thighs of cattle, on Ida and in the city of Troy." Similarly Athena, in the *Odyssey*, urges the gods to help Odysseus, because "he has given sacred things to the gods more than other men."[42] A more poignant formulation is put forth in the Old Babylonian epic *Atrahasis*. During the famine, people turn to the god of rain with exclusive veneration. They build a temple for him and make great sacrifices, in order that "the god shall be ashamed at the gifts"—and they succeed: the god is ashamed at the gifts, and he gives his help.[43]

The religious attitude so openly expressed over and over again has been characterized, even before the Mantiklos statuette was found, as the principle of *do ut des*: "I give in order that you shall give."[44] The most unabashed formulation comes from Vedic India: "Give to me, I give to you."[45] But also in Tanzania, at the libation of the first beer after harvest, this formula is spoken: "Accept this drink—give us bliss . . . grant life, life, life!"[46] In Near Eastern wisdom literature we read: "Give to the god all day long, you will receive your returns."[47] We even find the explicit term of "loan" or "investment": "Who has mercy for the low man makes a loan to Jahweh, and he will requite him," a Solomonian proverb says. Even Jesus, according to the Gospel of Matthew, encourages people to give alms by the promise that "the father . . . will give it back to you."[48] More cautious persons will prefer to invest their promise in the form of vows. "You will get back in exchange double and triple," the chorus promises Zeus in Aeschylus' Oresteia—a capitalist's plea to an investor, as it were.[49] Often it is the sacrificer who thinks of making a profitable investment. Sacrifice to the gods will bring a hundred cattle—this is the original sense of hecatomb, "a hundred-cows-sacrifice."[50] "Give more, and you will get more."[51] In the practice of votive religion, we often find the idea of a continuous circle of exchange, to give to the god because he has given and in order that he may give again. "Virgin Athena, Telesinos has dedicated a statue on the Acropolis. Be glad at this, and give him the chance to set up another one." "Menander, fulfilling his vow, dedicates the tithe, returning his thanks; daughter of Zeus, save him, returning your thanks."[52] In Rome, at the Ara Maxima, the Vertulei give their tithe as a gift to Hercules and pray that he might "often condemn them to pay for a vote."[53] For the farmer, the agricultural year is a cycle of giving. Grain is the gift of Demeter; it is collected at harvest, when first-fruit offerings to the gods are due immediately to guarantee continuation. It must have been difficult for the early farmers to throw eatable grain to the ground when winter is about to come[54]—but equally, sowing must be done to guarantee riches in the next year.[55] Reality and ideology concur in the concept of cyclic exchange.

The *do ut des* principle, as has been seen, allows for variations: for Mantiklos, it is *da quia dedi,* for Athena in the *Odyssey, date quia dedit,* and it is *do quia dedisti ut des* in the votive circle.[56] This finally ensures stability: King Ptolemy and his queen, the

Euergetai, "continue to bestow many and great benefices on the sanctuaries in the country, and to enlarge the honors of the gods . . . In return for this the gods have given them their kingdom in a continuing good state, and they will give them all the other goods forever."[57]

Protests against such blatant reciprocity are not lacking. The foremost one was by Jesus: "To give is more blessed than to receive."[58] God gives without symmetry, and men should not ask for it.[59] Yet the Christian tradition has more or less succeeded in restoring retributive justice and economy of exchange. A most sublime version of the principle is found in Islam: "Allah has bought from the faithful their lives and belongings, in order to give them paradise instead."[60] The transaction has been fixed, men have paid through their faith and may expect the appropriate return.

From the perspective of anthropology and religious phenomenology a double problem emerges: (1) How did the principle of reciprocal gift-giving arise and become one of the universals of human culture, alongside the famous "struggle for survival" among greedy and cunning individuals who are much more moved by the desire to get and not to give back? In a way, this is a question about the origin of collaboration and morality in general. (2) How could such a principle become dominant in religion, where one side of the deal must necessarily remain unseen? This seems to imply a third question: Why are both phenomena, social giving and religious giving, so closely bound together?

Genealogy of Morality?

Reciprocity is a form of morality. The question how morality could ever have evolved in a world dominated by the Darwinian struggle for survival has been refocused in the light of game theory and computer simulation. These studies have not only exploded the older idea of group selection in what was called social Darwinism at the beginning of this century but also the approach of Durkheim and Mauss, who, in explicit opposition to Darwin, wished to prove the priority of society as against the individual.[61] It is clear that justice and cooperation give an advantage to the "group" and thus should mark survival fitness and success; the greater advantage, however, will usually go to those who cheat and get emoluments without investments; it is the "selfish genes" that prosper.[62] One illustration of the alternative of cooperation versus cheating has become famous, the so-called Prisoner's Dilemma.[63] If you do not know what your partner is going to do, and if cheating pays more in a single case, which is the more promising decision? In one set of computer games based on these presuppositions the result has been that in the long run "nice" strategies turn out to be more successful than aggressive strategies based on cheating as soon and as often as possible. One should start with cooperation but react to cheating immediately by returning like for like. This has been called "a grudger's strategy," or "TIT for TAT"; it could equally be called the strategy of "pleasant return."[64] Should we assume that in the long run cooperation, reciprocity, and retribution have been found to be more advantageous and have therefore been turned into values of cultural tradition? And going further, assume that strategies of this kind would reproduce themselves and multiply as a result of their success? This is not to forget that games of this kind are highly simplified models of a multifactorial process going on in human society for thousands of years.

"Silent trade," which has been called the earliest form of foreign trade, calls for attention in this context.[65] Its classical description can be found in Herodotus. In Africa, south of Gibraltar, Phoenician merchants anchor their ships upon arrival,

> take out their goods and deposit them in order at the beach. Then they retreat to their ships and make a smoke signal. Then the natives, seeing the smoke, come to the beach and deposit gold, and they retreat again from the merchandise; then the Karchedonians come back and examine the amount of gold, and if the gold is seen to match the value of the goods, they

take it and depart; otherwise they retreat to their ships and remain there, and then the natives come and bring more gold, until they accumulate a convincing quantity. There is no cheating.[66]

Later authors relate that the trade of silk with the Chinese was also effected in this way.[67] Similar forms have been found everywhere in the world. They seem to arise spontaneously, especially in situations of utter distrust and quite limited communication. The principle of reciprocity is recognized from the start, even without direct contact, let alone discussion; it makes continued cooperation possible. It is certainly reinforced by practical experience; the system will break down, of course, if excessive cheating or violence takes over. In other words, it is a matter of course for humans to try out "nice" strategies, and these are found to succeed. The returns of continued trade are greater than the profit collected by cheating or robbing in a single case. Note that the phenomenon is anthropologically universal; it comes into being in different times and places even without continuous tradition; it is exclusively human. You cannot do it with chimpanzees.

The procedure of silent trade has evident analogies to certain forms of gifts to the gods. Offerings are deposited at some place outside the normal habitat; the giver retreats, sometimes without looking back, and waits for the "gracious return." In Greece such practice is especially common in the context of first fruit offerings. In the course of the seasons, *horaia,* seasonal products, are regularly deposited at some simple altar or just on the ground in honor of local heroes or nymphs, or of the respective gods. This is to uphold the circle of gifts and expectations on which life is found to depend. What is distinctive though, as against silent trade, is the *charis* usually involved in offerings to gods, some flowers added to the tribute, for instance.[68]

But the unmistakable analogy brings back the "prisoner's dilemma" with special force. How can the practice of gift offerings prevail when the return is not at all obvious? The principle of reciprocity, which is seen to control the dealings with the sacred again and again, is not based on unambiguous experience, let alone statistical evidence; nor should we understand giving as expression of individual feelings of gratitude, because these are taught and strengthened by traditional beliefs. The principle of reciprocal giving is not verifiable in relation to gods—nor in relation to the dead, the other sphere where giving, often lavish giving, occurs in practically all human societies. And it is definitely not "natural," that is, biological. Nonetheless it appears to dominate religion, especially in primitive and archaic civilizations.

Failing Reciprocity: Religious Criticism

"Look at all these votive gifts," Diagoras the atheist was told in the sanctuary of Samothrace, which houses the great gods who were famous for saving people from the dangers at sea. "There would be many more votives," the atheist unflinchingly retorted, "if all those who were actually drowned at sea had had the chance to set up monuments."[69] There is no statistical proof for the relevance of religious giving; statistics might rather prove the contrary.

In fact there are drastic counterexamples in individual cases that have resulted in bitter complaints. The catastrophe of the pious is set out in the example of Job, and Near Eastern parallels are not lacking.[70] In Greek literature we find similar laments that giving to the gods has been in vain. "Oh my father's sacrifices before the walls, prodigal in slaughter of the grazing flock: they availed not any cure."[71] Concerned discussion seems to have followed the misfortune of King Croesus of Lydia, in 547 B.C., who had "given to the immortal gods" more than any other mortal and still met a violent fate through Kyros, king of Persia. Herodotus has him send envoys to Delphi to ask "whether it is the custom of the god to cheat his benefactors";[72] the god should have been "ashamed of the gifts."[73] The god's answer was that the catastrophe had been ordained by fate, that there was the forefather's offense, the crime of Gyges, and that the god had still provided a three years' delay. These are three problematic excuses instead of one good one; but *charis* seemed to be saved in some small measure.

This indeed is the counsel of piety: to take a selective yet optimistic view. It is also what the anecdote of Diagoras finally teaches: the living count, the drowned do not. The Athenians must sacrifice as their ancestors did "because of the good luck that has come from those sacrifices."[74] "It is good to give gifts to the immortals," Priamos ends up saying in the *Iliad*.[75] The gods have not forgotten the pious men; if Zeus did not save Hector despite all his sacrifices, he has yet intervened to secure him a noble funeral. The exchange, *amoiba*, has been effected.

Disappointments thus do not stop people from believing that all the good things they need and may get in their lives—food and health and success—are gifts of the gods, the "givers of good things," or gifts "from above," as the apostle says. "Man, do not be ungrateful . . . but for seeing and hearing and, by Zeus, for life itself, and for what helps for living, for corn, for wine, for oil, thank God," Epictetus proclaims.[76] The very cycle of the agricultural year is interpreted as a cycle of gift exchange.[77] In the practice of hunting, at a much earlier stage in the evolution of civilization, the game hunted down could be taken as a gift sent forth to men by some supernatural owners, a Master or Mistress of Animals, who of course demanded gifts in return; if annoyed, the master or mistress would deny their gifts, and catastrophe would ensue.[78]

Criticism of religious gift exchange has been more effective at other levels. For one thing, religion is expensive. The speech "Against Nicomachus," in the corpus of Lysias, claims that Nicomachus, charged with the job of collecting and inscribing the sacred laws of Athens, had worked out such a long list of sacrifices that the city would go bankrupt if it kept to the code.[79] "Look at the gods," the cynical and cunning citizen says in Aristophanes while refusing to give his private property to the community in compliance with the communist law just passed by the

Women's Assembly, "look at the hands of the statues: if we pray to them to give us good things, the god stands there, stretching out his hollow hand, not as if to give, but in order to get something."[80] "It is not allowed to know the gods for nothing: they are for sale," *non licet deos gratis nosse: venales sunt,* Tertullian scornfully comments on the pagan gods.[81] It is true that Christianity developed as a "cheap" religion; but remember Jahweh, who dislikes the "empty hands" of worshipers. One line of Aeschylus became famous in this regard: "Alone among gods, Death is not desirous of gifts."[82] Normal gods, by contrast, are greedy, exacting gifts at every occasion.

Thus injustice seems to prevail in the face of expectation of a just and "pleasant recompense." The ancients raised the problem in these terms: how can a "trade" of interests go together with the rule of absolute justice as postulated of the gods? If returns count, the rich man will have much better chances in his dealings with the gods, since splendid rituals involve costly sacrifice.[83] Reflections on this problem go far back. Wise Hesiod already said that one must sacrifice "according to one's means."[84] Other anecdotes point out how the gods prefer the simple offerings of a poor and pious man, be it first-fruits or frankincense, to the lavish sacrifice of the rich.[85] Ever since prehistory we find cheap and simple objects, usually made of clay, as votive gifts in sanctuaries; they evidently are humble substitutes for what might be a real gift. Should this be called symbolism, fiction, or cheating? "And you must know that in sacred dealings fakes are accepted for the real things," Servius wrote; indeed, the god Mēn accepted a stele instead of a bull's sacrifice, and Heracles even enjoyed it when children "sacrificed" an apple for a ram.[86] A more advanced morality claimed that the god only looks at the thoughts or the "heart" of the worshiper, not at the cost of the gift; this is found in the Bible as well as in Greek ethics.[87]

A more thorough criticism of religious gift-giving, advanced notably by Plato, is that gifts to the gods constitute a form of bribery. With the advance of city organization directed by written laws, and with money ruling the market, the old forms of mutual obligations became suspect; *dorodokia,* "accepting gifts," came to mean "corruption."[88] Thus Plato is shocked at the principle which Hesiod accepted, that "gifts persuade the gods, gifts [sway] the respectable kings,"[89] or that "even the gods are flexible," as Homer had it.[90] Could punishments in the netherworld be avoided by offering the proper gifts to Persephone, as the old hymn had stated?[91] In his later works Plato is adamant that the gods, representing the principle of the good, cannot be influenced by either gifts or prayer.[92] This would abolish the central forms of cult, leaving only a philosophical "assimilation to god," *homoiosis theoi.*[93]

Ending the gift-giving also eliminates another disturbing conclusion to be drawn from this commerce, whereby the recipient becomes dependent upon the donor, the god becomes dependent on men's gifts. The Hittite hymn to Ishtanu the Sun God says: "Be gracious to this man, your servant, then he will go on sacrificing to you bread and beer." "Where will you get a sacrificer like this man to honor you?" is the question put to Zeus in Aeschylus.[94] A Christian prayer goes: "Lord, give us grace; for if thou givest us not grace, we will not give thee glory—and who will win by that, Lord?"[95] Aristophanes, in his *Birds,* has the gods starving after the birds' empire has blocked the sky and the traffic of sacrifices has come to a stop. The same idea occurs in even more drastic terms in the Orient. Because of the deluge, the gods have long missed the sacrifices, hence at the first offering they hasten to assemble "like flies."[96] "If you annihilate mankind, they will no longer give their supplies to the gods, nobody will offer bread or libation," a Hittite mythical text explains.[97] "You can make your god run after you like a dog," claims a text from Mesopotamian wisdom literature.[98]

Despite the attempts of philosophers to strive for a more sublime theology, based on gods who are self-sufficient and not dependent on anything human, giving has not been ousted from the practice of religion, on the contrary. Practically everywhere it is understood that communication with the divine should be through exchange, through mutual giving, which is reflected in the circulation of gifts within the community or hierarchy of believers. One might indeed be tempted to say that every form of religion is, among other things, an organization to elicit gifts. Some of the so-called new religions or sects provide the most striking examples.

Failing Reciprocity: The Facts of Ritual

If it seems paradoxical that giving is so important in all forms of religion, this is followed by another paradox: in the realm of reality, religious giving will never reach the addressee. There is a striking divergence between religious ideology and ritual practice. Whereas the vocabulary of offerings consciously and constantly invokes the principle of reciprocity, this is not at all enacted in ritual. The question asked before, how the principle of giving could become dominant in religion in spite of the otherworldly partners' "unclearness" or "nonevidence" *(adelótes)*, is transformed by this observation and finds a partial and preliminary answer: reciprocity, nonobvious from the side of the gods, is not even enacted from the human side. The commerce with the divine is executed by formulas and symbolism that, from a distanced view, may come close to tricks. The dialectical coexistence of practice and ideology must go back to most remote times, and there is no reason to suppose that primitive man did not realize the divergence. Deception does not postdate piety in the human mind.

In fact there never was a possibility of sending gifts to the gods in a direct way. There are two contrasting ways of handling them: they can be definitely withdrawn from human consumption or redistributed within human society. In other words, gifts presuppose some sort of economic surplus; in dealing with gods as in dealing with the dead such surplus changes hands. It can be ceremoniously destroyed, or it can be recycled. One of these practices strikes us as irrational, the other as rational. Instead of flowers, send money to Amnesty International or to some other humanitarian organization, we are asked in modern obituary notices. Still, we cannot do without flowers at burials. Indeed, both forms of practice have evidently been around for thousands of years, and we should beware of simple evolutionary patterns.

The ceremonial destruction of valuables undergoes one of three impressive forms of ritual: dumping in water, burning by fire, and just pouring out liquids.[99] In addition, gifts may be entombed with the dead. Customs of this kind took place ever since prehistory, possibly since the Upper Paleolithic. They are evident in civilizations all over the world and are especially notable in ancient religions. Immersion sacrifices abound, and they leave archaeological traces, especially if swamps have been chosen instead of ponds or rivers. Precious objects, animals, and even humans may be the objects of such "giving." In addition, objects may be made unusable, for example by breaking or twisting before deposition or immersion. The act of giving must be irreversible; it is seldom spelled out how the gift should actually reach the addressee.[100] There is a slight chance of recovery by humans of immersed objects; think of the coins in the Fontana Trevi at Rome, a late and playful case of immersion sacrifice. But it ought not to happen, as the example of Polycrates demonstrates.[101] If edible gifts or valuables are simply placed somewhere in the open, chances for recovery and reuse are high; this may be the beginning of "recycling." If humans keep away, animals will take advantage of such edibles. Interpretation can even make these animals the impersonation of divinity, as is the case with dogs and birds of prey in Iranian religions.[102] Greeks, by contrast, were more inclined to find the ravens at the altars committing sacrilege. Abraham too wards the birds off his sacrificial animals cut in halves, to let the god pass through them.[103]

The more brutal, obvious, and definite destruction is through burning; it can be visualized as if the smoke rising to heaven were directly reaching the god or gods. In West Semitic and Greek animal sacrifice only parts of the victims, including inedible parts, were burned.[104] Burning of whole animals, *holocaust*, came to special prominence in West Semitic religion, most of all in the daily service at the Temple of Jerusalem; there is also the burning of children, attributed to Phoenicians and Carthaginians in particular.[105] The more innocent form of worship was the burning of fragrant wood and especially of frankincense, a ritual which spread from the Semitic world all over the Mediterranean through trade with southern Arabia, always the sole source of production.[106] This was the smallest sacrifice that was finally required from citizens as a token of allegiance at the time of Diocletian; Christians refused to do it.

Another old and simple form of ceremonial waste is libation. It is an enactment of frustration, even if only plain water is poured out, for water does not gush from the faucet but must be laboriously brought from some distant well. But often more valuable liquids are used, poured from rare and beautiful vessels; a complicated agenda of what and where to pour can be constructed, always ending in the irretrievable waste.[107] The New Testament has the story of the "great sinner," traditionally identified as Mary Magdalene. Breaking the alabaster container she pours out her ointment, *nardos,* worth 300 denarii, as the more practically minded disciples quickly calculate. These riches should have been given to the poor, they protest, but Jesus endorses the ceremonial waste, with the partial rationalization that the offering anticipates his impending funeral.[108] Using perfumes on the dead is not much more rational than giving them flowers, which Neanderthal man already did.

Recycling pious gifts, as suggested by Jesus' disciples, is an old invention too. It is in fact basic for the temple system as it evolved in the ancient Near East and in Egypt and may be called the *condicio sine qua non* for these civilizations.[109] The temple personnel lives on the tribute brought to the god so that regular gifts to the temple resemble taxation. The "ten percent" principle seems to have evolved at an early date.[110] At a Mesopotamian temple the gods were regularly fed in a daily ceremony, with the statues moved to the dining room, tables set up, incense burners lit; happily the gods would leave the meal untouched, so the remains were left to the priests and their dependents for secondary consumption.[111] This system made it possible for specialists

148

to concentrate as a group at one place without having to worry about making their living; it implied access to coveted privileges, of course. The same was true in Egypt; even the food for the dead so prominent in ancient Egypt was in some form recycled to the living, although pious inscriptions are silent about this. The tithe owed to Jahweh is to be "eaten" at the temple "in front of Jahweh," without any direct share for the god, evidently.[112] At the Ara Maxima in Rome, people "sacrifice" their tithe to Hercules with lavish meals, inviting everyone.[113] Customs of meals for the dead survive to the present day, though it is the living who eat the meal. In all the sacrifices still performed today in Japan or South East Asia—for example on Bali, that island untouched by the expansion of Islam—sacrifices are mainly food offerings while the ceremonial act is in presenting and displaying the gifts, but de facto "recycling" covers almost 100 percent of the produce.[114] It must have been similar with food gifts placed on the offering tables in the Minoan and Mycenaean cultures, and the *trapezai* set up in Greek temples at sacrifice, laden with portions of meat that finally went to the priests. Even the meals offered to the dreaded goddess Hecate, to be deposited at the crossroads at night, were immediately snatched by the poor.[115]

In a more straightforward form of recycling, gifts are directly collected in the name of a god by the god's representatives. These are forms of sacralized begging, most prominent in the practice of Buddhist monks, who have to go around every day to have their bowl filled with offerings of rice. In the ancient world the most notable counterparts were the "beggars of the mother," *metragyrtai*, officiating in the name of the Anatolian Great Goddess, but there were many kinds of itinerant seers and purifiers, or *agyrtai*. Their returns, even "pleasant returns," were given by securing divine gifts for the giver's benefit through oracles, purifications, blessings, and prayers; if repelled, though, they might threaten with curses. The New Testament has the project of a similar organization for the apostles of Christ;[116] but in effect Christians soon declined to be *agyrtai*, "not taking anything from the pagans."[117]

A third way of handling gifts to the gods became fundamental in archaic Greece in particular. These gifts are neither destroyed nor recycled but transformed into durable monuments that belong to the deity in perpetuity, as they are ceremoniously set up in the god's precinct, *anathemata*.[118] Metals were among the scarcest goods, thus the most prestigious *anathemata* were big metal objects, especially tripod cauldrons that marked the early Greek sanctuaries—not too different from those at the Temple in Jerusalem.[119] Such gifts were demonstrations of the wealth and piety of the dedicants and of the skill of the craftsmen as well; through accumulation they also represented the power and prestige of the god and of the city in charge of the sanctuary. The temples and the divine statues themselves were *anathemata,* forms of costly communal dedication, including the most splendid and famous examples, the temple of Zeus at Olympia and the Parthenon. Economic surplus thus assumed a permanent function in the service of prestige and honor. This took place in a society mainly based on these values, but it was done in deference to the higher authority of the gods, who "rejoice if they are honored by mortals."[120] Profane use of temple properties was not excluded: Athena would generously grant loans to her people in Athens. But in principle, to set up *anathemata* in honor of the gods meant to put an end to the circle of exchange for the sake of permanent order. In the long run, however, reality hardly corresponded to the postulate. Whatever curses had been pronounced against *hierosylia,* in the end all temple treasuries and costly statues were robbed or plundered; the gold of Delphi went to finance a so-called holy war. We should hardly wonder at such violent endings; it is more amazing that "niceness," the *charis* of reciprocal giving, had ever prevailed.

Gift and Sacrifice

It has been impossible to avoid mentioning sacrifice in the preceding reflections. The concepts of gift to the gods and sacrifice largely overlap, but are not coextensive. The central ritual of ancient sacrifice is sacred slaughter introducing the common feast, in which the share of the gods is disconcertingly meager. Here, as in gift-giving, actual ritual and pious ideology diverge. Although sacrifice is wholly dedicated to the gods, even in Greece, it turns out not to be a real gift at all.[121] It celebrates the commensality of men in the presence of the sacred, while the gods receive mainly the inedible parts, bones and gall bladder. The Prometheus myth explained how the share of the gods had been defined by trickery, a deception wrought against the ruling god; if this did not go unpunished, the results persist. This was the "separation of gods and men," Hesiod says.[122]

Sacrifice not only includes but largely consists in the sacrificial feast. This ceremony seems to derive from the practice of hunters, acting out the concern for life and the anxiety of killing while providing the most valued food.[123] The feast constitutes the paradigm of food-sharing, which in turn is a basic form of collaboration among humans. Apes normally do not share food, even if an incipient practice of food-sharing has been observed at the rare occasions of chimpanzee hunt.[124] For humans, however, food-sharing had become central just because hunting had become so prominent by the Paleolithic epoch. Hunting was an exclusively male occupation, while a great percentage of food was gathered by the women. Both sexes were dependent upon mutual exchange, which accounts for the structure of the human family, too. Hence we are still dealing with the *universalia* of human civilizations. Many will share the outcome of a successful hunt, exchanging gifts and countergifts both within the family and among the members of a tribe. Recognition of equality and rank comes in from the start, as "parts" are distributed in due order; this is characteristic of the sacrificial feasts in primitive and in ancient societies alike. The Greek concepts of *moira* and *aisa,* constitutive of the Greek world picture, have been traced to this sharing of meat. The words simply mean "part, portion, share," but they came to designate the appropriate order in general, the world order, and Fate.[125]

In his "Reciprocity and the Construction of Reality," E. L.

150

Schieffelin has proposed that the principle of gift, *le don,* is in fact an extension of food-sharing.[126] This would derive gift exchange *in toto* from a simpler practice of similar importance. Certain mental prerequisites have to be met to make the progress from commensality to gift exchange in the full sense possible: recognition of the claims of partners not personally present at the moment, and recognition of the passage of time together with the ability to mark and to remember postponed retribution. This implies a stable mental world anchored to time and place; it also requires proto-mathematical concepts of measure and equality.[127]

If the discussion of the exchange of gifts with gods left irreducible problems, at this new level the question recurs in another form. What is the role of gods in human commensality? Why is the reference to unseen partners so frequent and important that the ceremonial feast regularly takes the form of sacrifice, of ritual legitimated by its relation to the divine or sacred? It is safe to assume that this must be quite an old tradition, although ideas about the actual participation of gods vary even within a single civilization. Do the gods take part in the eating? Yes, but only in the case of marginal Ethiopians and Phaeacians, Homer says.[128] Are they superiors who dine first and leave the rest to their servants, as in the Mesopotamian temple system; or is it enough if only the smoke reaches heaven, as Israelites and Greeks normally believed?[129] At any rate, consumption of meat and/or the previous slaughter is sacralized; it can even be forbidden in a profane context.[130] The rituals used to prepare and to accompany the slaughter and the feast—purification, offerings, appeasement, restitution—both increase and overcome special forms of anxiety. They entail the use of weapons, the drawing of blood, the enactment of death, and frequently propitiatory gifts to return the life force to the lord of life.[131] The integration of gods into the common meal serves the purpose of consolidating the group by establishing a superior authority, and ensuring continuity in the precarious transfer of life. Two constructions characterize the oldest Neolithic settlements and the earliest cities, the first forms of communal life that were able to achieve and retain stability for many generations: the granary and the place of sacrifice. Accumulation and consumption have to balance each other. In a way this still enacts the the law of reciprocity.

Aversion and Offerings: From Panic to Stability

The idea of reciprocity characterizes the act of giving. But some forms of giving reverse the link to the expectation of pleasant returns, and refer rather to situations of threat and violence. Forms of involuntary, compulsory "giving" abound in real life. Contributions may be exacted by barbarous neighbors or the local mafia, by marauding soldiers, pirates, thieves of all kinds; in more secure civilization they are replaced by taxation systems. Herodotus narrates how King Psammetichus of Egypt successfully pacified the invading Scythians "by gifts and prayers."[132] These are exactly the words used in religious ceremonies.

Even within a religious tradition, gifts to the gods may be regarded as a tribute exacted by their threatening power, which makes it necessary to "turn off" their impact. Remember the Indian myth about the origin of sacrifice to appease the devouring Fire God, *Agni*.[133] "I give in order that you go away," *do ut abeas,* is a formula coined by Jane Harrison for "apotropaic" sacrifice.[134] Gods may be oppressive. Hence it is not too strange that gods of pestilence and fever are worshiped too, in an effort to maintain good relations so as to keep them off.[135] "Erinys, clad in black, leave the house when the gods receive the sacrifice from the hands of the worshiper."[136] The sacred law of Selinus has an elaborate ritual to get rid of an oppressive demon, called *elasteros,* and concludes: "If he wishes to make sacrifice to the *elasteros,* he shall make sacrifice as to the immortal gods, but shall cut the throat with direction toward the earth."[137] It may be desirable to be on good terms even with the devil.

A related field of irrational offerings is the ubiquitous custom of gifts to the dead. Here too we find the explanation or illusion of familiarity continuing beyond the grave, and the belief that countergifts of various forms of prosperity come from the dead, including food that grows from the earth. Earth herself is a goddess who produces everything and is honored by appropriate gifts; birth and death become a great circle of getting and giving back.[138] At the same time there is a strong belief that the dead and the heroes become dangerous when angry; hence it is better to appease them with riches to keep them quiet and out of one's life. The horror of death is the clear background of these fears.

The tale which has been widely taken as the foundation of sacrifice in the Jewish, Christian, and Islamic traditions, the sacrifice of Isaac, is a story of yielding everything to threat rather than giving to express mutual familiarity. The demand of god is made without explanation, without any promise of compensation. Abraham is to "give" by destroying what is most dear to him. In the end the loss is modified by substitution, a ram for the burned offerings as they were practiced later in the Temple.

In West Semitic as in Greek ritual we repeatedly find the sequence of a burned sacrifice followed by a sacrificial feast. "Irrational" abandonment—that is, destruction—precedes commensality. A sheep or a pig is burned, and meat is consumed by humans; the relation is clearly to the profit of the worshipers, but the renunciation comes first.[139] The proceedings emphasize *charis,* the smiling face of the gods with whom we are familiar, and the joy of the meal is unmistakable. This does not, however, impeach the seriousness of sacrifice, the meaning of which is to acknowledge a higher authority.

In conclusion, giving to the gods or to the dead can also mean giving in to threatening powers. This brings back the prehuman anxiety reaction, throwing valuables away in a situation of pursuit and anxiety.[140] It must be earlier than food-sharing and before any calculations of equality and reciprocity. Still, giving achieves something: panic can be turned into controlled behavior and even a form of manipulation, with calculation of anticipated profit versus evident but limited losses, especially as substitution becomes possible. If one can get the god to "run after you like a dog," it makes quite an effect. In a way, this is what religious offerings undertake to do. A calculable loss turns into something like a bait. Anxiety is masked by a tentative smile, and hope for stability in the future remains. An early Christian inscription states that a benefactor has adorned a church "for release *(lytron)* from his sins and remission *(anesis)* for those who have died," and hopes at the same time that "he will get the gift of god as recompense *(antimisthia)*."[141] The donor of this expensive gift wants to use it both to pay up his debts and make an investment, reflecting the double aspect of giving something up and getting something back in return.

Reciprocity could develop from commensality within a circle of familiarity, protected from outside dangers—dangers that could still be controlled by vicarious giving. Thus is anxiety overcome. The principle of reciprocity in dealing with human partners as in dealing with gods is not only a "nice" and widely successful strategy but a postulate acted out to create a stable, sensible, and acceptable world, gratifying both intellectually and morally and bridging the gap of annihilation—something that still refuses to disappear completely from the horizon of that "intelligent and mortal animal," *zoon logikon thneton,* as the ancients defined "man." In relation to gods the practice of sacrificial gifts results in an interpretation of life's vicissitudes which is generally both rational and optimistic, Job and other exceptional cases notwithstanding. The postulate of cosmic sense overrides the evidence of deplorable examples of catastrophe. Thus teaching and rehearsing "nice" strategies has widely prevailed in religious tradition. Life is bound to optimism—even this may be called a biological necessity.

The strange fact remains that the postulate of equality and reciprocity appears to meet with "objective" laws of reality and has therefore been highly successful in the mathematical-physical interpretation of our world. Physics works through proportions—note the "portions"—and equations, the postulates of symmetry and equilibrium that are also the basis of mathematics. In this sense the principle of reciprocity is the very foundation of our rational, scientific world. It is not by chance that this is heralded right at the beginning of Greek philosophy in its most general terms: "All things are exchange *(antamoibe)* for fire, and fire for all things, as goods for gold and gold for goods," Heraclitus wrote, explicitly referring to commerce as the paradigm of the cosmic order.[142] And before Heraclitus, Anaximander said that things coming to be and being destroyed again are "paying penalty and retribution to each other for the injustice according to the assessment of time."[143] This formulation seeks to make destruction—even personal death—acceptable through the postulate of reciprocity. For Plato too it is the principle of giving back *(antapodidonai)* that guarantees the continuity of life. "If things that come into being did not give recompense to others, as if going around in a circle . . . everything finally would come to a stop."[144] The very constituents of the human body are "parts, borrowed from the universe, to be given back again."[145]

Should we apply the "evolutionary theory of knowledge" (in the sense of Konrad Lorenz) to explain the correspondence of the universal moral postulate of "equal exchange" with natural laws?[146] Did the principle of reciprocity become fixed in men's minds as a widely successful strategy for dealing with reality? Or is it just that the main mechanism of optimism is designed to circumvent or to hide the irreversible flux by concentrating on closed circles which indicate stability? The more trendy theories current today enthusiastically embrace chaos, and many contemporary observers have come to suspect the ideal of the mathematically ordered universe is more a projection of the mind in quest of stability than a reflection of what is at the heart of matter. In all this, biology is still at work. Life is *homoeostasis:* a transient stability depending upon the "just" exchange; a precarious equilibrium in the flux of matter and energy. The rational postulate of reciprocity fits the biological landscape, and it is duly inculcated through religious tradition.

The Reciprocity of Giving

7

✂️

The Validation of Signs

A COSMOS OF SENSE

Accepting Signs: Divination

The effective use of signs is fundamental in all functions of life, from that of primitive organisms to primates.[1] Interactions between single organisms and their environment can be indirect and selective as they are mediated by things that come into the environment, conveying physical or chemical information. A living being takes up the cues from its surroundings and reacts accordingly. In its turn, it gives signals to which other living beings of the same or of another species will react. Communication through this manner of signs has built-in risks: errors, misunderstandings, and forms of deceit are possible even at the level of plants, as signs can be doubled accidentally or falsified on purpose.[2] But complex adaptive evolution in the whole realm of life would be impossible without the use of signs.

In animals, all sensory perceptions work through the processing of signals, to be integrated into a well-structured if complex system of signs. To take a simple but obvious example: birds as well as humans cannot help seeing the stars as forming shapes and patterns—constellations, memorable icons rather than single unrelated dots—and they derive their orientation from them in the dark. If the ancients spoke of "animals" in the sky, the *zodia* of the zodiac, they were using the primitive hunter's eye, trained to distinguish, first of all, the different animals in the surroundings; they were also relating these "animals" to the main repertoire of meaning, to mythology. This is projection, in the sense of producing a world picture that is not "real" but that easily assumes the character of familiarity; it keeps the subject tied to the external world observed in its details.

In general, signs function to bridge the distance between the world and the individual, even if they remain intermediates and may even obstruct more direct access. Signs come from without but get their meaning from the living psyche; they refer to a reality which they represent in relation to the recipient. Some reactions to signs, in certain species, are innate, but there are programs of learning even at lower stages of evolution. Pavlov's dogs have become famous, as they learned to connect a particular perception to a special experience and reacted accordingly. Note the "signs"—and you will know what to expect.

In the wake of Saussure we are trained to think in terms of *l'arbitraire du signifiant:* signs are arbitrary, changeable, and replaceable. In an age of electronics we are all aware that signals can be remodeled in an infinite series of transformations. Modern psychology has studied the phenomena of psychic projection. In the standard Rorschach test, for instance, random sets of dots, marks, or blots are given shape by the person tested, who thus indirectly projects predilections and problems into the accidental arrangement. The meaning of signs is produced by the observer.

Yet this process is the opposite of solipsism. We experience meaning as flowing toward the conscious psyche from the outside. An external world presents itself through a multiplicity of media. The capacity to find orientation by understanding signs remains an achievement of empathy and intellect. Interpretation is called for, an adaptive attempt at integration with experience past and present to foresee eventual consequences. The human psyche excels in this ability to create sense. This is not merely self-reflective nor arbitrary *bricolage;* the process requires keeping in contact with external reality and being conscious of this connection.

"You know how to interpret the appearance of the sky, but

not the signs of the time?" Jesus chided his disciples.[3] A current and habitual interpretation of signs takes place in everyday life, but it is especially necessary to be alert to signs in situations of absolute seriousness. The true god, Jesus teaches, presents his advent through signs no less than pagan gods would do. In fact the interpretation of signs is fundamental in all of the ancient religions. In Latin, the art of interpreting signs was simply called "divine activity," *divinatio;* in Greek the word for god *(theos),* and hence the concept of god, are closely tied to the work of seers.[4] Divine signs were observed in Mesopotamia and duly reported to the king; whole libraries of relevant books are extant. Jahweh too spoke to Israel through signs.[5] In the Western Mediterranean, it was the Etruscans who acquired special fame for developing the interpretation of divine signs into a veritable science *(disciplina),* taught and passed on within families, even if some charismatic power remained indispensable.[6] It was left for Christianity and Islam to devalue divination decisively, at least at the official level; many forms nevertheless have persisted and keep reemerging even in modern societies, especially in times of crisis. Divination is hard to eradicate from the realm of human mental activity, because it rests on very old foundations.

The Romans distinguished "natural" signs encountered, for example, in the flight of birds, and "artificial" signs resulting from special actions such as slaughtering sheep.[7] The borderlines between them are fluid, however, since birdwatching may involve an elaborate apparatus while signs may be observed in the course of everyday butchering. In another sense of the word, John's Gospel consistently speaks of "signs" as "being done" by Jesus *(poiein semeia):*[8] His miracles and the amazement they cause are indications of divine reality. Signs should be uncommon, and at all events they must be unpredictable. Even in the simplest forms of divination, however artificial it may be, what is crucial is that the outcome cannot be predicted nor manipulated, that there is a moment of tension, uncertainty, and surprise—like a throw of dice.

Success is achieved when one is ready to accept the sign at the appropriate moment, integrate it into the particular situation, and thus create or recreate a meaningful *cosmos*. An example is the story Herodotus tells of the royal myth of Macedonia.[9] Perdikkas, from the Argeadai family that claimed Heracles as their ancestor, had been serving as a cowherd to a mischievous king; when he asked for his wages, the king scornfully offered the sun, which was just shining through the roof toward the hearth in the room. Perdikkas promptly said "I accept," and with a demonstrative gesture "took" the piece of sunshine into his lap. Through this acceptance, the king's arrogant utterance, by which he meant to give the boy nothing, turned into a sign of power, connecting Perdikkas and his offspring forever to the grand light that dominates the sky, the royal star of Macedonia. By accepting the sign of cosmic rank, Perdikkas received what it stood for: royalty.

Chance events could be turned into signs by "accepting" them. A name pronounced, a person encountered at a critical moment, words overheard accidentally, assume a certain meaning and determine the future. After the battle of Plataiai, an envoy from Samos comes to urge the king of Sparta to attack the Persians in Ionia; when he tells his name, Hegesistratos, which means "leading the army," the king says, "I accept," and starts the campaign.[10] But more subtle than that, the rustling of leaves or the glittering of water may also convey a message.[11] Most special is the role of birds. Birds are unpredictable in their flight and yet easy to spot and to describe. Birdwatching may have developed long ago through hunting experience, perhaps among carcass-eating hominids. It is the birds of prey, called *oionoi* in Greek, that give the important signs, from Mesopotamia to Italy. Twelve eagles appeared when Rome was to be founded, the greatest augury *(augurium maximum)* for Romulus. Homer's *Iliad* introduces Kalchas, "by far the best of birdwatchers," to lead the Greek army to Troy "through his divination." Older Akkadian textbooks specify what the sighting of a falcon will signify for an army on march, flying either to the right or to the left, forward or backward.[12] Later on, in the Hellenistic period, Jews made

The Validation of Signs

fun of this: the thing to do is to shoot the silly bird with an arrow to prove that it does not even know about its own fate.[13] Yet it remained difficult even for Christian emperors to abolish the *auspicia,* the "bird watching" ceremonies by which the Roman army had been guided through so many centuries.

Divination has its special place at sacrifice. In the serious context of sacred action, the *res divina,* all kinds of details acquire meaning: the soaring flames, the bursting of the gallbladder, the cracks in burning bones. The most important parts to watch at the butchering were the entrails, especially the liver; hepatoscopy is in evidence from Mesopotamia to Etruria, taking hold of Greece and Rome as well. There probably was cultural diffusion, but also great variety of local lore.[14] The tendency to observe signs in butchery comes up in other civilizations as well. Even in modern Greece and the Balkans, when a sheep has been slaughtered, some will try to "read" the shoulder blade.[15]

There are many more categories of signs used by diviners and even commonly observed by laypeople: a stumbling leg, quiverings of the body, objects floating or sinking in water, figures formed by the dispersion of oil or flour on water, but also drops of rain, thunder and lightning, or the silent movements and relative positions of the stars.[16] All these are watched and presumed to convey their meaning to those who "know."

☯

The fundamental form of communication for humans is language; hence signs are appropriated and translated into the experience of language. The abundance of signs turns into a plethora of voices. A feeling of universal empathy may prevail, as if every being, everywhere, were telling a message—to those who understand. Indistinct sounds tend to become speech for the charismatics. Some oracles worked directly through the voices of persons "possessed," whose speech was thought actually to emanate from unseen superior partners.

Speech presupposes speakers; signs seem to presuppose some great *signator,*[17] a universal signifier who has established the meanings we are summoned to understand. Relying on language, humans fit signs into a semantic structure with sender and reference; and if the reference of signs noted by special charismatic interpreters cannot be verified, it adds to those provinces beyond experience which have still come into existence in our common world.[18] Divination validates religion: important signs are believed to emanate from divine sources. At the same time, the signs appear in the ongoing context of human affairs. They belong in everyday life and even more so in uncommon situations, interfering, prohibiting or stimulating, giving directions and orientation. Private individuals and families,[19] along with public institutions, successfully participate in the actions and reactions the signs initiate, and thus uphold systems of divination according to various blends of cultural tradition.

161

What appears to be characteristic of a complex human world may be seen as a form of regression in a biological perspective. In more primitive organisms the sensorial apparatus is perfectly adapted to the needs of the species; hence "signs," all the signals processed by a simple brain, do have simple and unequivocal "natural" meanings. The frog does not see the whole of the colorful landscape at an evening sunset, but only the moving black dot which may be a fly, and it jumps for it.[20] The process can be analyzed and described by mathematical physics; tests are easy because the sensory apparatus is so easily deceived. Signs of this kind have meaning with direct survival value; they are bound to a closed system in which the less developed animals exist, instinctively reacting to specific signs and disregarding the rest of reality. This state has been left behind by the higher animals, and definitely by humans. By means of all the tools the human intellect can master, our world has widened immensely in scope and in diversity. This resulted in a loss of the immediacy of practical meanings. Women and men see landscapes in all their impractical beauty or ugliness; they are subject to a plethora of sense-impressions that stream from a vastly complicated universe. Human brains have no fixed program for structuring and selecting what can and should be known. Experience must be formed

The Validation of Signs

through long and intricate interactions of biological as well as cultural factors; culture becomes more and more important, especially because of the power of language; what should be experienced afresh has in fact been shaped by tradition and is being inculcated by the incessant influences and teachings of culture. Instinctive reactions to the overflowing multiplicity of signs are not possible; humans have to distinguish, to analyze, to combine, to interpret, to integrate details into a context to make some sense of it in the end.

As against this, the supposition that every incoming signal might be a sign conveying sense is regressive—a superstition in the very sense of the word. Characteristically, people tend to believe this especially in states of alarm or panic. As the self-sufficiency of a normal, closed cultural system is shattered, it gives way to uncommon openness to signs hitherto disregarded, which may offer a chance for reorientation. Heightened anxiety makes us watch out with fearful attention and shiver at every rustling leaf. Periods of crisis are the high time for oracles and seers. There are even recognized forms of frenzy and ecstasy, producing messages bearing a new divine content. The sensitivity born of anxiety leads to an enlargement of the recognizable world, directed by the premise that everything has meaning. This amounts to a reprise of the sort of closed world in which less developed animals exist, though at a higher level. While these animals are experiencing nothing but contacts that impinge directly upon their life, man may stand up to postulate a totality of sense within his universe. The dialectic of the widening of insight and the closing of the universe may be found in ancient philosophy: Plato, in his *Timaeus,* builds up a divine *kosmos* for humans in which every detail has its timeless correspondence, place, and function; nothing is meaningless. Stoics went on to draw the picture of a *kosmos* held together and pervaded by an intelligent *pneuma,* in which everything is held in "sympathy" with everything else; hence even the divinatory meaning of a bird's flight would be ratified. Ptolemy found that the "sympathy" of the *kosmos* fully justified astrology.[21] The *kosmos* is a universe of signs: a philosophical given that appears to be pre-determined by a more ancient biological heritage.

It is still the natural world which comes into direct view in these processes. They do not involve gods or abstractions but simply trees, flying birds, water, and stars, while uncommon phenomena such as comets and meteors are believed to be all the more portentous. Integrated in nature, interpreting incoming messages, humans construe their *kosmos* of sense. It hints at the divine.

Decision through Signs: The Ordeal

A special instrument to make gods speak out through nature in the context of impending conflict is the ordeal.[22] This procedure goes beyond divination insofar as it constitutes an intervention in a situation of social crisis, of imminent fight, or at least of a legal process, when high-ranking individual or group interests and even lives are at stake. The crisis has a special aura of seriousness and urgency. In consequence, the sign to be obtained must be realistic in the extreme. To reach beyond interpretation and arbitrary intellectual adaptation, it is necessary to work on the body.

One way to express utmost seriousness is to have a fight for life and death, be it single combat or battle.[23] But the more striking forms of ordeal entail submitting to a test from nature, the outcome of which decides between the rivaling claims. The result, as in normal divination, cannot be predicted or manipulated. In this way, language is imputed to nature in a cultural context, with the hypothesis of divine supervision. Quite diverse civilizations have recourse to very similar proceedings.

Two natural forces, the bases of life and of technology, are usually summoned for the ordeal: water and fire, both known to be potentially dangerous. A water test, "going to the river," appears in texts from Mesopotamia; details are unknown, but it may have been similar to the witch test applied in medieval and premodern Europe, when the person accused of magic was thrown into the water and considered guilty if he or she did not sink.[24] Touching melted metal is another very old practice; there seems to be in fact an unpredictable chance of not getting burns.[25] In Iran, this procedure came to dominate eschatological fantasy: at the end of time, streams of burning metal will flow over the earth and destroy the wicked but leave the just untouched.[26] Walking through fire was a dreaded test known also in Greece;[27] it was still practiced during the Crusades.[28]

Less spectacular and more common, but still affecting the basic process of life, was to make the person to be tested eat or drink some special and supposedly poisonous substance. Sickness would immediately strike the culprit, manifesting itself through a swollen body, pain, and swoon; the innocent would be left unharmed. Moderns will grant some psychosomatic efficacy to such a form of lie-detector. An elaborate description of the method is found in the Pentateuch. Hesiod describes a similar procedure, of "drinking Styx," forced upon a god caught in perjury.[29] The use of such an ordeal is also documented in the Near East and in Iran.[30] A simpler and more benign form, making the suspect swallow bread and cheese with the expectation that the culprit will exhibit swallowing difficulties, was generally practiced in the ancient church, even by a bishop.[31] The procedure is reported from other parts of the world too: "The Massai of East Africa bite off a few blades of grass, then exclaim 'May this grass prove poisonous to me if I have lied before God!' "[32]

As in divination, tricks may well enter the ordeal, "giving words" for truth; best known from medieval literature is the ordeal of Isolt in Gottfried's Tristan romance. The lovers contrive a trick whereby Isolt's proclamation is literally true though false in the sense required; thus Christ, the divine supervisor, is found to be "pliable as a windblown sleeve."[33] Real cases were less funny. During the first Crusade, the "sacred spear" of Christ was allegedly excavated at Antioch. Enthusiasm was soon followed by skepticism, and clerics made the happy discoverer walk through fire with his spear; he died of his burns.[34] The fire's testimony was efficacious. Death is irrevocable; the purported sacred spear ignominiously disappeared from history.

Creating Signs: Territory and Body

Action and passive acceptance come together in the use of signs. While humans tend to perceive signs from the environment and to credit them with hidden meanings, they are no less able and ready to change their environment to adapt it to the presuppositions and categories of their common mental world. This means that people create perceptible signs which act to stabilize the common world as it has been formed by language and cultural tradition. Processes of perception, as established through biological evolution, generally work by selection and adjustment of data taken out of a fluid and ambiguous assortment. In the same way, manmade marks, consciously applied, help make a world that is "good to perceive" because they reduce complexity.[35] Marks delete ambiguities and make reality correspond to instinctive needs and to conscious concepts.[36] Often they are applied both to the surroundings and to individual persons, marks of territory and marks of the body. As explanatory markings mingle with the opportunities for deception, there are overt as well as secret signs in both realms of application.

Marking territory is common to many mammals, usually by spreading scent marks. By analogy, humans follow these behavioral tracks in marking stones by oil libations.[37] There are many more ways to mark a landscape, especially by manipulating its most solid components, stones. Piles of stones or large stones set up in uncommon positions are signs of human presence throughout the world. The stone arrangements help people to find their way; and in general such marks evoke feelings of familiarity. It is striking how often and how easily such territory marks are drawn into a religious context. Stones bearing the marks of oil libation are sacred, and a single stone set upright is called the "house of god," *baitylos*, Beth-El.[38] Real estate is marked by stones which are themselves sacred. Babylonians set up phallus-shaped stones with inscriptions and divine symbols in relief to record property, *kudurrus*.[39] Roman boundary stones were supervised by a special god called "Boundary," *Terminus*. It is true

that visible signs, even big stones, can be moved or destroyed intentionally. Hence hidden signs can be introduced, secret markers to testify for the boundaries, relics of sacrifices and charcoal covered with earth.[40] There may be secret tombs referred to in local myth, uncovered at regular intervals by individuals who confirm their territorial power by arcane knowledge.[41] Sanctuaries of the gods are conspicuous in the landscape, marked by stone and tree and thus becoming markers themselves. Returning to Athens from the sea, you see first the temple at Sunion and sometime later the blinking tip of Athena's spear at the Acropolis.[42]

The production of figurines and pictures, which starts in the Upper Paleolithic, has created a new category of signs, icons whose visual modeling suggests a clear and seemingly direct reference to the object. In fact they create a second level of reality, a world of pictures more manageable than reality and subject to willful creativity,[43] with nonobvious references coming up immediately.[44] Later observers are left with the problem of interpreting these early representations, following the realistic or the fantastic indications, in a context of art, magic, or religion. In particular, the question of how far gods are represented can hardly be answered before the advent of high cultures, which speak to us through writing. At this stage no doubt is left that gods are represented through images, on which worship will concentrate. Much later, the Jews and Christians bitterly denounced the worship of manmade idols, and Islam remained adamant in the condemnation of images.[45] Yet originally it was not the images that created worship, but religious rituals that created images for common orientation—rituals of veneration made explicit and special by the visible "sign" produced by the artist. Note that in Latin a divine statue is just called the "sign," *signum*.

The link between the mental world and natural environment is the body. Rituals are strategies to control the body's behavior.

Hence the mental world tends to assert its seriousness by working its will on the body.

We may find it natural that special groups have their special signs or emblems, flags, mascots, or songs. Handling them may still be taken quite seriously, especially in situations of crisis: "The flag is more than death," a Nazi hymn proclaimed. And even when we do it unconsciously, nay unwillingly, we all react to clothing styles. But such signs can be dropped or exchanged, unless they are made corporeal. The mental world, which is changeable and fragile or excessively shaped by privacy and individual freedom, thus turns upon itself and seeks confirmation from the body. Body marking seems to have been invented at the same prehistoric period which saw the emergence of representative art, and this is hardly a coincidence.[46] Man was shaping his world through self-created signs.

Corporeal distinctions commonly apply to sex and to age classes as well as to secluded and closely knit societies. "Rites of passage" allow for recruitment while stabilizing cultural meanings and values even through the change of generations. As the crisis of transition is made manageable, the status attained must be irreversible, beyond some special attire or adornment, beyond language and imagination.

Some bodily markers are reversible, especially hairstyle. We all know how effectively hairstyle is used to mark "alternatives," whether for monks or rebellious juveniles. Hair is part of the natural body, and as it interacts with the individual face, its variations give the impression of a change of personal identity. While this can be undone in a few weeks, other marks cannot be undone. Branding, scarring, and tattooing are both common and old; other operations are also performed.[47] Many tribes in various parts of the world have or had the strict custom dictating that to become a full member of the group an individual must have some operation performed on the body, normally at an initiation ceremony; these include breaking of teeth, perforations of lips or nose, elaborate forms of scarification, and especially circumcision or subincision of genitals.

Initiation marks admit various codes of interpretation. Semiologists chart the system of "making differences," functionalists speculate about group solidarity, and psychoanalysts dwell on Oedipal conflicts and castration phobia. At any rate, it is not sufficient to establish a person's identity just by decision, pronouncement, or act of imagination. It does not even suffice to make an unforgettable imprint by psychic terror.[48] The nonobvious must become obvious, and what is inside must be turned outside. There must be visible differences that persist. Note that the other paraphernalia of initiation, the change of place and costume, dietary rules, tests, and maltreatments have their bodily reality too; initiatory beatings do hurt.

According to Herodotus, when Lydians and Medes make an oath of alliance, they "cut the skin of their arms and then lick each other's blood." Arabians make a pledge in this way: a man stands between the two people pledging, makes an incision at the inner side of their hands at the thumb, then takes a hem of the garment of each and anoints seven stones with their blood, invoking Dionysus and Uranie.[49] Intimacy mingles with pain and terror, scars will remain to remind them of the act, and the bloodied stones endure; language then adds the divine partners, names associated with regular worship. The instinctive shudder and conscious symbolism combine in another attempt at "imprinting," as it were, to create a definite and long-lived partnership, beyond the vagaries of imagination and language.

Marks, qua signs, are made to attract notice. Forms of scarification or mutilation of teeth cannot be disguised. Yet secret signs may become even more powerful. Common to Jews and Moslems—but not confined to them—is circumcision, which is "the sign of the covenant" made between Jahweh and Abraham.[50] This is an irrevocable mark which is invisible to the public because of the code of normal decency. But everybody knows about it, and it catches attention all the more once it comes to the fore. The process of turning the inside out is reversed superficially, gaining force by the disguise.

Goddesses in Mesopotamia, Anatolia, and Syria had groups

of eunuchs as their special worshipers, either at their sanctuaries or wandering abroad. Castration is a drastic, irreversible sign, normally hidden by decency but exhibited in uncommon presentations; it upsets the normal categories of male and female. The only Akkadian text which refers to the institution says that these men "changed their masculinity into femininity to make the people of Ishtar revere her," or rather "fear" her: awe confirms religion.[51] The more perplexing the sign, the more it is taken to refer to a higher, invisible authority.

The term *character indelebilis* was coined in the Christian tradition, from Augustine to Thomas, to describe the effect of sacraments, in particular of baptism.[52] Augustine took his metaphor from the way soldiers were marked. Christian tradition has taken recourse to metaphysical "sealings" without further operating on the body, though not without prescribing appropriate garments and hairstyle; and touching the body with water has still remained indispensable in Christian ritual.[53] The spiritual world articulated by verbal constructs does not exist as a closed system but is broken up and reconstituted by signs that affect reality beyond language.

Language Validated: The Oath

Why must people have religion? In the ancient world, the obvious answer would have been, for the validation of oaths.[54] Without gods there would be no oaths, and hence no basis for trust and cooperation, for legal action, or for business.[55] "Oaths are encountered among all peoples and in all cultures. They are a primal symbol of religion."[56] Oaths were indispensable in social interactions at all levels, economic and juridical, private and public, intra-tribal and international. No contract, no treaty, no administration of justice proceeds without an oath. This was the one place where religion, morality, and law definitely met.

Oath is a phenomenon of language which owes its existence to the very insufficiency of language. The weakness of the word is the possibility—the likelihood—of lying, of fraud and trickery in all of the social games. It is survival fitness regulated by selfish genes to outwit the others. There has been growing interest in these phenomena even at the prehuman level.[57] Chimpanzees, taught to use sign language, immediately tried to trick their trainers by lying.[58] It is safe to conclude that at the very beginnings of civilization, lying and language were there together. Tales of deceit and deception are favorites in many civilizations.[59] It may be natural that children are tempted to lie. But collaboration and interchange within society require trust and the means to prevent deception, to make fellow men predictable, and to give stability to a common world of values.

The purpose of an oath, sworn by responsible partners, has always been to exclude lying in all its forms, tricks, distortions, and fantastic elaborations. It is "to tell the truth and nothing but the truth," or to take on an obligation to be fulfilled without change or subterfuge. In other words, taking an oath means a radical "reduction of complexity," in an effort to establish univocal meanings and create a world of sense that is dependable, with clear divisions between true and false, right and wrong, friend and adversary, ally and foe.

It is true, and characteristic, that tricky humans immediately take the next step and make cheating by oaths a fine art.[60] Homer has it that Autolycus, Odysseus' grandfather, was "famous for thievishness and oath"; there are various tales about how well he managed that craft.[61] He was not alone. "To give words," *verba dare* in Latin, means to deceive; the very word "sense," *sensus,* means the opposite of *verba.* The formula "what I feel I am saying" was introduced to give weight to mere words.[62] But how to be sure about feelings?

To achieve reduction of complexity, to establish fixed and univocal meaning, acts of speech cannot suffice. To add to a statement that it is true and that alternatives are wrong and excluded is at best a rhetorical device to impress the naïve, but useless from a logical point of view; it will fail to convince the experienced. Add terrifying expressions to demonstrate seriousness and provoke hair-raising anxiety; even this will leave well-versed partners rather cool. It is necessary to get beyond the closed semantic universe of language.

For this purpose two concomitant strategies have been devised: the use of witnesses to guarantee a shared mental world, and the use of ritual to create realistic signs, to affix an ineradicable seal by the imprinting function of awe. At both levels reduction of complexity is met by a "surplus" from the supernatural sphere.[63] Unseen partners share the knowledge, and nonobvious causality wields coercive power. Both are accepted in an atmosphere of absolute seriousness.

As our mental world is controlled by common knowledge, so do independent witnesses guarantee the truth. Note that the same Indoeuropean root *wid-*, meaning "to see" and hence "to know," is used both in the English word *witness* and in the ancient Greek word *histor*. But humans are frail, both physically and mentally; they are likely to forget or even to lie in the future. A first step to attain a higher level would be to invoke "the oath of the king"—which makes monarchy itself indispensable.[64] But how will the king "know"? A common expedient is to choose what is most evidently present, even if this imputes knowledge to inanimate objects. Thus Odysseus, in disguise, swears "by the host's table and the hearth of Odysseus."[65] International treaties ever since the Bronze Age refer to the most permanent phenomena of the natural surroundings, the sun and the sky, heaven and earth. The sun "who sees everything" holds special rank: for Babylonians Shamash is the main guarantor of oaths. Hittite treaties routinely invoke "the mountains, the rivers, the springs, the great sea, heaven and earth, the winds and the clouds—let these be witnesses to this treaty and to the oath."[66] Homer has the Trojans offer one sheep to the Sun and one to the Earth at their oath ceremony and invoke the sun, the rivers, the earth, and the punitive powers of the netherworld.[67] Through an ingenious language game of personification, the most obvious object is provided with functions that are anything but obvious.

The accepted language game goes further in postulating ever higher-ranking witnesses, more reliable than those actually present, to represent inflexible truth. This is when gods enter the scene. It would not be correct to say that gods are just invented in this context. Rather, it is that all the gods and powers venerated by established tradition who guarantee hierarchical order, who are made partners in gift exchange, who are experienced in terror and held responsible for the well-being or illness of the individual, the family, tribe, or country, are used in the context of oath-taking and prove to be useful indeed. The guarantee of absolute truth is with god.[68]

It is better still when obvious reality and superior gods can both be integrated in the proceedings. The sun is a brilliant phenomenon in the sky and held to be a god in many civilizations. If for the Greeks Helios is a lesser god, Zeus the preserver of oaths, called *horkios* in this function, originally was a designation of the shining sky, a fact which Greeks did not totally forget. It is to Zeus that the Achaeans sacrifice, according to Homer; likewise, Odysseus gives Zeus the first place in his oath, to be followed by the table and hearth.[69] The Athenian youngsters who enter military service, the ephebes, take their oath by a series of gods of the city and end it by "the boundaries of the fatherland, wheat, barley, vines, olives, and fig trees."[70] This evokes a meaningful, familiar world in which the citizens live and for which they will have to fight. The boundaries of the fatherland, with all that the soil provides for the sustenance of life, are summoned before the young men's eyes and named witnesses to validate the pronouncement, together with the gods for whom sanctuaries and temples have been installed.

Gods are powerful, and if annoyed, they will retaliate with relentless punishment. They are expressly summoned to do so in the oath formulas, in Mesopotamia as in Egypt, Greece, or Rome. "Their power will kill," an Egyptian oath formula holds.[71] "Zeus throws his thunderbolt at the perjurers," the Athenians are wont to believe.[72] In Akkadian, the oath itself is said to turn into a demon and "grasp" the transgressor.[73] Special demons are summoned to watch the oath and to punish perjury; for the Greeks these are the Erinyes, personifications of the curses that accompany an oath. They "circle around the Oath as he is born," Hesiod warns, and will chase the transgressor and exact punishment even beyond the grave.[74]

All this is not enough. The unseen, with all those superhuman witnesses, gods, and avenging powers, must be bound back again to obvious reality. Beyond the word is action, in the form of ritual to enact what is meant or felt in the linguistic exercise, to give validity to the assertions, imprecations, and curses, and to demonstrate irreversibility. In traditional religious ritual, the verbalized culture structures the environment in order to modify human lives accordingly and to secure dependable behavior.[75] If the formulas reach for the fantastic, the sense of reality is never lost in the process.

Oath rituals principally enact irreversibility. At Alalakh in Syria, a transaction of property is accompanied by slaughtering a sheep: "Let me die in this way if I take back that which I gave you."[76] Sheep are slaughtered also in the oath ceremony in the *Iliad*, and as Agamemnon cuts their throats, the other participants pour wine to the ground from their goblets and pray: "Whoever does wrong against the oath, his brain shall flow to the ground as does this wine, his and his children's, and their wives shall be given to others."[77] Flowing blood, flowing wine, flowing brain are brought together; as the one is enacted, the other is conjured to follow suit. Actions and prayers of this kind are quite common. In an Assyrian treaty from the middle of the eighth century B.C., we read: "If Mati'ilu sins against this treaty, then just as the head of this spring lamb is torn off, and its knuckle placed in its mouth . . . so may the head of Mati'ilu be torn off."[78] Bronze-Age Hittites, in the soldiers' oath, spill wine while saying "this is not wine, this is your blood."[79] The Roman *fetiales*, performing their treaty ritual, proclaim: "If the Roman people should fail (to fulfill this treaty) . . . then you, Jupiter, shall hit this Roman people just as I here and today shall hit this pig; you shall hit it all the more the more able and potent you are." Then they kill the pig with a stone.[80] "When the Molossians make an oath, they bring forward an ox and a drinking vessel

The Validation of Signs

filled with wine; they then cut up the ox into tiny pieces and pray that the transgressors may be cut in this way; they pour the wine from the drinking vessel and pray that the blood of the trans-

gressors may be poured out in this way."[81] Another way to represent the threat of destruction in a graphic form is to burn images of wax or asphalt, with accompanying curses: as the wax melts down, annihilation shall befall the transgressor. This practice too is known from the ancient Near East as well as from Greece.[82]

These are clear cases of symbolism, but the symbols are made as real as can be: wine and blood, wax and fire, and animals expiring in agony. Touch is important. The entrails of the victims are taken in hand—this is done in Mesopotamia as in Greece[83]— weapons are dipped into the blood,[84] or a ring is dipped into the blood and held during the swearing of the oath.[85] One gory detail commonly enacted in Greek oaths was to cut the genitals of the sacrificial victim and to step on them. Biological continuity shall be abolished if the oath is violated, so that perjury will extinguish a whole family.[86] At the Athenian Areopagus, the court that tried cases of intentional homicide—with Orestes as the most famous mythical example—the priests slaughtered a boar, a ram, and a bull and the defendant had to tread on the severed genitals and recite the oath in which he called down utter destruction on his house and on his line if he failed to speak the truth.[87]

Less spectacular is the ritual of throwing an object away. Achilles swears an oath to retreat from battle "by the wooden scepter" he is holding in his hand, which will never grow leaves again—and he throws it to the ground.[88] In the Roman oath "by Jupiter the stone," *per Iovem lapidem,* which evidently harks back to very old tradition, the oath-taker grasps a stone and speaks the usual formula. "If I hold to the oath, good things shall come to me; if I should plan or act differently, all the others shall be safe . . . but I alone shall fall off as this stone does now," and he throws the stone away. In a strange way, by its name this oath seems to identify stone and god.[89] The unseen is bound to objective reality. Assyrians, for example, have to tear out a god's symbol.[90] Absolute irreversibility is graphically demonstrated by sinking iron bars into the sea. In this way Ionians and Athenians sealed their alliance against Persia in 478 B.C.; Phocaeans had used the same ritual when they left their home for good.[91] Such an action can develop into pure magic, as the curse is emancipated from the oath and used with direct intent. Jeremiah writes all the evil that shall befall Babylon on a sheet of leather and orders his servant Seraia to take it to Babylon, to recite what it says, and then tie it to a stone and throw it into the Euphrates: "In this way shall Babylon sink and not rise."[92]

Oaths are primitive and sophisticated at the same time. Oath rituals have been called pre-deistic—a stone taken for Jupiter!—and attributed to primitive mentality. But at the same time they are strategies of tricky humans endowed with language, who will match every attempt at validation with new attempts at deception. Gods have been part of the proceedings since time immemorial, in the most diverse cultural systems. Somehow the proper use of oaths must have outweighed the misuse.

Some religious reforms or revolutions have tried to reduce or even to forbid the use of oaths, as Pythagoras is said to have done.[93] Jesus explicitly did forbid them, but the prohibition failed to guide later Christian practice.[94] Oaths have been kept up to the present day; there are oaths of allegiance and oaths at court (which even preserve some of the ritual by touching the Bible), and perjury is subject to legal prosecution. The use of written documents should have made the oath superfluous long ago, but that did not happen. Already Akkadians referred to the "oath of the tablet," without ever disregarding "the god of the oath."[95] Roman oath ceremonies, for the sake of precision, were executed "from tablets or wax," but they still used the stone instead of a knife for ritual slaughter. The age of literacy employs Stone Age implements.

The practice of oaths may be a model example of attempts at imprinting by construing a common cosmos of meaning, with anxiety lurking at the fringe. They are based on the belief in unseen superiors and make use of these powers while binding

The Validation of Signs

them to practical life through signs of utmost realism. The use of oaths entails the necessity of religion. "Those who deny the existence of the Deity are not to be tolerated at all. Promises, covenants and oaths, which are the bonds of human society, can have no hold upon or sanctity for an atheist. For the taking away of God, even only in thought, dissolves all." These are words of John Locke, at the threshold of the Age of Enlightenment.[96]

Conclusion

Religion has emerged in this study as an aboriginal tradition of serious communication with powers that cannot be seen. The problem of validation of the "worlds beyond" does not seem to have a single answer. Neither autonomous expression of a genetic heritage nor direct imprinting of parental attitudes nor arbitrary transfer of information can account for it. Instead, I propose the existence of biological patterns of actions, reactions, and feelings activated and elaborated through ritual practice and verbalized teachings, with anxiety playing a foremost role. Religion offers solutions to various critical situations recurring in individual lives. Through manifold forms and functions of ritual behavior and cultural interpretations, religion can still be seen to inhabit the deep vales of the landscape of life. Religion follows in the tracks of biology, even if it is closely related to the aboriginal invention of language, which brought the great opportunity for a shared mental world. At this level, what matters is not the success of "selfish genes" in procreation, but coherence, stability, and control within this world. This is what the individual is groping for, gladly accepting the existence of nonobvious entities or even principles. Baffling details of experience thereby fall into place, and reality itself can "have speech," *logon echein,* as the Greeks would say. This is the creation of sense.

If language brought decisive progress in sharing, storing, and processing information, the next momentous step occurred with the invention of writing some 5000 years ago. With it was created a new form of objectivity beyond the spoken word as encoded in individual brains. Rituals of validation and oaths in particular could have lost their function as against the use of written documents. With Judaism, Christianity, and Islam, literacy attained its most salient triumph. The sacred scriptures guarantee once and for all the words of god spoken to his prophets and envoys. Writing drastically reduced the need for interpreting signs and for recourse to paranormal experiences of ecstasy and mysticism, but it gave rise to interpretation in a new quest for making sense amidst the gaps of the evidence. Yet most elements of more ancient religions have subsisted both at the official and the subcultural level, including the use of oaths and omens. It is difficult for humans to get off the old tracks of construing sense in a world full of disconcerting events, scandal, and trickery.

It could be the case that the third step of information processing we are experiencing just now is about to bring the most crucial changes. With the electronic network of a computerized society, shared information and corresponding programs become ubiquitous and definitely independent from the individual. This is experienced, for instance, as the "loss of the subject" discussed in literary circles. The individual finds herself or himself in the solitude of arbitrariness while being controlled by new and ineluctable dependencies so subtle and efficient that the older forms of communication look awkward and antiquated by comparison. Admission and exclusion now depend on bits or bytes, on access numbers and codes, and validation occurs by pressing a key on a keyboard.

If this is to be the future, religion, stuck between nature and network, might cease to function—that is, religion in the sense of serious, nonobvious communication based on the antecedent sense-structures of life. Collective ritual may be supplanted by electronic self-engendering games within the brave new world of virtual realities. Still, insofar as the biological basis of life can hardly be abolished, "real" reality will make itself felt time and again as against its virtual counterfeits. Perhaps more disquieting are the likelihood and dangers of regression, of fundamentalism or even primitivism revived. The contents and prospects of religion remain thoroughly problematic—and fascinating. Even within a world dominated by self-created technology, humans still will not easily accept that constructs of sense reaching out for the nonobvious are nothing but self-created projections, and that no other signs from the universe around are there to be perceived except for the irregularities resounding from the first big bang.

Abbreviations
Notes
Bibliography
Index

❧❧

Abbreviations

Abh.	*Abhandlungen der Akademie der Wissenschaften . . .*
AC	*L'Antiquité classique*
AHw	W. v. Soden, *Akkadisches Handwörterbuch*, Wiesbaden 1965–1981
AJA	*American Journal of Archaeology*
AK	*Antike Kunst*
ANEP	J. B. Pritchard, ed., *The Ancient Near East in Pictures Relating to the Old Testament*, 2nd ed. with supplement, Princeton 1969
ANET	J. B. Pritchard, ed., *Ancient Near Eastern Texts Relating to the Old Testament*, 3rd ed. with supplement, Princeton 1969
ANRW	H. Temporini and W. Haase, eds., *Aufstieg und Niedergang der römischen Welt*, Berlin 1972 ff.
ARW	Archiv für Religionswissenschaft
ASNSPisa	Annali della Scuola Normale Superiore di Pisa
BABesch	*Bulletin Antieke Beschaving*
BCH	*Bulletin de correspondence hellénique*
BICS	*Bulletin of the Institute of Classical Studies of the University of London*
BphW	*Berliner philologische Wochenschrift*
CAD	I. J. Gelb et al., eds., *The Assyrian Dictionary of the Oriental Institute of the University of Chicago*, Chicago 1956 ff.
CCCA	M. J. Vermaseren, *Corpus Cultus Cybelae Attidisque* I-VII, Leiden 1977–1989

CEG	P. A. Hansen, ed., *Carmina Epigraphica Graeca saec. VIII-V a. Chr. n.*, Berlin 1983
CEG II	P. A. Hansen, ed., *Carmina Epigraphica Graeca saec. IV a. Chr. n.*, Berlin 1989
CIL	*Corpus Inscriptionum Latinarum*, Berlin 1869 ff.
CIMRM	J. Vermaseren, ed., *Corpus Inscriptionum et Monumentorum Religionis Mithriacae* I-II, The Hague 1956/60
CRAI	Comptes Rendues de l'Académie des Inscriptions et Belles Lettres
EdM	K. Ranke et al., ed., *Enzyklopädie des Märchens*, Berlin 1977 ff.
ER	M. Eliade et al., ed., *The Encyclopedia of Religion* I-XVI, New York 1987
FGrHist	F. Jacoby, *Die Fragmente der griechischen Historiker*, Leipzig 1922 ff. Leiden 1950–1958
GB	J. G. Frazer, *The Golden Bough* I-XIII, London 1911–1936
GRBS	*Greek, Roman and Byzantine Studies*
HAL	L. Koehler and W. Baumgartner, *Hebräisches und Aramäisches Lexikon zum Alten Testament*, 3rd ed., enlarged by W. Baumgartner, Leiden 1967–1990
HDA	H. Bächtold-Stäubli, ed., *Handwörterbuch des deutschen Aberglaubens* I-X, Berlin 1927–1942
HRR	H. Peter, ed., *Historicorum Romanorum Reliquiae*, Leipzig I² 1914, II 1906
HrwG	H. Cancik, B. Gladigow, and M. Laubscher, eds., *Handbuch religionswissenchaftlicher Grundbegriffe*, Stuttgart 1988 ff.
HSCP	Harvard Studies in Classical Philology
IG	*Inscriptiones Graecae*, Berlin 1903 ff.
JCS	*Journal of Cuneiform Studies*
JDAI	Jahrbuch des Deutschen Archäologischen Instituts
JHS	*Journal of Hellenic Studies*
JNES	*Journal of Near Eastern Studies*
JRS	*Journal of Roman Studies*
KAI	H. Donner and W. Röllig, *Kanaanäische und aramäische Inschriften* I-III, Wiesbaden 1966–1969
KHM	J. and W. Grimm, *Kinder- und Hausmärchen*, original text (1857) ed. by H. Rölleke, Stuttgart 1980
LAMA	Centre de Recherches Comparatives sur les Langues de la Méditerranée Ancienne, Nice

LIMC	L. Kahil, ed., *Lexicon Iconographicum Mythologiae Classicae*, Zürich 1981 ff.
LSAM	F. Sokolowski, *Lois sacrées de l'Asie mineure*, Paris 1955
LSCG	F. Sokolowski, *Lois sacrées des cités grecques*, Paris 1969
LSJ	H. G. Liddell, R. Scott, H. S. Jones, *A Greek-English Lexicon*, Oxford 1925–40
LSS	F. Sokolowski, *Lois sacrées des cités grecques*, Supplément, Paris 1962
MDAI (Athen)	Mitteilungen des Deutschen Archäologischen Institutes, Athenische Abteilung
OF	O. Kern, *Orphicorum Fragmenta*, Berlin 1922
OGI	W. Dittenberger, ed., *Orientis Graeci Inscriptiones Selectae* I-II, Leipzig 1903–1905
PGM	*Papyri Graecae Magicae*, ed. K. Preisendanz, 2nd enlarged ed. by A. Henrichs, Stuttgart 1973–74
RAC	*Reallexikon für Antike und Christentum*, Stuttgart 1941 ff.
RE	*Paulys Realencyclopädie der classischen Altertumswissenschaft*, Stuttgart 1894–1980
RhM	Rheinisches Museum
RlAss	*Reallexikon der Assyriologie*, Berlin 1932 ff.
RML	W. H. Roscher, ed., *Ausführliches Lexikon der griechischen und römischen Mythologie*, Leipzig 1884–1937
SAHG	A. Falkenstein, W. v. Soden, *Sumerische und Akkadische Hymnen und Gebete*, Zürich 1953
Sitzungsber.	*Sitzungsberichte der Akademie der Wissenschaften . . .*
ThWbNT	*Theologisches Wörterbuch zum Neuen Testament*, Stuttgart 1933–1979
TAPA	Transactions and Proceedings of the American Philological Association
TrGF	B. Snell et al., eds., *Tragicorum Graecorum Fragmenta*, Göttingen 1971 ff.
ZPE	Zeitschrift für Papyrologie und Epigraphik

Notes

Preface

1. See S. L. Jaki, *Lord Gifford and His Lectures: A Centenary Retrospect* (Edinburgh, 1986). The term *theologia naturalis* goes back to Augustine, *Civ. D.* 6,5–8, discussing Varro's "tripartite theology"; it was used in a positive sense by Marsilio Ficino, who tried to harmonize Platonism and Christianity, see B. Gladigow, "Religio docta bei Marsilio Ficino," in S. Haug and D. Mieth, eds., *Religiöse Erfahrung* (Munich, 1992), 277–285, esp. 279 f; by the Enlightenment, the concept of "natural religion" emerged to confront "supernatural" revelation.

2. For "deconstruction" of "ontotheology" see Ruf 1989.

3. Similar forms may still be studied in folk religions of India, Indonesia, China, or Japan. The author keeps to his field of expertise, though he takes the risk now and then to throw glances elsewhere.

4. For a discussion of these problems see Versnel 1990.

1. Culture in a Landscape

1. Rappaport 1971, 23.

2. Cic., *Nat. Deor.* 2,5; cf. A. S. Pease, *Marci Tulli Ciceronis De Natura Deorum Libri Tres* (Cambridge, Mass., 1955) *ad loc.* Artemidor, 1,8, 17: "No tribe is without religion *(atheon)*"; Strabo 3,4,16 mentions one tribe which "according to some" was *atheon,* but that judgment was wrong; see J. M. Blásquez, *Imágen y Mito* (Madrid, 1977) 451f.

3. Williams 1981, 207, cf. 13: "culture as the *signifying system* through which necessarily . . . a social order is communicated, reproduced, experienced, and explored."

4. This term is used by Reynolds 1981, 13–18. Note that it was Plato who first pointed out the two ways of human procreation through which mortal individuals have their chance to partake in immortality: biological begetting and conscious teaching, or, in other words, the continuity of life and of the cultural tradition, *Symp.* 206c–209e. He was elaborating on the antithesis *physis-nomos* (nature—custom) as proclaimed by the sophists.

5. Geertz 1973, 35 f; cf. D. Freeman in Montagu 1980, 211: culture is an "accumulation of chosen alternatives." Historical studies pursue cultural relativism through the concept of "mentalities." See V. Sellin, "Mentalität und Mentalitätsgeschichte," *Historische Zeitschrift* 241 (1985) 555–598; G. E. R. Lloyd, *Demystifying Mentalities* (Cambridge, 1990).

6. B. Malinowski, *Argonauts in the Western Pacific* (1922); E. E. Evans-Pritchard, *Witchcraft, Oracles and Magic among the Azande* (Oxford, 1937); id., *Nuer Religion* (Oxford, 1956); A. R. Radcliffe-Brown, *The Andaman Islanders* (Glencoe, Ill., 3rd ed. 1948[3]).

7. Geertz 1973, 35 ff; cf. Boon 1982. For criticism see Fleming 1988, 37–43.

8. See Durkheim 1912.

9. See van Baal 1971; Leach 1976.

10. See Vernant 1974; 1991; Vernant and Vidal-Naquet 1972–1986; cf. Versnel 1990.

11. Cf. Taub 1984; Hewlett 1992.

12. Psalm 52 (53) 2.

13. Ps.-Liban. *Characteres, epist.* 1, ed. V. Weickert (Leipzig, 1910), 15, 11; cf. Eurip. *Heracl.* 904 f: "Close to madness steers he who denies that the city must honor the gods."

14. Van Baal 1971, 3. The term "empirical" is problematic. The existence of antipodes, for instance, could not be verified empirically in antiquity, yet this was not a religious notion but a scientific hypothesis.

15. Geertz 1973, 90.

16. See L. Richter and C. H. Ratschow, *Die Religion in Geschichte und Gegenwart* V (3rd ed., Tübingen, 1961) 968–984; W. L. King *ER* XII (1986) 282–292; K.-H. Kohl *HrwG* I 217–262; *Historisches Wörterbuch der Philosophie* VIII (Basel, 1992), 632–713.

17. Saler 1993 pleads for the concept of "family resemblances," that is, "more or less" rather than "yes or no," and refers to "a pool of

elements that more or less tend to occur together in the best exemplars of the category," 225; cf. 213.

18. Diels-Kranz 80 B 6. Likewise Ptolemy, in the preface to his *Syntaxis* (1,1), says theology is characterized by "the absolute invisibility and incomprehensibility of its object."

19. Rom. 1,19 f. Cf. Cic. *Nat. Deor.* 2,4 f; Min. Felix 17. In I Cor. 1,21, however, Paul acknowledges that men fail to recognize god.

20. I Epistle of John 4,1, cf. Paul I Cor. 12,10 on "distinguishing spirits" and "interpretation" of glossolaly. Spiritism became a fashion in the 1920s and produced a host of "mediums" through whom the dead spoke; they disappeared with the decline of interest. Cf. E. R. Dodds, *Missing Persons* (Oxford, 1977) 98–111.

21. "No sacrifice works without prayer," Plin. *Nat. Hist.* 28,10. Yet the role of language must not be overestimated: It is forbidden to translate the Quran from Arabian, hence that sacred text is unintelligible to Persian, Turkish, Indian, or Indonesian Moslems, but this does not impeach its sacredness; the pre-Reformation church hardly found it necessary to translate the Latin Gospel.

22. Buddhism is atheistic in theory but comparable to other religions in ritual practice.

23. Spiro, quoted in C. Renfrew, *The Archaeology of Cult* (London, 1985) 12. This formula insists on culture; the basic mechanism is supracultural.

24. For the concept of "social tool" see Sommer 1992, 85–88; 111 f; see at n. 95.

25. H. Popp, *Die Einwirkung von Vorzeichen, Opfern und Festen auf die Kriegführung der Griechen im 5. und 4. Jh. v. Chr.* (Ph.D. diss., Erlangen, 1957). I Maccabees 2,29–41; the Maccabees, though, decided to fight for survival even on the Sabbath.

26. *Senatus consultum de Bacchanalibus,* CIL I² 581, line 4.

27. See Psalm 1,1 warning people not to sit "among the scornful" (the word was misunderstood in the Septuagint and hence in the Vulgate). Likewise, Apollonius of Tyana or St. Peter subjects a laughing boy to exorcism; Philostr. *Vit.Apoll.* 4,20; *Actus Petri cum Simone* 11, *Acta Apostolorum Apocrypha* ed. Lipsius I p. 58 f. This does not exclude laughter, ribaldry, and comedy from having a place within a religious system.

28. The evidence for human sacrifice is viewed more and more critically today; for Phoenicians, see Chapter 2 at n. 76; for Aztecs, P. Hassler, *Menschenopfer bie den Azteken?* (Bern, 1992); for antiquity, D. D. Hughes, *Human Sacrifice in Ancient Greece* (London, 1991). No doubt

there are phenomena of black magic or "voodoo death" which use religious symbolism and achieve the absolutely realistic effect of killing.

29. See Ehalt 1985.

30. Lorenz 1963; his model case was the aggressive display of a pair of greylag geese. See also Eibl-Eibesfeldt 1984.

31. Burkert 1972, 1983.

32. See, among others, F. M. A. Montagu, *Man and Aggression* (New York, 1968); J. Rattner, *Aggression und menschliche Natur* (Frankfurt, 1970); A. Plack, ed., *Der Mythos vom Aggressionstrieb* (Munich, 1973); *Sevilla Statement on Violence* (Middletown, 1986) (cf. de Waal 1989, 9).

33. Wilson 1975; cf. Wilson 1978; Lumsden and Wilson 1981.

34. Cf. Sahlins 1976; Caplan 1978; Gregory, Silvers, and Sutch 1978; Montagu 1980; Baldwin and Baldwin 1981; see "The Sociobiology Controversy," Lumsden and Wilson 1983, 23–50. See also Reynolds 1981; Fischer 1988; Fleming 1988; Slobodkin 1992, 36–39.

35. W. Irons in Chagnon 1979, 258; Fleming 1988, 110–113, 112 with reference to E. O. Wilson: "culture is shaped by biology." For the concept of "inclusive fitness" see Hamilton 1964.

36. Dawkins 1976. For the evolution of cooperation, see Chapter 6.

37. Cf. Eigen 1987, 59 f.

38. On "fulguration" as a breakthrough to new dimensions see Lorenz 1973, 48–50.

39. Cf. Reynolds 1981, 71 f.

40. Chagnon 1988.

41. For centuries Europeans enforced the law that thieves must be hanged, but did not succeed in reducing the human tendency towards stealing. The more modern trend in cultural studies is to stress discontinuities even in primitive civilizations.

42. Wilson 1978, 175, cf. 169–193; he did not, however, investigate religious phenomena in any detail.

43. Cf. Plato *Prot.* 322a: "man alone among animals has made the belief in gods mandatory."

44. Cf. Burkert 1979, 33 f; 88–94.

45. Gruppe 1921, 243. Otto Gruppe is best known for his huge compendium, *Griechische Mythologie und Religionsgeschichte* (Munich, 1906).

46. The exact text is: "We are made more numerous as often as we are cropped by you; the seed is the blood of the Christians," *plures efficimur quotiens metimur a vobis; semen est sanguis Christianorum,*

Tert. *Apol.* 50,13. Iustinus *Dial.* 110,4 has the metaphor of the vine which, being pruned, thrives all the more.

47. John 12,24.

48. See Hamilton 1964.

49. Cf. Hamilton 1964, 1: "no possibility [exists] of the evolution of any characters which are on average to the disadvantage of the individuals possessing them."

50. K. Marx, "Einleitung zur Kritik der Hegelschen Rechtsphilosophie," *Deutsch-französische Jahrbücher 1844, Marx-Engels-Werke* I 378, cf. K. Marx and F. Engels, *On Religion* (New York, 1964); see *Historisches Wörterbuch der Philosophie* VIII 687.

51. A close and direct interrelation between religion and drug use has repeatedly been advocated. In the case of the Vedic soma cult, the texts leave no doubt that soma must have been a kind of drug. But ever since the move of Indoaryan tribes into India, more than 3000 years ago, the drug has been replaced by absolutely innocuous plants—and still the form of religion has been kept alive; a ceremony of the kind described was filmed in 1964, see F. Staal, *Agni* (Berkeley, 1983). The ritual secures a marked advantage for the practitioners, the Brahmans, who hand it on through their families. Within the institution, their "fitness" has replaced the "opium effect."

52. Cf. Burkert 1983, 26 f.

53. A Christian sect that presents the best conditions for raising many children may double within 20 years and increase by the factor 40 within a century, cf. R. W. Brednich, *Mennonite Folklife and Folklore* (Ottawa, 1977), on the Hutterers in Canada.

54. Rappaport 1984, 233.

55. See C. Malone, A. Bonamo, and T. Gonder, "The Death Cults of Prehistoric Malta," *Scientific American* 269, 6 (December 1993) 76–83, esp. 83; in general, J. Diamond, "Ecological Collapses of Past Civilizations," *Proc. Amer. Phil. Society* 138 (1994) 363–370.

56. Or rather, less, if we accept that the danger of certain diseases, for example trichinosis, is modified by dietary rules.

57. See Chapter 7 at n. 50.

58. See below at nn. 111–114.

59. The basic work was M. Foucault, *Histoire de la sexualité* (Paris, 1976–1984); cf. D. M. Halperin, J. J. Winkler, and F. E. Zeitlin, *Before Sexuality: The Construction of Erotic Experience in the Ancient Greek World* (Princeton, 1989).

60. Ditfurth 1976, 45.

61. Lumsden and Wilson 1983, 20.

62. Lorenz 1963, 259–264.

63. See below at nn. 116–122.

64. There is not much prospect that mankind's "original" language could be reconstructed; cf. P. E. Ross, *Spektrum der Wissenschaft* 6 (1991) 92–101. The most successful reconstruction of a lost language, Indoeuropean, reaches back to perhaps 2000 years before the first documents, that is, 5000/4000 B.C.—but human language must go back more than 40,000 years.

65. For speculations about a spontaneous rise of language, mainly influenced by Herodotus 2,2, the "Psammetichus experiment," see A. Borst, *Der Turmbau von Babel* (Stuttgart, 1957–1963), esp. I (1957) 99–101.

66. Chimpanzees can be taught some fairly advanced form of language, mostly in the form of sign language; see Fouts-Budd 1979. Whether this is to be regarded as real language or something else, one should admit that their performance is much more human than expected. In contrast to their human partners, however, chimpanzees are not very interested in using and passing on their "language." See also Chapter 3 at n. 32.

67. Bar-Yosef and Vandermeersch 1993; R. White, "Bildhaftes Denken in der Eiszeit," *Spektrum der Wissenschaft* 3 (1994), 62–69.

68. See Dissanayake 1988.

69. See P. Mellars, "Archaeology and Modern Human Origins," *Proc. Brit. Acad.* 82 (1992) 1–35; Bar-Yosef and Vandermeersch 1993.

70. Bar-Yosef and Vandermeersch 1993, 64.

71. This was the thesis of P. Lieberman, "On the Evolution of Human Language," *Proc. of the 7th Int. Cong. of Phonetic Sciences* (Leiden 1972), 258–272; cf. J. N. Spuhler, "Biology, Speed and Language," *Annual Review of Anthropology* 6 (1977) 509–561; G. S. Kruntz, "Sapienization and Speech," *Current Anthropology* 21 (1980) 772–792; further discussions in *Nature* 338 (1989) 758–760; *Spektrum der Wissenschaft* 7 (1989), 34; Bickerton 1990, 176 f; *Spektrum der Wissenschaft* 6 (1991), 100. Most think Lieberman has been refuted, which means that speech may be older than contemporary homo sapiens.

72. For the concept and function of ritual see Burkert 1979 and 1983. For an epicritic study of the concept of ritual, see Bell 1992.

73. See Slobodkin 1992, 35.

74. See also n. 112.

75. Lévi-Strauss, *Les Structures élémentaires de la parenté* (Paris, 1949), associated the incest taboo with the exchange of women, with exchange as such, and even with binary logic.

76. See Bischof 1985.

77. Ibid.

78. The landscape metaphor was used by Burkert 1979, 58, with reference to the myth-and-ritual tradition: "dug those deep vales of human tradition in which even today the streams of our experience will tend to flow," and earlier by Friedman 1974, 34: "Evolution has dug the major channels through which the river of experience runs"; in a negative sense it has been anticipated by Frazer GB I xxvi, who claimed that traditional religion was built "on the sands of superstition rather than on the rock of nature."

193

79. Ditfurth 1976, 165–167.

80. T. Struhsaker, "Auditory Communication among Vervet Monkeys (Cercopithecus aethiops)" in S. A. Altmann, ed., *Social Communication among Primates* (Chicago, 1967). On chimpanzees' reaction to leopards and snakes see Wilson 1978, 83; Lumsden and Wilson 1983, 96. For cross-cultural "knowledge" about life and body, see Atran 1987; Johnson 1987.

81. See Chapter 7 at n. 1.

82. Hence nothing is established or hypothesized in this study at the level of either genes or structure of the brain. A venture in this direction is V. Turner, "Body, Brain, and Culture," in his *On the Edge of the Bush* (Tucson, 1988), 249–273. The attempt of J. Jaynes, *The Origin of Consciousness and the Breakdown of the Bicameral Mind* (Boston, 1976), has failed to convince scientists.

83. The Latin translation, *animal rationale,* catches only part of this concept.

84. For the evolutionary theory of knowledge see Lorenz 1973; Vollmer 1994.

85. See Sommer 1992.

86. Sommer 1992, 80; he adds that the intruder normally takes part in the alarm and gives up aggression.

87. This too has an antecedent in ritual, defined as "action pre-done or re-done" by J. Harrison, *Epilegomena to the Study of Greek Religion* (Cambridge, 1921), xliii.

88. See Burkert, "Elysion," *Glotta* 39 (1961) 208–213; a mythical personality, Linos, arose from the ritual cry *ailinon;* there is a fairy or witch Befana in Italy—comparable to Santa Claus—who takes her name from the festival Epiphanias; further examples in Burkert, *Museum Helveticum* 38 (1981) 203f.

89. What has made the phoenix so permanent is the memorable paradox of annihilation reversed, the circle of death and rebirth, adopted and reinforced by Christianity.

90. Cf. Burkert 1983, 76.

91. See G. R. Levy, *The Gate of Horn* (London, 1948), 22 f; pl. II b.

92. See W. Helck, *Betrachtungen zur Grossen Göttin* (Munich, 1971).

93. Luhmann 1977.

94. Lord Gifford found "natural theology" (see Preface at n.1) equivalent to "the knowledge of God, the Infinite, the All, the First and Only Cause, the One and the Sole Substance, the Sole Being, the Sole Reality, and the Sole Existence."

95. The expression "good to think" is from Lévi-Strauss.

96. In consequence, "god is dead" has been proclaimed as the founding proposition of modern semiology: M. Casalis, *Semiotica* 17 (1976) 35 f.

97. To formalize: a:b is made an equation, x:a = a:b, see Chapter 4 at n. 107. Primates tend to react to threat from a dominant partner by bullying an inferior in turn, a:b = b:y, Sommer 1992, 85.

98. a > b is made into the equation $a - x = b - y$. See Chapter 5.

99. See Lorenz 1973; Vollmer 1994.

100. Richard Gordon, "Reality, Evocation and Boundary in the Mysteries of Mithras," *Journal of Mithraic Studies* 3 (1980) 19–99, p. 22, with regard to the Mithras mysteries.

101. Cf. Cic. *Nat. Deor.* 2,5.

102. For such an attempt see Gordon n. 100.

103. Within language, resonances within the *signifiant,* namely rhythm, assonance, and rhyme, account for stability. Dawkins 1976 suggested that there may be self-replicating "memes" corresponding to self-replicating genes, that is, sentences or commands that engender themselves in the mind. This is hardly more than a metaphor; another metaphor would be the analogy to computer viruses. Their existence and function remain to be demonstrated.

104. L. L. Cavalli-Sforza et al., "Theory and Obeservation in Cultural Transmission," *Science* 218 (1982) 19–27.

105. See Lorenz 1963, 23; cf. Lorenz 1978, 95 ff.

106. Cf. J. Assmann, *Das kulturelle Gedächtnis* (Munich, 1992).

107. Cf. Durkheim 1912.

108. For a discussion of myth and ritual, see Burkert 1979, 56–58.

109. A striking example is Hebr. 12,4–11 on violent education *(paideia)* conducted by a father and by god.

110. Plat. *Leg.* 887de.

111. See J. E. LeDoux, "Das Gedächtnis für Angst," *Spektrum der Wissenschaft* 8 (1994) 76–83.

112. See Lorenz 1963, 65–67. The greylag goose, Martina, got frightened in the unaccustomed situation and instinctively ran towards the window and only then back to the stairs which she was supposed to climb; henceforth she made it a habit for a whole year to make the detour to the window. Once, in a hurry, "she deviated from her habitual path and chose the shortest way." Yet "arrived at the fifth step" she showed signs of horror, "hesitated a moment, turned around, ran hurriedly down the five steps and set forth resolutely, like someone on a very important mission, on her original path to the window and back. This time she mounted the steps according to her former custom" and exhibited all the signs of relief. A disquieting experience gives rise to a fixed behavior pattern, a well-established sort of ritual. Accidentally forgetting it causes grievous anxiety, while going back and repeating the ritual from the start brings back relief. It seems that every Roman pontifex would agree with Lorenz' goose.

113. On the circumcision ritual see Chapter 2 at nn. 50, 51; Chapter 7 at n. 50; Bloch 1986; cf. Bischof 1985, 133 f; see also Dowden 1989, 36. In antiquity the suspicion was often voiced that secret cults practiced human sacrifice or even cannibalism; see A. Henrichs, "Pagan Ritual and the Alleged Crimes of the Early Christians," in *Kyriakon. Festschrift Johannes Quasten* (Münster, 1970), 18–35; Chapter 7 n. 87.

114. *HDA* III 1141; E. v. Künßberg, "Rechtsbrauch und Kinderspiel. Untersuchungen zur deutschen Rechtskunde und Volkskunde," *Sitzungsber* (Heidelberg, 1920), 7.

115. On initiation at Samothrace, see Burkert, in N. Marinatos, R. Hägg, *Greek Sanctuaries: New Approaches* (London, 1993), 184 f; cf. Chapter 7 n. 87.

116. Stat. *Theb.* 3,661.

117. R. Borger, *Die Inschriften Assarhaddons Königs von Assyrien* (Osnabrück, 1967), 9 §7, cf. §2 I, §11 etc.; Sargon II in E. Ebeling, *Die akkadische Gebetsserie "Handerhebung"* (Berlin, 1952), 98f. (Rs.3): "servant, fearing your [god Adad's] divinity." Cf. Lambert 1960, 104: "He who fears the gods is not slighted by anyone."

118. S. Parpola, *Letters from Assyrian and Babylonian Scholars* (Helsinki, 1993), 155 nr. 188 (672 B.C.), cf. Lambert 1960, 104, line 143 f. Isocrates *Bus.* 25 concurs, even if alluding to the atheistic text of Kritias *TrGF* 43 F 19: "Those who, in the beginning, wrought this fear (of the divine) in us, have caused us not to behave totally in the way of beasts towards each other."

119. Prov. 1,7; Eccles. 12,13.

120. C. Austin, *Nova Fragmenta Euripidea* (Berlin, 1968), nr. 81,48 = *TrGF* Adesp. 356; cf. Theognis 1179: "Respect the gods and fear them." For hair-raising shivers see at n. 62.

121. R. R. Marett, *The Threshold of Religion* (London, 1909, 4th ed. 1929), 13: "Of all English words awe is, I think, the one that expresses the fundamental religious feeling most neatly." Cf. *HrwG* I 455–471 s.v. Angst. On anxiety and ritual, see also the discussion in Homans 1941; H. v. Stietencron, ed., *Angst und Gewalt. Ihre Präsenz und ihre Bewältigung in den Religionen* (Düsseldorf, 1979).

122. R. Otto, *Das Heilige* (Munich, 1917), transl. *The Idea of the Holy* (2nd ed. Oxford, 1950), chap. IV.

123. Cf. Ditfurth 1976, 269: sexuality ceases in times of famine. In certain species the importance of procreation overrides self-preservation: procreate and die.

124. Alexander Marshack has found the symbols of killing among the first notations of paleolithic man; he links "time-factored death" to the "cognitive beginnings" of mankind. See Marshack 1972, esp. 235 ff. In a Babylonian myth, Sea, the primeval mother, has to be killed to allow for the creation of a stable world out of her body, *Enuma elish* IV-VI, *ANET* 67–69.

125. Cf. Burkert, "Eracle e gli altri eroi culturali del Vicino Oriente," in C. Bonnet and C. Jourdain-Annequin, eds., *Héraclès d'une rive à l'autre de la Méditerranée* (Brussels, 1992), 111–127.

126. Aesch. *Hik.* 479. Cf. Matth. 10,28, Luke 12,4 f.

127. Hieronymus *Chron.*, *praefatio: timor enim dei hominum timorem expellit.*

128. Cf. Burkert 1983; Bloch 1992.

129. See also the more general finding of E. Becker, *The Denial of Death* (New York, 1973), 3: "society everywhere is a living myth of the significance of human life, a defiant creation of meaning."

130. H. Huber in H. J. Braun and K. Henking, eds., *Homo religiosus* (Zürich, 1990), 158.

131. St. Paul, Rom. 9,26; II Cor. 3,3; 6,16 etc.; Mt. 16,16; 26,63 etc.; see Bultmann and von Rad in *ThWbNT* II (1935) 833–877.

132. John 14,19.

133. It can be reformulated in philosophy to postulate timelessness, the ultimate freedom from change. This is the "werttheoretische Fundamentalsatz" in O. Weininger, *Geschlecht und Charakter* (Vienna, 1903; repr. Munich, 1980) 168 f: "Der Wert ist also das Zeitlose."

134. In Ziusudra, Atrahasis, Gilgamesh, Noah, Deukalion, Manu. Cf. J. Rudhardt, "Le Mythe grec relatif à l'instauration du sacrifice," in his *Du mythe de la religion grecque et de la compréhension d'autrui* (Geneva, 1981), 209–226; G. Caduff, *Antike Sintflutsagen* (Göttingen, 1986).

2. Escape and Offerings

1. Report of R. Françillon, Zaire 1962.

2. Sen. *Nat. Qu.* 4,6 f; blood of a "blind-rat," or menstrual blood is used against hail according to Plut. *Quaest. Conv.* 700e; cf. the sac-   197 rifice of a black lamb in expectation of a tempest in Aristophanes, *Ran.* 847 f; sacrifice of white lambs in a storm to summon the Dioscures, Hom. *Hymn.* 33,8–11. Agamemnon has to slaughter Iphigeneia to stop the winds. A priestess of the winds is attested as early as Mycenaean Knossos, cf. Burkert 1985, 175. See Chapter 5 at n. 20.

3. Cf. E. R. Dodds, *Pagan and Christian in an Age of Anxiety* (Cambridge, 1965), 39–45; on Aristeides' chronology, see A. Humbel, *Ailios Aristeides, Klage über Eleusis* (Vienna, 1994), 45–52.

4. Aristid. *Or.* 48, 26–28; Burkert 1981, 123 f; H. S. Versnel, "Polycrates and His Ring: Two Neglected Aspects," *Studi Storico-Religiosi* 1 (1977) 17–46; "Self-Sacrifice, Compensation and the Anonymous Gods," in *Le Sacrifice dans l'antiquité. Entretiens sur l'antiquité classique 27* (Geneva, 1981), 135–185, esp. 163 ff.

5. On votive religion see Burkert 1987b, 12–14.

6. Paus. 8,34,1–3. At Selinus there is sacrifice first to the dirty *(miaroi)*, then to the clean *(katharoi)* Tritopatreis, Jameson 1993, 29 f; 61–64.—According to Ptolemaios Chennos, the Nemean Lion bit off one of Heracles' fingers, "and there is a tomb of the chopped-off finger," Phot. *Bibl.* 147a37-b2.

7. Ed. A. Hilka, *Historia septem sapientium* II (Heidelberg, 1913). Cf. J. G. Frazer, *Apollodorus, The Library* II, Loeb C. L. 1921, 409–422; D. Page, *The Homeric Odyssey* (Oxford, 1955), 8 f.

8. Frazer 1898, IV 355–357; cf. id., *GB* IV 219; III 161; see also Levy 1948, 49; E. M. Loeb, "The Blood Sacrifice Complex," *Memoirs of the Anthropological Association* 30, 1923; *KHM* nr.25; *EdM* IV 1143 s.v. Finger.

9. Frazer 1898, IV 356.

10. Levy 1948, 93.

11. *GB* IV 219.

12. Pindar dissented: "If property is being robbed, it is better to be dead than to be a coward," Fr. 169a 16 f.—heroic values versus rational choice.

13. Aesch. *Ag.* 1008–1016, a simile for prudent sacrifice to avert catastrophe.

14. *Dedet tempestatebus aide mereto[d]*, Sarcophagus of L. Cornelius Scipio, *CIL* I 9; R. Wachter, *Altlateinische Inschriften* (Bern, 1987), 301–342.

15. One is reminded of the phrase in Mark 14,51 f: "and he left his linen cloth and escaped naked."

16. See Chapter 1 n. 61.

17. Cf. K. Lorenz, in H. v. Ditfurth, ed., *Aspekte der Angst* (Stuttgart, 1965), 40; Baudy 1980, 101–118; on animal and *daimon* see also R. Padel, *In and Out of the Mind* (Princeton, 1992), 138–147; cf. Ditfurth 1976, 168 on ghost appearances.

18. See Chapter 1 nn. 79–80.

19. See, in general, F. T. Elworthy, *The Evil Eye* (London, 1895); S. Seligmann, *Der böse Blick und Verwandtes* (Berlin, 1910); O. Koenig, *Kultur und Verhaltensforschung* (Munich, 1970), 183–260, esp. 194–200: "Die Ritualisierung des Auges in der Ornamentik"; Burkert 1979, 73; Baudy 1980, 133 f; A. Dundes, "Wet and Dry, the Evil Eye," in V. J. Newall, ed., *Folklore Studies in the XXth Century* (Woodbridge, Suffolk, 1980), 37–63. For Mesopotamia, see E. Ebeling, "Beschwörungen gegen den Feind und den bösen Blick aus dem Zweistromlande," *Archiv orientalni* 17 (1949) 172–211; M. L. Thomsen, "The Evil Eye in Mesopotamia," *JNES* 51 (1992) 19–32; for Islam, see *ER* V 383 f; for antiquity, see O. Jahn, "Über den Aberglauben des bösen Blicks bei den Alten," *Berichte der Sächsischen Gesellschaft der Wissenschaften, Phil.-hist. Cl.* 7 (1855) 28–110, cf. R. Schlesier, *Kulte, Mythen und Gelehrte* (Frankfurt, 1994) 33–64; Plut. *Q. Conv.* 5,7, 680c-683 b; a Roman mosaic: *CCCA* III pl. CVII nr. 210 (cf. Harrison 1922, 196 f.), cf. pl. CVI nr.207; on phallus see Diod. 4,6,4; Herter *RE* XIX 1734 f., cf. phallic guardians, Fehling 1974, 7–14; Burkert 1979, 39–41; for associations of "eye" and "female" see G. Devereux, "The Self-Blinding of Oidipous in Sophokles: Oidipous Tyrannos," *JHS* 93 (1973) 36–49; on Attic eye-cups see N. Kunisch, "Die Augen der Augenschalen," *AK* 33 (1990) 20–27; in general, Faraone 1992, 45–48; 58 f. Hunters treat the eyes of their quarry in special ways, Meuli 1975, 970 f; we shut the eyes of the dead.

20. Aristoph. *Pax* 279.

21. Šatapatha Brahmana, see W. Doniger O'Flaherty, *Hindu Myths* (Harmondsworth, 1975), 32 f.

22. Lambert 1960, 104 line 144.

23. Harrison 1922, esp. 8–10; see R. Schlesier in *HrwG* II 41–45. Otto Jahn coined the term "apotropaic."

24. This injunction is common in Akkadian, Hittite, Greek, and Roman rituals, e.g. Castellino 1977, 625; 674; 679; *ANET* 348 iv 3; Aesch. *Cho.* 96–99; Soph. *OC* 490; Ov. *Fast.* 6,164 (infra n.72).

25. Liv. 8,6,11: *placuit averruncandae deum irae victimas caedi.*

26. Plut. *Q. Rom.* 284c; cf. Wissowa 1912, 60; 420 f; at Mycenaean Pylos, apparently in a situation of crisis, individuals were sent to the sanctuary *(hieto)*—was it a case of human sacrifice? PY Tn 316, see A. Heubeck, *Aus der Welt der frühgriechischen Lineartafeln* (Göttingen, 1966), 100–103; S. Hiller, O. Panagl, *Die frühgriechischen Texte aus mykenischer Zeit* (Darmstadt, 1976), 309; Hughes 1991, 199–202.

27. A. Aarne, *Die magische Flucht* (Helsinki, 1930); cf. Campbell 1949, 196–207; *KHM* 79. The oldest poem of pursuit seems to be the Sumerian "Inanna and Enki"; in it Inanna conveys the divine decrees from Eridu to Uruk; the bearer is pursued by messengers of Enki and confronted at seven stops; see Bottéro-Kramer 1989, 230–256; but there is no magical act of throwing away.

28. Meuli 1975, 847; 868; 873; 878. Cf. Chapter 3 at n. 41.

29. Pomponius Mela 3,43; *RE* VI A 951.

30. Cf. the story about robbing gold from gold-digging ants in India, Hdt. 3,102–105; Megasthenes *FGrHist* 715 F 23.

31. See Burkert 1979, 41–43; Chapter 7 at nn. 37–40.

32. Apollod. 1,133.

33. Aristoph. *Ach.* 350 f., *Eq.* 1057, *Av.* 66, *Ran.* 479–493; cf. Juvenal 14,199.

34. Annals of Sennacherib, battle of Halule: enemies in flight "let their dung go into their chariots," Luckenbill 1927 §254, II 128.

35. Used by his enemies to ridicule Aratus of Sicyon, Plut. *Arat.* 29,7 f.

36. Lumsden and Wilson 1983, 96; De Waal 1982, 57 f; Goodall 1990, 63 f.

37. *HDA* III 1178–1180 s.v. *grumus merdae*. An example appears also in A. Lorenz, *Wenn der Vater mit dem Sohne* (Munich, 1978), 150–153.

38. *PGM* IV 1402. Cf. Hippocr. *Morb. Sacr.* 1, VI 360 f. Littré: excrements indicate Hekate *Enodia*.

39. Ael. *Nat. An.* 6,34, from Sostratos, cf. *Schol.* Nik. *Ther.* 565; Aesopus 118 Perry.

40. The terminology is Dawkins'; see Dawkins 1976, 49 ff.

41. Cf. Burkert 1979, 104 f; see also Chapter 7 at n.51. There are various modern constructs to explain the ritual: Assimilation to the "Mother," Farnell 1896/1909 III 300 f; asceticism, A.D. Nock, *ARW* 23 (1925) 25–33 Nock 1972, 7–15; fecundation of Mother Earth, Cook 1914–1940 I 394–396; R. Pettazzoni, *I Misteri* (Bologna, 1924), 105 ff; H. Herter, *Gnomon* 17 (1941) 322 f. It is a "disease sent by a god," according to Arrian *FGrHist* 156 F 80, an act of irrational frenzy in Catullus 63.

42. *Erra* 4,56: Dalley 1989, 305.

43. Hellanikos *FGrHist* 4 F 178 (Atossa); Amm. Marc. 14,6,17 (Semiramis); Claudian. *In Eutrop.* 1,339–345.

44. Luc. *Dea Syr.* 19–26, cf. M. Hörig, *Dea Syria* (Neukirchen-Vluyn, 1979); *ead.*, "Dea Syria-Atargatis," *ANRW* II 17,3 (1984) 1536–1581.

45. Cf. T. Mitamura, *Chinese Eunuchs* (Tokio, 1970); see also Bertolucci's film, *The Last Emperor.*

46. The local name of the goddess at Bambyke was Atargatis. Kybebos occurs as a name for Kybebe's priests, Semonides Fr. 36 West. The name Kombabos has also been associated with Humbaba, the demon of the cedar forest in Gilgamesh mythology (see Chapter 3 n. 22).

47. Species *callithrix jacchus*, Bischof 1985, 316–319.

48. Luc. *Dea Syr.* 51.

49. Ex. 4,24–26. The word translated as "private parts" literally means "feet," but this is generally assumed to be a euphemism; see Kautzsch 1922–1923, I 104, *HAL* 1106.

50. Cf. Noth 1962, 49 f; Childs 1974, 95–101; Bloch 1992, 93: "to submit to the conquest of God . . . to co-operate with His apparently murderous intentions." The Septuagint translation makes the mother's exclamation a charm for clotting blood: "The blood of the circumcision of my little boy has stopped running."

51. A. M. Hocart, *Kingship* (London, 1927), 136 gives a comparable report of circumcision at Fiji: "The operation is said to be performed as a sacrifice to the recently dead"; the term applied is also "used of a human victim buried with a chief, of a little finger cut off at his death, of funeral gifts, and finally of the people who stay in the house for a time after death" (that is, left there as if belonging to death). For more modern observations on circumcision see Bloch 1986.

52. Ch. Belger, *BphW* 12 (1896) 640; Hitzig-Blümner 1895–1910, III 236 on Paus. 8,34,1–3.

53. *RML* V 317 f; cf. 324; H. Herter, *De Priapo*, Giessen 1932, 193, with doubts as to the identification of these statuettes.

54. Arnob. 5,14.

55. John 11,50, cf. Mark 10,45 "to give his life as ransom, instead of many"; J. N. Bremmer, "The Atonement in the Interaction of Greeks, Jews, and Christians," in J. N. Bremmer F. García Martínez, ed., *Sacred History and Sacred Texts in Early Judaism* (Kampen, 1992), 75–93.

56. In a ritual context the formula appears in Sophocles. To appease the Eumenides at Kolonos by libation sacrifice, "one soul atoning for all will be enough," *Oedipus at Colonus* 498 f.

57. *Enuma elish* 6,14 (*ANET* 68; Dalley 1989, 261).

58. Above, n. 13.

59. Cf. L. Röhrich, "Die Volksballade von 'Herrn Peters Seefahrt' und die Menschenopfer-Sagen in Märchen, Mythos, Dichtung," in *Festschrift F. von der Leyen* (Munich, 1963), 177–212.

60. Verg. *Aen.* 5,815; 835–871.

61. Procilius in Varro *Ling. Lat.* 5,148 *HRR* I 313 *(dehisse terram)*; Liv. 7,6,1–6 *(vorago; donaque ac fruges super eum a multitudine virorum ac mulierum congestas)*; Hülsen *RE* IV 1892 f; *stipes* thrown into the lake by Roman *equites* on the birthday of Augustus: Suet. *Aug.* 57.

62. Above, n. 2.

63. *LSS* 115,5–7 (§1).

64. G. Graber, *Sagen und Märchen aus Kärnten* (Graz, 1944), 85; W. Kohlhaas, *Das war Württemberg* (Stuttgart, 1978), 21; D. Sabean, "Das Bullenopfer," *Journal für Geschichte* 1 (1985), 20–25.

65. *HDA* I 963.

66. See Burkert 1979, 59–77; J. Bremmer, "Scapegoat Rituals in Ancient Greece," *HSCP* 87 (1983) 299–320.

67. The basic text is OT Isaiah 53, applied to the passion of Jesus.

68. It has been dealt with in an original way in several books by René Girard (see Girard 1977 and 1982; Burkert 1987a), who makes it the basis of sacrifice, of the organization of a "unanimous" society and of human civilization as such. Instead of competition and "mimetic desire" as construed by Girard, I prefer to emphasize the situation of anxiety and the characteristic reaction to it of "abandoning."

69. *Lev.* 16; Burkert 1979, 64; see Janowski and Wilhelm 1993.

70. O. Eissfeldt, *Kleine Schriften* III (Tübingen, 1966), 85–93; Janowski and Wilhelm 1993, 119 f.

71. Meissner 1920, 222; Furlani 1941, 285–305. For the concept of substitute *(puhu)* in Mesopotamian magic see *AHw* 877 f.

72. Ov. *Fast.* 6,131–168, esp. 158–167, cf. Burkert 1992a, 58 f; for a Hittite parallel see H. Kronasser, *Die Sprache* 7 (1961) 140–167; V. Haas, *Orientalia* 40 (1971) 410–430; H.S. Versnel, *ZPE* 58 (1985) 266–268.

73. Cf. also Verg. *Aen.* 5,483 f., sacrifice of a bull instead of killing an adversary in boxing, *hanc tibi, Eryx, meliorem animam pro morte Daretis persolvo.* Jahweh accepted a ram instead of Isaac, Gen. 22.

74. M. Leglay, *Saturne africain*, Paris 1966.

75. Lev. 18,21; II Reg. 23,10; cf. *HAL* 560.

76. Diod. 20,14,4–7. Cf. Plat. *Minos* 315bc; Demon *FGrHist* 327 F 18 (Sardinien); Theophrastus in Porph. *abst.* 2,27,2; Diod. 13,86 cf. 5,66,5; Dion. Hal. ant.1,38,2–3; Porph. *abst.* 2,56; Philon Bybl.

FGrHist 790 F 3b = Euseb. *P.E.* 4,16,11; there were legal counteractions by Dareios (Iustin 19,1,10), Gelon (Theophrastus Fr. 586 Fortenbaugh = *Schol.* Pind. Pyth. 2,2; Plut. *Reg. et imp. apophth.* 175a, *De Sera* 552 a), finally Tiberius (Tert. *Apol.* 9,2). Cf. Hughes 1991, 115–130. "Tophets" in Carthage, Motye-Mozia, Sardinia, see L. E. Stager, *Oriental Institute, Annual Report* (1978–79) 56–59; A. Ciasca, "Sul 'tofet' di Mozia," *Sicilia Archeologica* 14 (1971), 11–16; R. Pauli, *Sardinien* (Cologne, 1978), 134–139. All of the evidence has been called into question by Sabbatino Moscati, who claims the children had died a natural death: S. Moscati, "Il sacrifico punico dei fanciulli: Realtà o invenzione?," *Quaderni dell' Accademia Nazionale dei Lincei* 261 (Rome, 1987); S. Moscati and S. Ribichini, "Il sacrificio dei bambini: Un aggiornamento," *Quaderni dell' Accademia Nazionale dei Lincei* 388 (Rome, 1991).

77. *FGrHist* 790 F 3b. Cf. Plutarch on human sacrifice in Rome, above, n. 26.

78. Above, n. 21.

79. *Or.* 48,44; 51,19–25; Burkert 1981, 122 f.

80. Hdt. 7,114; J. de Vries, *Altgermanische Religionsgeschichte* (2nd ed. Berlin, 1957), 421; Elisabeth Bathory, brought to court in 1611, Burkert 1981, 122.

81. Caesar, *Gallic War* 6,16.

82. *Descent of Inanna* 277; 284–288 (Bottéro-Kramer 1989, 286 f).

83. Cass. Dio 59,8,3; Suet. *Calig.* 14,2; 27,2.

84. Aur. Victor *Caes.* 14,8; cf. Cass. Dio 69,11,3.

85. Cf. Bloch 1992. See also Faraone 1992, 47 on animal trophies as amulets, with the threatening message: "Look what we have done to these powerful animals and monsters."

3. The Core of a Tale

1. Schapp (1884–1965) 1953; two other volumes have followed, *Philosophie der Geschichten* (Leer, 1959; 2nd ed. Frankfurt, 1981), and *Wissen in Geschichten* (2nd ed. Wiesbaden, 1976).

2. *Tractatus logico-philosophicus* 1.1: "Die Welt ist, was der Fall ist."

3. Mainly due to F. G. Heyne; cf. Burkert 1980 and 1993; F. Graf, *Greek Mythology. An Introduction* (Baltimore, 1993), 9–34.

4. J. and W. Grimm, *KHM* 1812–1815; *Deutsche Sagen* (Berlin, 1816–1818); J. Grimm, *Deutsche Mythologie* I-III (4th ed. Berlin, 1876).

5. J. A. MacCullock and I. H. Gray, *Mythology of All Races,* 13 vol. (New York, 1922).

6. Suffice it to refer to Kirk 1970.

7. For myth as "tale applied" in its social function see Burkert 1979, cf. Burkert 1993.

8. Aarne-Thompson 1964; the first edition was A. Aarne, *Verzeichnis der Märchentypen* (Helsinki, 1911).

9. Cf. Burkert 1979, esp. 10–14 for a discussion of the structuralist approach.

10. V. Propp, *Morfologija skaski* [Morphology of the Tale] (Leningrad, 1928); translated as *Morphology of the Folktale* (Bloomington, 1958); see Propp 1968; see also the interesting elaborations of Dundes 1964; Jason 1984; Milne 1988.

11. A. J. Greimas, "Eléments d'une grammaire narrative," in *Du sens* (Paris, 1970), 157–183, takes Propp's pattern as model of *le récit,* the tale *tout court.*

12. Dundes 1964; for Greimas cf. n. 11.

13. Isidor Levin *EdM* I 135: "So hat sich das Stilempfinden A[fanas'iev']s bzw. des Bauern Zyrjanov ein Jahrhundert später in den USA, Frankreich und Deutschland bei Erzählforschern als 'Tiefenstruktur' jeder Erzählung, ja des 'homo narrans' überhaupt, geltend gemacht." A. N. Afanas'ev (1826–1871), *Narodnye russkie skaski* (Moscow, 1855–1863, 2nd ed. 1873).

14. Propp's functions 23–28 (the hero unrecognized in his own house, the test, recognition and punishment) suspiciously reproduce the *Odyssey.* Parallels to the *Odyssey* had been collected ever since W. Grimm, "Die Sage von Polyphem," *Abh.* (Berlin, 1857), cf. Burkert 1979, 33; see Chapter 2 at n. 7.

15. E. S. Hartland, *The Legend of Perseus. A Study in the Tradition in Story, Custom, and Belief* I-III (London, 1894–1896). See also at n. 85.

16. Cf. Burkert 1991.

17. Burkert 1979, 83–85; a newly discovered 7th century representation: Ph. Brize, *MDAI(Athen)* 100 (1985) 53–90; Schefold 1993, 107–109; see also C. Jourdain-Annequin, *Héraclès aux portes du soir,* Besançon 1989.

18. *Od.* 12,70.

19. Meuli 1975, 594–610 (originally *Odyssee und Argonautika,* (Ph.D. diss. Basel 1921), 2–24); the type is called Helfermärchen, Aarne-Thompson 1964, 180–182 nr. 513.

20. Cf. Chapter 2 at n. 27.

21. Cf. G. Crane, *Calpyso: Backgrounds and Conventions of the Odyssey* (Frankfurt, 1988).

22. D. O. Edzard, "Gilgameš und Huwawa," *Zeitschrift für Assyriologie* 80 (1990) 165–203; 81 (1991) 165–233; this text is more complete now than its reelaboration in the Gilgamesh epic, Tablet V.

23. Traditionally called *Lugal-e:* J. van Dijk, *LUGAL UD ME-LAM-bi NIR-GAL*, I (Leiden, 1983); Bottéro-Kramer 1989, 339–377. The text still presents many difficult problems of interpretation.

24. Cf. W. Burkert, "Eracle e gli altri eroi culturali del Vicino Oriente," in C. Bonnet and C. Jourdain-Annequin, eds., *Héraclès d'une rive à l'autre de la Méditerranée* (Brussels, 1992), 111–127.

25. Bottéro-Kramer 1989, 276–300 (Sumerian versions). The Akkadian version (*ANET* 106–109; Dalley 1989, 154–162; Bottéro-Kramer 1989, 318–330) is much abridged in comparison to the Sumerian version. Cf. W. Burkert, "Literarische Texte und funktionaler Mythos. Ištar und Atrahasis," in J. Assmann, W. Burkert, and F. Stolz, *Funktionen und Leistungen des Mythos* (Freiburg, 1982), 63–82.

26. The Akkadian version has *asinnu*, a certain kind of priest.

27. Cf. Chapter 2 at n. 82.

28. *Gilgamesh* IX-XI; *ANET* 88–97; Dalley 1989, 95–120. The quest that fails in the end is a favorite pattern of movies. An original inversion of the quest tale has also been invented by J. R. R. Tolkien, *The Lord of the Rings* (London, 1954–55). The quest is not to get but to get rid of a powerful object.

29. Arist. *Poet.* 1450a38.

30. Burkert 1979, 15.

31. Burkert 1979, 16. Cf. Gans 1981, 98–107; 99: "the imperative is not a 'defective' form of the declarative but its ancestor."

32. Sullivan et al. 1982, 410. I am grateful to Professor Fouts for having made this publication available to me. On the language of apes see also Bickerton 1990, 106–110; Chapter 1 at n. 66.

33. See Bickerton 1990, 122–126; here 116, about a genie who never learned to speak.

34. Critics might point out that this language of chimpanzees is not their own invention; they have been taught it by a superior species. We are not dealing with the invention of language, however, but with the use made of it once it is acquired.

35. "Functions" 12–14. Cf. M. Lüthi, *Die Gabe im Märchen und in der Sage*, (Ph.D. diss., Bern, 1943).

36. Hom. *Od.* 10, 277–307, a model case for Propp's pattern: the loss (8) of comrades, the hero decides to go (9–10); leaving his home

base (11) he meets Hermes (12), who provides the *pharmakon* (14); he gets to the place required (15), and the loss is made up (19).

37. Hom. *Od.* 13,221; 352.

38. Morris 1967, 202–206, has coined the term "grooming talk" for noninformative conversation as a form of social activity.

39. For the impact of hunting on human body building, behavior, family structure, use of weapons, and religious sacrifice, see Morris 1967; Lee and DeVore 1968; cf. Burkert 1983; 1987a.

40. K. Hoffmann, *Der Injunktiv im Veda* (Heidelberg, 1967). Its functions are to mention, to describe by evoking memory ("erwähnend," "memorativ," "erwähnende Beschreibung"). See also M. L. West. "Injunctive Usage in Greek," *Glotta* 67 (1989) 135–138.

41. H. M. Chadwick and N. K. Chadwick, *The Growth of Literature* III (Cambridge, 1940), 192–226. Cf. K. Meuli, "Scythika," in Meuli 1975, 817–879 (originally 1935). See also Burkert 1979, 88–94.

42. Phrixos: Pind. Pyth. 4,159; Iason acts as a healer in the Phineus story, see the vase picture in Schefold 1993, 267 fig. 287.

43. Cf. n. 25.

44. On myth and ritual see Burkert 1983, 29–34; Burkert 1993. Myth and ritual continue to have different rules. The sense of the tale is dependent on the unity of structure, from beginning to end; you cannot leave a tale "without its head," the ancients said (Plato *Leg.* 752a). In ritual action details can be isolated and repeated over and over again.

45. Tales of deceit-deception are put in a special category of tales by Dundes 1964. Stories about deception appeal to and presuppose intelligence. But even deception is not a prerogative of humans, cf. Sommer 1992.

46. Aarne and Thompson 1964 nr. 425; Apul. *Met.* 4,28–6,24; J. Oe. Swahn, *The Tale of Cupid and Psyche* (Lund, 1955) (documentation of variants); the thesis of a purely literary filiation is presented by D. Fehling, "Amor und Psyche," *Abh.* (Mainz, 1977) 9; see also R. Merkelbach, *Roman und Mysterium* (Munich, 1962), 1–53; G. Binder and R. Merkelbach, eds., *Amor und Psyche* (Darmstadt, 1968) (Wege der Forschung); D. Fehling, "Die alten Literaturen als Quelle der neuzeitlichen Märchen," in Siegmund 1984, 79–92; J. Oe. Swahn, "Psychemythos und Psychemärchen," ibid. 92–102.

47. See, as to *KHM,* H. Rölleke, *Die älteste Märchensammlung der Brüder Grimm* (Geneva, 1975), and in Siegmund 1984, 125–137.

48. R. Förster, *Der Raub und die Rückkehr der Persephone in ihrer Bedeutung für die Mythologie, Litteratur- und Kunstgeschichte* (Stuttgart, 1874); Richardson 1974, 74–86; Burkert 1979, 138–140 (not

treated in Dowden 1989). The initiation context of the Kore myth has been stressed by Lincoln 1981, 71–90.

49. Burkert 1979, 6 f; Dowden 1989.

50. Dan 1977.

51. O. Rank, *Der Mythos von der Geburt des Helden* (Vienna, 1909).

52. Hes. Fr. 135; *LIMC* s.v.; cf. n. 15.

53. *LIMC* s.v. Auge.

54. Burkert 1983, 161–168; Dowden 1989, 117–146.

55. Dowden 1989, 182–191.

56. Burkert 1979, 6.

57. *Popol Vuh. The Maya Book of the Dawn of Life,* trans. D. Tedlock (New York, 1985), 114–120; cf. Burkert 1979, 147 n. 19.

58. *ANET* 119: I try to give a more literal rendering. For *entu* = High Priestess ("changeling" *ANET*) see *AHw* 220 s.v. *entu*. For the celibacy of *entu*, see *Atrahasis* III vii 6 f., p. 102 f. Lambert-Millard; Dalley 1989, 35. Note that the preserved forms of the text are hundreds of years later than the dates of the historical King Sargon.

59. See Binder 1964.

60. Moses in Ex. 2; Rhea Silvia: Liv. 1,4 cf. Ennius, *Ann.* 35–51 Vahlen = Fr. I xxix Skutsch.

61. *KHM* 12; for the French original "Persinette," by Mlle. de la Force, 1698, see M. Lüthi, *Volksmärchen und Volkssage* (Bern, 1961, 3rd ed. 1975), 62–96, 187–190.

62. *KHM* 53.

63. S. Hirsch, "Das Lied 'Een ridder ende een meysken ionck,'" *Zeitschrift für deutsche Philologie* 79 (1960) 155 ff.

64. Cf. L. Koenen, "Eine Hypothesis zur Auge des Euripides," *ZPE* 4 (1969) 7–18, esp. 14–18 on the festival Plynteria. Cf. Nausikaa washing clothes in anticipation of her marriage.

65. See Bischof 1985 pass.

66. A convenient collection of material is in *GB* X 22–100.

67. J. Harrison, *Mythology and Monuments of Ancient Athens* (London, 1890), xxvi–xxxvi, on *arrhephoroi,* cf. below n. 72. See A. Brelich, *Paides e Parthenoi* (Rome, 1969); Dowden 1989.

68. See/H. Jeanmaire in Binder-Merkelbach 1968, 313–333; O. J. Brendel, "Der grosse Fries in der Villa dei Misteri," *JDAI* 81 (1966) 206–260; Merkelbach (see n. 46) made Amor and Psyche the key text for mysteries as reflected in Greek romances, especially the Isis mysteries; cf. Burkert 1987, 95 f.

69. A. van Gennep, *Les Rites de passage* (Paris, 1909).

70. S. L. La Fontaine, "Ritualization of Women's Life Crises in Bugisu," in J. S. La Fontaine, ed., *The Interpretation of Ritual* (London, 1972), 159–186; see also the short report on Yaos (Africa) in *Anthropos* 30 (1935) 875; cf. Burkert 1979,16.

71. Today the operations of female circumcision are the most controversial.

72. On Arrhephoria W. Burkert, "Kekropidensage und Arrhephoria," *Hermes* 94 (1966) 1–25; K. Jeppesen, *AJA* 83 (1979) 381–394; L. van Sichelen, "Nouvelles Orientations dans l'étude de l'arréphorie antique," *ACl* 56 (1987) 88–102 (no collective initiation); Brulé 1987, 11–175 (initiation); divergent interpretation in N. Robertson, "The Riddle of the Arrhephoria at Athens," *HSCP* 87 (1983) 241–288.

73. L. Kahil, "L'Artémis de Brauron: Rites et mystère," *AK* 20 (1977) 86–98 cf. L. Kahil in W. G. Moon, ed., *Ancient Greek Art and Iconography* (Madison, 1983), 231–244; Brulé 1987, 177–283; R. Hamilton, "Alkman and the Athenian Arkteia," *Hesperia* 58 (1989) 449–472; Chr. Sourvinou-Inwood, *Studies in Girls' Transitions,* Athens 1988; Dowden 1989, 25–33.

74. It is possible to place the Arcadian myth of Kallisto, which conforms to the pattern, at Brauron, but this is not usually done. There is another myth of girls carried off at Brauron by Pelasgian pirates and rescued by Hymenaios, "marriage" personified, Schol.A *Il.* 18,493; Eustath. 1157,20; Proklos, *Chrestom.* in Phot. *bibl.* 321 a 22. The normal cult myth of Brauron is about a bear killed by Athenian youths and expiation of this crime by offering the girls to Artemis. W. Sale, "The Temple Legends of the Arkteia," *RhM* 118 (1975) 265–284. Offerings of garments of women who died at childbirth are in Eur. *Iph.Taur.* 1464–1467.

75. Eur. l.c.; cf. C. Wolff, "Euripides' *Iphigenia among the Taurians:* Aetiology, Ritual, and Myth," *Classical Antiquity* 11 (1992) 307–334.

76. The Locrian maiden tribute was interpreted as a kind of vicarious sacrifice in antiquity, whereas moderns find the initiatory motifs in it; see Hughes 1991, 166–184.

77. Judges 11, 30–40.

78. Eur. *Hippol.* 1425–1430; U. v. Wilamowitz-Moellendorff, *Griechische Tragödien* I[10], (Berlin, 1926), 100–104 made this the origin of the Hippolytos myth.

79. See C. Koch *RE* VIIIA 1732–1753; cf. Chapter 2 at n. 26.

80. Myths tell that a virgin was impregnated right at the hearth: it was Ocresia, the mother of King Servius Tullius. Rhea Silvia, mother of Romulus and Remus, was a Vestal virgin, above n. 60. Certain Mesopotamian priestesses were forbidden to bear children, above n. 58.

81. For Greek "phallocracy," see E. Keuls, *The Reign of the Phallus* (Berkeley, 1985).

82. See R. D. Griffith, *JHS* 189 (1989) 171–173; Krummen 1990, 168–204.

83. Ephoros *FGrHist* 70 F 149; see K. Dover, *Greek Homosexuality* (New York, 1978), 189 f; H. Patzer, *Die griechische Knabenliebe* (Wiesbaden, 1982).

84. Akusilaos *FGrHist* 2 F 22; bronze relief from Olympia, 7th cent., Schefold 1993, 122; E. Laufer, *Kaineus,* Rom 1985, and *LIMC* V 884–891.

85. M. H. Jameson, "Perseus, the Hero of Mykenai," in R. Hägg and G. C. Nordquist, eds., *Celebrations of Death and Divinity in the Bronze Age Argolid* (Stockholm, 1990), 213–222.

86. V. Propp, *Istoriceskije korni volsebnoj skaski* (Leningrad, 1946); *Die historischen Wurzeln des Zaubermärchens* (Munich, 1987).

87. Plato *Gorg.* 574b; *Resp.* 350e; *Tht.* 176b.

4. Hierarchy

1. F. Schleiermacher, *Der christliche Glaube nach den Grundsätzen der evangelischen Kirche* (Berlin, 1821–22; new ed. Berlin 1984) §3/4.

2. His earlier, influential publication was entitled *Über die Religion. Reden an die Gebildeten unter ihren Verächtern* (Berlin, 1799); English transl., *On Religion. Speeches to Its Cultured Despisers* (New York, 1958).

3. H. Steible, *Rimsín, mein König. Drei kultische Texte aus Ur mit der Schlußdoxologie ^{d}ri-im-^{d}sîn lugal-mu* (Wiesbaden, 1975); M.-J. Seux, *Epithètes royales akkadiennes et sumériennes* (Paris, 1967); id., "Le Roi et les dieux," *RlAss* VI 166–172; cf. J. G. Griffiths, *Atlantis and Egypt* (Cardiff, 1991), 252–265.

4. Psalm 95,3.

5. John 20,28.

6. The second part of the name remains elusive; see F. Gschnitzer, *Serta philol. Aenipontana* (1962), 13–18; Burkert 1985, 136.

7. Burkert 1985, 44.

8. On *anax* see B. Hemberg, *"Anax, anassa* und *anakes* als Götternamen," *Acta Univ. Uppsal.* (1955), 10; J. T. Hooker, "The wanax in Linear B Tablets," *Kadmos* 18 (1979) 100–111. For Paphos see O. Masson, *Inscriptions chypriotes syllabiques* (Paris, 1961, rev. ed. 1983), nr.4; 6; 7; 10; 16; 17; 90; 91; *Éléments* (1960) 135; for Perge, *SEG* 30, 1517; Head 1911, 702.

9. Persephone and Cybele are often called *despoina,* cf. A. Henrichs, *HSCP* 80 (1976) 253–286; sanctuary of Despoina at Lykosura, Paus. 8,37; *despotes* for Zeus and Poseidon: Pindar, *Nem.* 1,13, *Ol.* 6,103 etc.; see also L. Robert, *CRAI* (1968) 583,5; *RPh* 33 (1959) 222. Eur. *Hippol.* 88 seems to presuppose a distinction between divine *anax* and human *despotes. Zeus basileus* Hom. *hy. Dem.*358, Theogn. 285, Solon 31 etc., cf. *Schol.* Aristoph. *Nub.* 2. Zeus the King can be understood mythologically as the king of the gods, Hes. *Theog.* 886, *Erga* 668, *Kypria* F 7,3 Davies. The Moon-God Mēn in Asia Minor is routinely called *Menotyrannos,* see E. Lane, *Corpus Monumentorum Religionis Dei Menis,* Leiden 1971–1978; *Men basileus SEG* 29,1288. See, in general, Pleket 1981.

10. Zeus "whose *kratos* is greatest" is the formula in *Iliad* and *Odyssey.*

11. Aesch. *Sept.* 255, *Hik.* 815, *Eum.* 918; cf. W. Kiefner, *Der religiöse Allbegriff des Aischylos* (Hildesheim, 1965).

12. Eur. *Hippol.* 8.

13. But *rex Gradive* was used for Mars, Verg. *Aen.* 10,542.

14. Cic. *Verr.* II 4,128; Liv. 6,29,8; *CIL* VI 30935.

15. *CIMRM* 1017; *rex Iuppiter* 1419.

16. The Iranian provenience and etymology of the god *Shadrapa/Satrapes* has finally been proved by the trilingual inscription of Xanthos, which equates Aramaean *hstrpty* with Greek Apollo; see *Fouilles de Xanthos VI: La stèle trilingue du Létoon* (Paris, 1979); Semitic etymologies had long been favored. See also *KAI* 77; *ANRW* II 17, 698. A God Satrapes at Elis is mentioned by Paus. 6,25,5 f.

17. By etymology, "lord" is the "warden of bread."

18. This is central in the New Testament, *ThWbNT* V 981–1016; but *Dyaus pitar* (father of heaven) is Indoeuropean; El (god) is *ab adam* (father of men) in Ugaritic. In the royal ideology of Egypt and Mesopotamia, the ruling god is designated the father of the king.

19. See *ER* VII 303. The word root means "wholeness," or "integration"; Salman Rushdie, in his *Satanic Verses,* tendentiously translates it as "submission."

20. For Akkadian (*re'um, AHW* 977 f.) see *RlAss* VI 162 f; prologue to the Laws of Hammurapi, *ANET* 164 f; Old Testament: Psalm 23; New Testament: John 10,2; 10,11. King Agamemnon is "shepherd of men" in Homer; gods are shepherds in Plato, *Polit.* 271de, 274e.

21. G. Simmel, *Die Religion* (2nd ed., Frankfurt, 1918) 57 f: "das Ausbleiben der Konkurrenz in der religiösen Erfahrung."

22. See Frankfort 1948; cf. Gladigow 1981, 13 f.

23. Freud 1912 found the origin of religion in posthumous worship of a father murdered by the hominid horde; on the relation of these ideas to Robertson Smith see Burkert 1983, 73 f.

24. For a general survey see Dunbar 1988; cf. Freedman 1979, 27–43; Popp and DeVore 1979.

25. Freedman 1979, 36–39: 36, referring to M. R. A. Chance, C. Jolly, *Social Groups of Monkeys, Apes, and Men* (New York, 1970).

26. De Waal 1982; see also de Waal 1989.

27. Baudy 1980, 78 and in *HrwG* II (1990) 109–116.

28. The Sumerian Gudea has a "tree of life" in his temple "which touches heaven," *RlAss* I 435; the Akkadian epic of Erra (1,150; Dalley 1989, 291) has a *mesu* tree, the roots of which reach down to the netherworld, the top of which rests in heaven. Nordic mythology has the ash tree Yggdrasil, O. Huth, "Weltberg und Weltbaum," *Germanien* 12 (1940) 441–446; for Greek see Pherecydes A 11 DK, cf. West 1971, 55–60; H. S. Schibli, *Pherekydes of Syros* (Oxford, 1990), 69–76.

29. Cult at high places and mountains is widespread; see W. F. Albright, "The High Place in Ancient Palestine," *Vetus Testamentum* Suppl. 4 (1957) 242–258; for Minoan Crete, Marinatos 1993, 115–122; for Hittites, V. Haas, *Hethitische Berggötter und hurritische Steindämonen* (Mainz, 1982); Aphrodite, merging with the Phrygian goddess, gets her sanctuary "at a lookout-place, visible all around," Hom. *hym. Aphr.* 100.; see also Fehling 1974, 39–58. On the "world mountain," see R. J. Clifford, *The Cosmic Mountain in Canaan and in the Old Testament* (Cambridge, Mass., 1972).

30. Greek Olympos is originally the mountain's name, but assumes the meaning of heaven, see E. Oberhummer, J. Schmidt *RE* XVIII 258–310.

31. Zeus adressed as highest in Hom. *Il.* 8,31; *Od.* 1,45 etc.; for Akkadian *elū* and *šaqû*, "high" with reference to gods, see *AHw* 205 f; 1179 f; Hebrew *'l* and esp. *'ljn*, *HAL* 780; 787 f; cf. *ib.* for equivalent expressions in Ugaritic and Aramaean; *summe Juppiter* Plaut. *Amph.* 780; *summe deum . . . Apollo* Verg. *Aen.* 11,785. A special cult of Zeus Hypsistos existed in Hellenistic times, often merging with Jewish worship, see Cook 1913–1940, II 876–890; A. D. Nock, C. Roberts, and T. C. Skeat, "The Gild of Zeus Hypsistos," *HThR* 29 (1936) 39–88 (partially reprinted in Nock 1972, 414–443); A. T. Kraebel, "Hypsistos and the Synagogue at Sardis," *GRBS* 10 (1969) 81–93. The concept of "highest" is taken up in philosophical religion, [Arist.] *De mundo* 397b24–28; 400a5–21: "This is attested by the whole of common life, which assigns to god the place above; and we all stretch our hands up to heaven when praying." (15–18); cf. n. 61; 87.

32. Menander Fr.223,3 Koerte; Menander is protesting against this principle.

33. On this concept, Freedman 1979, 36–39 (above at n. 25).

34. In a lighthearted way Morris 1967, 178–182, suggests that religion rose from the apes' hierarchic society; 180: a "fundamental biological tendency . . . to submit ourselves to an all-powerful, dominant member of the group."

35. See Chapter 1 at n. 93.

36. Ceremonial vase from Uruk, end of 4th millennium, Strommenger 1962, fig. 19–22; cf. F. Lämmli, *Vom Chaos zum Kosmos* (Basel, 1962), 142–144.

37. David *Prol.* 38,14 Busse. See also P. Lévêque, *Dieux, hommes, bêtes* (Paris, 1985).

38. Col. 1,16 *thronoi, kyriotetes, archai, exousiai,* cf. 1. Petr. 3,22 *angeloi, exousiai, dynameis.*

39. Cf. P. Lévêque, *Aurea catena Homeri* (Paris, 1959).

40. Seneca *Quaest. Nat.* 7,30,1: *in omne argumentum modestiae fingimur.*

41. Morris 1967, 179 takes this to be the essence of religion, "to perform repeated and prolonged submissive displays"; see 156–158 on "characteristic submissive displays."

42. Above, Chapter 1 at n. 62.

43. Cf. Eibl-Eibesfeldt 1970, 199 f.

44. See Chapter 2 at n. 19.

45. On *hiketeia* see J. Gould, "Hiketeia," *JHS* 93 (1973) 74–103; Burkert 1979, 43–47; G. Freyburger, "Supplication grecque et supplication romaine," *Latomus* 47 (1988) 501–525. I am indebted to an unpublished study by Thomas Kappeler, "Hiketeumata."

46. See the black obelisk, Strommenger 1962 fig. 208; J. Reade, *Assyrian Sculpture* (London, 1983), fig. 94 (from Assurbanipal's palace). For *labanu appa* see *AHw* 522.

47. The Greek word *proskynesis* is ambivalent, it can also mean "throwing kisses"; see J. Horst, *Proskynein,* Gütersloh 1932; A. Delatte, "Le Baiser, l'agenouillement et le prosternement de l'adoration *(proskynesis)* chez les Grecs," Acad. roy. de Belgique, *Bull. de la Classe des Lettres* 5,37 (1951) 423–450; *ThWbNT* VI 759–761; E. Bickerman, "À propos d'un passage de Chares de Mytilène," *Parola del Passato* 18 (1963) 241–255.

48. Caes. *b.g.* 1,27,2 (Helvetii: *se ad pedes proicere, suppliciter, flentes);* Liv.7,31,5 (Campanians: *manus ad consules tendentes, pleni lacrimarum procubuerunt*); 44,31.13 (Illyrians: *lacrimae, genibus . . . accidens*).

49. Streck 1916, II 74 f; Hom. *Od.* 14,273–279; in both cases it is a god who inspires the decision. Assurbanipal put his prisoners in fetters, however, whereas Odysseus started a successful career in Egypt.

50. Cf. n. 43.

51. Two forms of behavior seem to mingle here, which is perplexing to interpreters; see W. Pötscher, "Die Hikesie des letzten Ilias-Gesanges (Hom., *Il.* 24,477 ff.)," *Würzburger Jahrbücher* 18 (1992) 5–16.

52. Burkert 1979, 46 f; the same gesture appears in Egyptian representations: E. Swan Hall, *The Pharaoh Smites His Enemies*, Berlin 1986, fig. 9, cf. fig. 8 (the "Narmer Palette"); I owe these references to Thomas Kappeler.

53. *ThWbNT* VI 759–767 s.v. *proskyneo*, cf. n. 47; Hebrew *hišta-hawa*, HAL 284, a term for prayer, but also describing behavior before a powerful person; Akkadian *šukenu* before king and god, *AHw* 1263; *laban appi* see n. 46; cf. Schrank 1908, 58 f.

54. Gen. 17,2; 17.

55. F. T. van Straten, "Did the Greeks Kneel before Their Gods?" *BABesch* 49 (1974) 159–189; M. I. Davies, "Ajax at the Bourne of Life," in *Eidolopoiia. Actes du Colloque sur les problèmes de l'image dans le monde méditerranéen classique* (Rome, 1985), 83–117, esp. 90–96.

56. See Aesch. *Sept.* 95; Soph. *Trach.* 904; OC 1157.

57. For Assurbanipal, see Streck 1916, 346 f; cf. *AHw* 431 s.v. *kamasu*; Schrank 1908, 59–65.

58. Euseb. *Hist. eccl.* 5,5,1.

59. Christians take off their hats in church (hats make people taller), whereas Jews cover their heads at prayer.

60. The Sun God accepts Gilgamesh's tears as a "becoming gift" in *Gilgamesh und Huwawa*, see D. O. Edzard *Zeitschrift für Assyriologie* 80 (1990) 184, line 34; for Assurbanipal, see Streck 1916, 40 f; 116 f; Josiah is blessed by God because he has wept before him, II Kings 22,19. Demonstrative weeping seems to be uncommon in Greek religion. But the Septuagint has "he wept" instead of Hebrew "he invoked" (god) at least twice, Jud. 15,18; 16,28.

61. In Sumerian, this is "lifting the hand," *šu ila* = *našu qat* in Akkadian, *AHw* 762, *ns' jd* in Hebrew, *Psalm* 28,2; the Homeric formula is *cheiras anaschon*; Latin *manus tendens*. Cf. [Arist.] *De mundo* 400a15–18, above n. 31.

62. In such a context, the strange Roman ritual of a procession to Fides with veiled hands (Wissowa, 1912, 133 f.) is more understandable.

63. Luke 18,13.

64. Bottéro-Kramer 1989, 276–295; cf. Chapter 2 at n. 82; 3 at n. 25.

65. See also Plato *Leg.* 715 e = *OF* 23; A. Dihle *RAC* III (1957) 735–778 s.v. Demut.

66. Psalm 111,10; Aesch. *Hik.* 479. See Chapter 1 at n. 116–122.

67. See Chapter 2 at n. 72.

68. Menander *Sam.* 503, Theocr. 6,39 with Gow *ad loc.;* Lucian *Apol.* 6.

69. Menander Fr.754 = Porph. *abst.* 4,15; hence Plut. *superstit.* 168c. For the context of guilt and confession, see Chapter 5 at n. 85.

70. H. Zimmern, *Babylonische Hymnen und Gebete in Auswahl* (Leipzig, 1905) 27 nr.8.

71. For example, the priests of Baal, I Kings 18,28; cult of Ishtar at Uruk, *Erra* IV 57 f., Dalley 1989, 305; cult of Meter and Bellona, note 73.

72. A. Lebessi, *BCH* 115 (1991) 99–123; I doubt whether this can be interpreted as belonging to a context of initiation.

73. For *galloi,* see Burkert 1987, 36 with n.31; relief of an archigallus with his scourge, Cumont 1931 pl. I 3; for Bellona, see R. Turcan, *Les cultes orientaux dans le monde romain* (Paris, 1989) 48 f.

74. Parody in Luk. *Asin.* 37 f. / Apul. *Met.* 8,27–29.

75. Plut. *qu. Gr.* 304c.

76. Burkert 1983, 284 n. 46.

77. J. Boese, *Mesopotamische Weihplatten* (Berlin, 1971), 290 f. pl.XXXI,1, cf. *ANEP* 597; M. Müller, *Frühgeschichtlicher Fürst aus Iraq* (Zürich, 1976).

78. The monkeys' sign of submission, the presentation of the posterior, has been inverted by humans to become a sign of contempt against the weak, cf. Fehling 1974, 27–38; *HDA* IV 62 f; H. P. Duerr, *Obszönität und Gewalt* (Frankfurt, 1993), 148–152.

79. D. Arnaud, *Emar. Recherches au Pays d' Aštata VI 4: Textes sumériens et accadiens* (Paris, 1987) 326–337, nr. 369.

80. K. Koch in P. Frei, and K. Koch, *Reichsidee und Reichsorganisation im Perserreich* (Freiburg, 1984), 79–90, 98–105. A different structure, through reversal, appears in Maya civilization. The Maya king was not allowed to touch the ground and was lifted up and carried by his subjects; but in iconography he is represented carrying mankind—a human figure—on his own shoulders.

81. Isaiah 6; cf. Ezekiel 1,26. For the enthronement of Mesopotamian kings, see *RlAss* VI 148; *AHW* 515 s.v. *kussu.*

82. See Marinatos 1993, 206.

83. V. K. Müller, *Der Polos. Die griechische Götterkrone* (Berlin, 1915); Hepat at Yazilikaya, E. Akurgal, *Die Kunst der Hethiter* (Munich, 1961) pl.76/77; the Hittite rock sculpture, badly weatherworn, at Mt. Sipylus, the so-called Niobe, ib. pl. XXIII.

214

84. Callim. *Hy. Apoll.* 102 f.

85. Mark 11, 9 f. with parallels, following Psalm 118,25.

86. Luke 2,14; *hosanna in excelsis* Matth. 21,9; *ThWbNT* VIII 604 f.

87. Aeschylus Fr. 70 *TrG f*; cf. n. 31.

88. See *SAHG* 1953; J. Assmann, *Aegyptische Hymnen und Gebete* (Zürich, 1975); Lebrun 1980; M. Lattke, *Hymnus. Materialien zu einer Geschichte der antiken Hymnologie* (Fribourg, 1991); *L'inno tra rituale e letteratura nel mondo antico*. Atti di un colloquio Napoli (Rome, 1991) (A.I.O.N. 13); W. Burkert and F. Stolz, eds., *Hymnen der Alten Welt im Kulturvergleich* (Freiburg, 1994).

89. See, e.g., the Hittite hymn to Ishtanu, Lebrun 1980, 93–111; the Akkadian hymn to Shamash, *SAHG* 240–247; Psalm 19, 6 f; Akhen-Aton's great hymn, Assmann (n. 88) 215–221.

90. See S. Sahin, *Epigraphica anatolica* 9 (1987) 61–72; *SEG* 37, 957–980; cf. *SEG* 33,1056.

91. Hymn to Ishtanu, Lebrun 1980, 102, lines 32–38. Cf. the Roman centurion who sees Jesus ruling the demons in strict parallel to his own command within the Roman army: "I am subject to my superiors," as "soldiers [are] subject to me," Luke 7,8; Matth. 8,9.

92. Psalm 19.

93. Cylinder inscription §74, Luckenbill 1927, II 66; on fear of god see Chapter 1 at nn. 116–122.

94. Polyb. 6,56,6–12. Cf. Burkert 1985, 247.

95. Arist. *Met.* 1074b3: The divine encompasses the whole of nature, "the rest is addition in the form of myth, in order to persuade the multitude and to be useful for laws and (private) interest."

96. A model case is the Rosetta inscription of Ptolemy V, *OGI* 90,26 f: The king "conquered the city and annihilated all the godless inhabitants in it, as Hermes and Horos, son of Isis and Osiris, subdued the rebels in the same place before"; cf. E. Hornung, *Geschichte als Fest* (Darmstadt, 1966).

97. *ANET* 164 f; *ANEP* 246.

98. Weissbach 1911, 10 f. §5; cf. G. Ahn, *Religiöse Herrscherlegitimation im achämenidischen Iran,* Leiden 1992. On the Bardiya problem see Frye 1984, 96–102; J. M. Balcer, *Herodotus and Bisitun* (Wiesbaden, 1987).

99. R. Ghirshman, *Iran, Parther und Sassaniden* (Munich, 1962), 132 fig. 168; cf. 131 fig. 167; 167–8 fig. 211; 176 fig. 218; Frye 1984, 371–373.

100. Hom. *Il.* 1,279.

101. Hdt. 1,60; taken seriously e.g. by F. Kiechle, "Götterdarstellung durch Menschen in der altmediterranen Religion," *Historia* 19 (1970) 259–271; cf. W. Connor "Tribes, Festivals and Processions; Civic Ceremonial and Political Manipulation in Archaic Greece," *JHS* 107 (1987) 40–50; criticism in J. Beloch, *Griechische Geschichte* I 2² (Strassburg, 1913) 288.

102. Cf. Christian Habicht, *Gottmenschentum und griechische Städte* (Munich 1970, 2nd ed.).

103. See J. R. Fears, *Princeps a Diis Electus. The Divine Election of the Emperor as a Political Concept at Rome* (Rome, 1977); idem, *RAC* XI (1981) 1103–1159 s.v. Gottesgnadentum; bibliography on emperor's cult by P. Herz in *ANRW* II 16,2 (1978) 833–910.

104. Palermo, Martorana Church.

105. Ambros. *epist.* 17,1; J. Wytzes, *Der letzte Kampf des Heidentums in Rom* (Leiden, 1977), 214. Cf. Liban. *or.* 22,41, about a high official at the emperor's court "who, just as the emperor follows the gods, is himself following the emperor."

106. Formulation of Assurbanipal, Streck 1916, 300 f.

107. x:a = a:b, see Chapter 1 n. 97. Cf. M.-J. Seux, *RlAss* VI 168: "Le Roi d'Assyrie a donc, par rapport au dieu national, la position qu'avait un gouverneur par rapport à son roi." It is less edifying to find that already in monkey societies an individual that feels threatened will threaten another of lower rank.

108. *ANET* 268.

109. II Samuel 7; the word used by David is ʿäbäd = *doulos*.

110. Psalm 110, cf. Matth. 22,44.

111. The famous text is Thureau-Dangin 1921, 127–148; *ANET* 334.

112. Dan. 4.

113. Hor. *carm.* 3,6,5.

114. Solon in Diog.Laert. 1,60; Arist. *Pol.* 1277b14. From a:b = b:a, there follows a = b.

115. Ps.-Phokylides *Sent.* 8. Cf. in the *Avesta, Gatha* 9,7 = *Yasna* 44,7: The obedience of a son towards his father ranks immediately after cosmic order. See also Chapter 1 at nn. 109–110.

116. Hebr. 13,17.

117. See Chapter 3 at n. 31.

118. Sommer 1992, 83–88.

119. [Arist.] *De mundo* 398a.

120. Cf. Burkert in F. Stolz, ed., *Religion zu Krieg und Frieden* (Zürich, 1986), 67 ff.

121. For texts from the temple of Ishtar at Arbela, see *ANET* 449 f.

122. *RE* Suppl. III 101–114 s.v. Angelos; *ThWbNT* I 72–86; J. Michl *RAC* V (1962) 53–258 s.v. "Engel."

123. John 5,23; 6,44; 12,44; 14,24 etc.

124. John 1,33.

125. John 20,21; cf. 17,18.

126. A. Boehlig, *Die Gnosis* III (Zürich, 1980) 155 cf. 83; A. Adam, *Texte zum Manichäismus* (Berlin, 2nd ed. 1969) nr.3a.

127. *Quran,* Sura 33,40 etc.

128. Hes. *Erga* 253–255.

129. The crucial text is Plato, *Symp.* 202d-203a; Plato's expression for communication between men and gods that occurs through demons is "encounter and speech," *homilia kai dialektos.*

130. Aesch. *Eum.* 19 "Loxias is prophet of Zeus, the father."

131. Jonah 1,1.

132. II Sam. 12.

133. Aristoph. *Pax* 1070 f.

134. Diod. 36,13; Plut. *Marius* 17,8–11; cf. Chapter 5 n. 41.

135. See also Chapter 1 at n. 86, on the "monster in the corner."

136. See Chapter 1 at n. 100.

137. See Chapter 7.

138. Words of Maximilla, Epiphan. *Panar.* 48,13,1; Bishop Epiphanius criticizes this constraint; but St. Paul's experience was quite comparable: "Woe to me if I do not preach the gospel" (I Cor. 9,16).

139. Aesch. *Ag.* 1562.

5. Guilt and Causality

1. *Il.* 1,62–64: *mantin, hierea, oneiropolon;* see on the proceedings Parker 1983, 207–234. Cf. Delbos-Jorion 1981.

2. Hdt. 9,93,4: At Apollonia "they asked the prophets (of the oracles) about the cause of the present evil"; cf. 6,139,1: Pelasgians ask Delphi for "riddance *(lysis)* of the present evils."

3. Persians declare that whoever gets leprosy must have committed some fault against the Sun; hence the culprit is driven from the town, and nobody enters into contact with him; the rational but brutal means to control infection is made acceptable by the declaration of nonobvious guilt, Hdt. 1,138,1.

4. I Sam. 5.

5. *Kohanim* and *qosemim;* on this term, with special reference to arrow-oracles, see *HAL* 1041 f; *hiereis, manteis, epaoidoi* in the Septuagint, I Sam. 6.2.

6. ʿ*opel, HAL* 814; the Septuagint has *hedrai,* "buttocks." A votive offering of buttocks *(glouthron)* is in *SEG* 29 (1979) nr.1174.

7. T. Dothan, *The Philistines and Their Material Culture* (New Haven, 1982); J. F. Brug, *A Literary and Archaeological Study of the Philistines* (Oxford, 1985); L. E. Stager, *Ashkelon Discovered* (Washington, 1991).

8. *ANET* 394 ff; Lebrun 1980, 192–239, esp. 203–216, the second version; here 212,29 f; 32′; 38′.

9. Lebrun 1980, 211,12′; 213,8′;13′;19′.

10. *Tages-Anzeiger,* Zürich, Jan. 21, 1986.

11. Already Homer has it that "the gods made known" the deeds of Oedipus, *Od.* 11,274.

12. Cf. Burkert, *Oedipus, Oracles, and Meaning. From Sophocles to Umberto Eco* (Toronto, 1991).

13. Apollod. 2,130 f. The quarrel about the tripod is one of the earliest mythological motifs to appear in Greek art, see Schefold 1993, 47 fig. 20. Orestes too gets sick after killing his mother, and he recovers with the help of Apollo's oracle. Cf. Burkert 1992a, 56 f.

14. Verg. *Georg.* 317–558, possibly going back to Eumelus, T 2 Davies; *morbi causam* 4,397; 532; cf. Varro *r.r.* 2,5,5; the ritual of *bugonia* is described in *Geoponica* 15,2,22–29; cf. *RE* III 431–450 s.v. Biene.

15. See F. Graf, *ZPE* 92 (1992) 267–279, esp. 275–277.

16. Lanternari 1994, 262 f.

17. Livy 8,18.

18. Cf. Sullivan 1988; *ER* s.v. "Diseases and Cures," "Healing."

19. Livy 2,36, 390 B.C. (comments by Arnob.7,39–43): Titus Latinius is summoned by Jupiter in his dream to announce that the Roman games *(ludi Romani)* had been polluted by the spectacular punishment of a slave just before the games in the arena and must be repeated; because he does not heed the divine command, his son dies and he himself falls ill. He then delivers his message to the Senate and recovers at once. Cf. a story in *Tages-Anzeiger,* Zürich, Feb. 27, 1990: during the building of a highway in Indonesia, a worker was told in a dream that a buffalo must be sacrificed to the spirits of the dead dwelling in that region; he fell seriously ill and recovered only when the sacrifice had been made—along with the celebration of a Christian Mass.

20. Aesch. *Ag.* 188–217. Aeschylus does not tell which fault is imputed to Agamemnon; the parallel accounts give various reasons.

21. *Od.* 4, 351–586; for the obvious suspicion of "missing" sacrifices see also *Il.* 5,177 f.

22. Jonah 1,7; cf. Chapter 2.

23. H. W. Parke, *The Oracles of Zeus* (Cambridge, 1967) 261 f. nr.7; *SEG* 19,427.

24. Nikolaos *FGrHist* 90 F 45 cf. 15, probably from Xanthos.

25. A. Livingstone, *State Archives of Assyria IV: Court Poetry* (Helsinki, 1989), nr. 33, p. 77 (I do not indicate lacunae and restorations). One might compare Kroisos' method of testing Greek oracles, Hdt. 1,46, or the suggestion to verify a dream oracle at Amphiaraos by inquiring at Delphi, Hypereides 4,14 f; a Greek general too will "assemble" the seers at sacrifice and accept the verdict on which they agree, Eurip. *Heracl.* 340; 401–407.

26. Diod. 20,14 (*zetesis* §4). On Moloch sacrifices see Chapter 2 at n.76.

27. Thuc. 1,128,1; cf.2,17, below, n. 47.

28. Herakleides Fr.46a Wehrli = Strab. 8 p. 384 cf. Diod. 15,48; Paus. 7,24,5–12; R. Baladié, *Le Péloponnèse de Strabon* (Paris, 1980) 145–157.

29. Paus. 7,17,13 f.

30. A.R. 2,463–489.

31. Apollod. *Bibl.* 100–102; Pherekydes *FGrHist* 3 F 33 = *Schol.* Od. 11,287; Eust. p. 1685,33; *Schol.* Theokr. 3,43 cf. *Od.* 11,291–297; 15,231–238; Hes. Fr. 37.

32. Criticism of Freud's diagnosis by Grünbaum 1984. A characteristic difference is that psychoanalysis rejects guilt in favor of trauma inflicted from outside.

33. Hdt. 9,93,4 cf. n. 2.

34. Eur. Fr. 912,9–13. Hdt. 6,91 has a story about the Aeginetans who were not able to "expiate by sacrifice" the "pollution incurred" *(agos)*, "although they tried to do so."

35. Plato *Phdr.* 244 de, cf. Burkert 1987b,19.

36. In Greek, this is the question for *prophasis,* a word much discussed in relation to Thuc. 1,23,6, but more clearly seen in its original function in Thuc. 1,133; see H. R. Rawlings III, *A Semantic Study of Prophasis to 400* B.C. (Wiesbaden, 1975); A. A. Nikitas, "Zur Bedeutung von *Prophasis* in der altgriechischen Literatur," *Abh.* (Mainz, 1976) 4.

37. Dundes 1964 has a tale pattern of interdiction-infraction-consequence-attempted escape.

38. Livy 5,51,8.

39. Meyer 1962; F. García Martinez, *The Dead Sea Scrolls Translated* (Leiden, 1994) 289.

40. See above at n. 21.

41. See above, Chapter 4 at n. 69; 134; in general, Delbos-Jorion 1981. A catalogue of how a herdsman might violate taboos is given in Ov. *fast.* 4,747–762: sitting under a sacred tree, entering a sacred grove, etc.; *da veniam culpae* 755. Syrians hold fish sacred, and if they eat fish they immediately fall ill, Menander Fr. 754. The typical Greek word for a religious fault committed is *aliteîn* (on which see H. Vos, *Glotta* 34 [1955] 287–295; E. Tichy, *Glotta* 55 [1977] 160–172). Cf. also the death of the Roman official in 102 B.C. who had insulted a priest of Magna Mater, Diod. 36,13; Plut. *Marius* 17,8–11.

42. Burkert 1985, 235 f; Krummen 1990, 108–116; M. Petterson, *Cults of Apollo at Sparta* (Stockholm, 1992) 57–72.

43. Burkert 1983, 136–143.

44. Plut. *mus.* 42, 1145 BC, referring to Pratinas *TrGF* 4 F 9; cf. L. Käppel, *Paian. Geschichte einer Gattung* (Berlin, 1992), 349–351.

45. Ceres: Dion.Hal. *ant.* 6,17; 6,94,3; Apollo: Liv. 4,25,3; 4,29,7.

46. Above, n. 14.

47. Thuc. 2,17: He does not accept that the breaking of a taboo was the cause of the pestilence, but does not question divine wisdom and foreknowledge. See also S. B. Aleshire, *The Athenian Asklepieion* (Amsterdam, 1989).

48. Hdt. 1,19–22; cf. the erection of a temple to Namtar, the god of pestilence, in *Atrahasis* I 401, Dalley 1989, 19. For the principle "two for one" see Thuc. 1,134,4; the inscription on a vase refers to vases set up in a sanctuary: "having broken one, two for Aphrodite." G. A. Koshelenko et al., eds., *Anticnye gosudarstva Severnogo Pricernomorja* (Moscow, 1984) 142 nr.4.

49. *Od.* 12,345–347.

50. Luk. *Syr.D.* 19, cf. Chapter 2 at n. 44.

51. *SEG* 33, 736; IC II xxviii 2, Hermes Tallaios.

52. Below, n. 85.

53. Hdt.1,167. The Romans derived *caerimonia* from Caere.

54. Hdt. 1,105 cf. Hippocr. *aer.* 22; see D. Margreth, *Skythische Schamanen? Die Nachrichten über Enarees-Anarieis bei Herodot und Hippokrates* (Ph.D. diss., Zürich, 1993).

55. Lanternari 1994, 256 f.

56. In Plato *Resp.* 364bc "beggars and seers" claim the "power" *(dynamis)* to "make good" *(akeîsthai)*.

57. Cf. the Hittite hymn to the Sun God, Lebrun 1980, 104 f: "qu'il me dise mon péché." See also van der Toorn 1985, 94–97: "in search of the secret sin."

58. Daniel 2,12 f; 24; "magicians, exorcists, sorcerers, and Chaldaeans" 2,2.

59. See at n. 25.

60. Hdt. 4,68.

61. Hdt. 6,66; 6.75,3; 5,66,1; cf. 5,90,1.

62. Soph. *OT* 380–389.

63. Eur. *Phrixos A,* Apollod. *Bibl.* 1,80–82, Hyg. *fab.* 2, cf. C. Austin, *Nova Fragmenta Euripidea* (Berlin, 1968) p. 101 f.

64. Cf. Burkert 1979, 88 f.

65. *Divinatio oblativa* and *impetrativa,* see Chapter 7 n. 7.

66. Psalm 124,7.

67. Hdt. 6,139,1, cf. above note 2.

68. Soph. *El.* 447.

69. Soph. *OT* 100 f. *(lyein).* Latin *luere,* related to Greek *lyein,* has assumed the meaning "to expiate."

70. K. Tsantsanoglou, G. M. Parassoglou, "Two Gold Lamellae from Thessaly," *Hellenika* 38 (1987) 3–16; *SEG* 37,497; cf. Burkert 1987, 19; F. Graf, "Dionysian and Orphic Eschatology: New Texts and Old Questions," in T. H. Carpenter and C. A. Faraone, eds., *Masks of Dionysus* (Ithaca, 1993) 239–258.

71. Above, n. 35.

72. First "Merseburger Zauberspruch," cf. M. Wehrli, *Geschichte der deutschen Literatur* I (Stuttgart, 1980) 22–24.

73. See esp. the series *Shurpu* (Reiner 1958) tablets II–III; the term is *pašaru,* "to release," *AHw* 842, in contrast with *rakasu* and *kamû* "to bind," *AHw* 946; 433.

74. Akkadian incantation text in Ebeling 1931 nr. 30 A III 63, p. 132 f.

75. A. Audollent, *Defixionum Tabellae* (Paris, 1904); R. Wünsch, *Defixionum Tabellae Atticae, IG* III 3 (Berlin, 1897); D. R. Jordan, "A Survey of Greek Defixiones Not Included in the Special Corpora," *GRBS* 26 (1985) 151–197; see also C. A. Faraone, "The Agonistic Context of Early Greek Binding Spells," in C.-A. Faraone and D. Obbink, eds., *Magika Hiera. Ancient Greek Magic and Religion* (New York, 1991) 3–32; F. Graf, *La Magie dans l'antiquité gréco-romaine* (Paris, 1994) 139–198.

76. Sophronius, *Narratio miraculorum SS Cyri et Ioannis sapientium Anargyrorum, PG* 87,3, 3541–3548 (see Audollent, n. 75, p. cxxii).

77. Liban. *Or.* 1,243–250; C. Bonner, "Witchcraft in the Lecture Room of Libanius," *TAPA* 63 (1932) 34–44.

78. Hdt. 6,12,3.

79. See Chapter 4.

80. Plut. *Superst.* 168 d: "Often he rolls naked in the mud as he confesses his various faults and errors"; cf. Chapter 4 n. 69.

81. Arnob. 7,5 (this is said to be the hypothesis of his adversaries, the pagans). This comes close to the program described in Chapter 2. 221

82. *AHw* 716.

83. Cf. the Pythagorean saying in Iambl. *V.P.* 85: "those who have come (into this life) to be punished must be punished."

84. *ANET* 395; Lebrun 1980, 214,24–28; above, n. 8. In the Christian tradition the parent-child relationship comes more to the fore than the lord-servant relation.

85. F. Steinleitner, *Die Beicht im Zusammenhang mit der sakralen Rechtspflege in der Antike* (Ph.D. diss., Munich, 1913); R. Pettazzoni, *La confessione dei peccati,* 3 vol. (Bologna, 1929–1936); H. Hommel, "Antike Bußformulare," in *Sebasmata* I (Tübingen, 1983) 351–370; the growing corpus of inscriptions from Western Asia Minor has now been collected by Petzl 1994; see also G. Petzl, "Lukians 'Podagra' und die Beichtinschriften Kleinasiens," *Métis* 6 (1991) 131–145. Examples from Mesopotamia are in Schrank 1908, 46 f; M. Jastrow, *Die Religion Babyloniens und Assyriens* II, Giessen 1912, 71 ff; S. Langdon, *Babylonian Penitential Psalms* (Paris, 1927); *SAHG* 18–19; from Egypt, in Roeder 1915, 58; H. I. Bell, *Cults and Creeds in Greco-Roman Egypt* (Liverpool, 1953), 13.

86. For example, A. I. Hallowell, *Culture and Experience* (New York, 1967), 266–276 (on Saulteaux Indians).

87. Aristoph. *Peace* 668 cf. *Clouds* 1478; *Wasps* 1001.

88. Pind. *Pyth.* 3,82 f.

89. See *Guilt or Pollution and Rites of Purification.* Proceedings of the XIth International Congress of the International Association for the History of Religions II (Leiden, 1968); *ER* XII 91–100 s.v. purification; a standard work is M. Douglas, *Purity and Danger* (New York, 1966).

90. Parker 1983. Cf. also Pfister *RE* Suppl.VI (1935) 146–162 s.v. Katharsis.

91. M. L. West in his review of Parker, *CR* 35 (1985) 92–94.

92. Epimenides *FGrHist* 457 T 1; 4; Burkert 1992a, 60; 62 f.

93. Plut. *De Sera* 560 ef (*Italias* corrected to *Phigalias* by Mittelhaus *RE* XIX 2084); Fr. 126 Sandbach; Thuc. 1,134,4. The mention of ghosts brings to mind the third model, demoniac wrath. The models are also mixed up in the rhetorical exercise of Antiphon 4,1,3: a victim of murder "leaves behind . . . the hostility of the avenging spirits," and those who fail to administer justice "bring this hostility of the avenging spirits, a defilement *(miasma)* which ought not to be, into their own

houses." See J. D. Mikalson, *Athenian Popular Religion* (Chapel Hill, 1983), 50–52.

94. Nadig 1986, 223, cf. 220 f., 225–229, 381 f.

95. Latte 1920/1.

96. Dodds 1951, 28–63 following R. Benedict, *The Chrysanthemum and the Sword. Patterns of Japanese Culture* (Boston, 1946), 222 ff. Note that for Latte the idea of impurity and the corresponding practice of purification was primitive and hence very old, whereas Dodds associates the discovery of guilt with the interest in purification in the archaic, post-Homeric age. It has always been noticed that in the *Iliad* and the *Odyssey* there is very little about purification, and definitely no purification from murder; this second category makes its appearance in the *Aithiopis*, p. 47 lines 11–13 Davies.

97. See now Cairns 1993, 27–47.

98. See Chapter 2; esp. Girard 1972 and 1982.

99. Aristoph. *Fr. dubium* 940 Kassel-Austin; Menander *Dysc.* 114; Theokrit 5,119; Hsch. s.v. *katharthenai: mastigothenai*. Prov. 20,30: "A good beating purifies the mind" (the interpretation and translation, though, is controversial).

100. See Parker 1983, 378.

101. Cf. Eur. *Ion* 367: Ion, servant to Apollo's sanctuary, says to Kreusa, who had been violated by the god: "He is ashamed of the act: do not condemn him."

102. See also Kelsen 1982.

103. M. P. Nilsson, "Religion as Man's Protest against the Meaninglessness of Events," *Opuscula Selecta* III (Lund, 1960), 391–464.

6. The Reciprocity of Giving

1. *CEG* 326; Jeffery 1990, 90 f; 94 nr.1; *LIMC* "Apollon" nr.40.

2. *Od.* 1,187 f; 311–318; *doron* 311, 316; *axion . . . amoibes* 318. See Scheid-Tissinier 1994, 165 f.

3. Mauss 1923–24 (Eng. tr. 1967); see also K. Polanyi, *Primitive, Archaic, and Modern Economy* (Garden City, 1968); Cheal 1988, who calls giving "a system of redundant transactions within a moral economy, which makes possible the extended reproduction of social relations" (19).

4. Satirically stressed by Martial 5,59,3: *quisquis magna dedit, voluit sibi magna remitti*, "whoever has presented great gifts wanted that great gifts be sent back to him."

5. Gregory 1980; cf. Schieffelin 1980; Gouldner 1960; Sahlins 1970.

6. See Mauss 1967, 72f.

7. M. Finley, *The World of Odysseus* (New York, 1954; 2nd ed. 1978) 61–65 (qualifications in J. T. Hooker, "Gifts in Homer," *BICS* 36 [1989] 79–90); J. N. Coldstream in R. Hägg, ed., *The Greek Renaissance of the Eighth Century* B.C. (Stockholm, 1983), 201–206; Scheid-Tissinier 1994. See also L. Gernet, "Droit et pré-droit en Grèce ancienne," in Gernet 1968, 175–260; S. Humphreys, *Anthropology and the Greeks* (London, 1978); Herman 1987; Ulf 1990, 211 f.

8. See M. Weinfeld, "Initiation of Political Friendship in Ebla and Its Later Developments," in H. Hauptmann and H. Waetzoldt, eds., *Wirtschaft und Gesellschaft von Ebla* (Heidelberg, 1988) 345–348.

9. Hom. *Il.* 6,230–236: *epameipsomen* 230; the standard of *axion* is violated in this case, as gold is exchanged for bronze, 235–237. A grotesque account of a gift exchange among friends, including the wife of one of them, appears in Hdt. 6,62.

10. Prov. 18,16. On bribery, *dorodokia* in Greek (acceptance of gifts), see at n. 88.

11. C. F. A. Schaeffer, *Le Palais royal d'Ugarit* VI (Paris, 1970) 9–11, A 12–14, *RS* 17.148. Cf. Liverani 1990, esp. 211–217.

12. Bourdieu 1972, 227–243: "Le Capital symbolique."

13. Aside from giving objects, there are also other forms of interaction to express friendship, solidarity, and rank: play of eyes, bowing down, or caressing—common among apes too. For humans language has added further possibilities, such as "verbal stroking" (see Chapter 4 at nn. 86–91). We speak of giving and exchange even in this context and measure "units of caressing" *(Streicheleinheiten)*.

14. On Homeric *eedna* see S. West, *A Commentary on Homer's Odyssey* I (Oxford, 1988) 110 f.

15. "Give me part of your virginity" Ps.-Plato *Anth.Pal.* 5,79,2. See also M. I. Finley, "Marriage, Sale and Gift in the Homeric World," *Revue Internationale des droits de l'antiquité* III 2 (1955) 167–194, repr. in M. Finley, *Economy and Society in Ancient Greece* (London, 1981), 232–245; J. P. Vernant, *Mythe et société en Grèce ancienne* (Paris, 1974; repr. 1981) 57–81.

16. The root of the word is *pera-*, transaction.

17. Cf. Burkert 1994. See also Seaford 1994 on two forms of reciprocity, gift and revenge.

18. This is the "justice of Rhadamanthys" executed through transmigration, Arist. *EN* 1132b25. P. Marongiu, G. Newman, in their book *Vengeance: The Fight against Injustice* (Totowa, N.J., 1987), understand reciprocity basically in this sense, "vengeance" taking the place of "obedience" out of an "elementary sense of injustice."

19. See e.g. Ex. 21,23–27.

20. This is the expression of the penitent culprit at the cross, NT Luc. 23,41. In Akkadian the relevant expressions are *gamalu, gimillu* and *riabu,* "to retribute," used both in friendly interactions and in the situation of revenge, *AHw* 275 f; 978 f.

21. Deut. 25,2 f; Ioseph. *Ant.Iud.* 4,8,21,238; NT II Cor. 11,24; Plat. *Leg.* 845a.

22. *epieike' amoiben, Od.* 12,382.

23. Aristoph. *Nub.* 245 cf. 118.

24. See below at n. 124.

25. See de Waal 1989, 38 f; Burkert 1994, 12.

26. See S. A. J. White, "Gift Giving," *ER* V 552–557; Linders and Nordquist 1987; F. T. van Straten, "Gifts for the Gods," in Versnel 1981, 65–151. In Greek, *anatithenai* prevails, but *didonai* is not absent; for Latin, the normal votive formula is DDD, *dedit donavit dedicavit.* For "giving sacrifice" in Akkadian, see *AHw* 1525 s.v. *zibu.*

27. Corinth: *CEG* 359/60; with variation, *aphorman* for *amoiban,* "a pleasant fresh start" *CEG* 358; Smyrna: *CEG* 426. Cf. Lazzarini 1976 and 1989–90.

28. Hom. *Od.* 3,58 f; Hom. *Hymn. Dem.* 494.

29. Plato *Euthyphro* 14 ce. See also *Leg.* 716e: the god does not accept gifts from polluted givers.

30. Plato *Symp.* 202e.

31. Hippocr. *Aer.* 22, quoting Eur. *Hippol.* 8.

32. R. Schmitt, *Dichtung und Dichtersprache in indogermanischer Zeit* (Wiesbaden, 1967), 142–149.

33. MY V 659,4; A. Morpurgo, *Mycenaeae Graecitatis Lexicon* (Rome, 1963), 324.

34. Persepolis inscription g, Weissbach 1911, 85.

35. Democr. B 175.

36. James 1,17. Cf. also *theon eis anthropous dosis* Plat. *Phil.*16cd.

37. *SVF* II nr.1081: The *Charites* (traditionally worshiped as goddesses) are the personification of "our first fruit offerings and returns *(antapodóseis)* for the gods' good deeds."

38. Sallustios 16,1; cf. below, n. 121.

39. Ex. 23,15; Psalm 96, 7 f; the Hebrew term for the gift accompanying sacrifice is *minhah.* See also Akkadian *kurbanu* and *muhhuru.*

40. Stele of Fekherye, A. Abou-Assaf, P. Bodreuil, A. R. Millard, *La statue de Tell Fekherye et son inscription bilingue assyro-araméenne* (Paris, 1982) 17 (Assyrian version line 2 f.) cf. 24 (Aramaic version lines 2–4).

41. Plato *Euthyphro,* see above n. 29.

42. Hom. *Il.* 22,169–172 f; *Od.* 1,66 f.

43. *Atrahasis* II ii 14; 20, Lambert-Millard 1969, *libašma ibiš,* cf. Dalley 1989, 21. For Kroisos' reproach to Apollo in Herodotus, see infra n. 72.

44. See G. van der Leeuw, "Die Do ut des-Formel in der Opfertheorie," *ARW* 20 (1920/1) 241–253; Widengren 1969, 280–288; *ER* VI 197–214; Grottanelli 1989–90; for qualification, see Festugière 1976, 418: "beaucoup plus complexe que la notion du contrat."

45. *Tittiriya-Samhita,* Widengren 1969, 284; *ER* V 554.

46. See Chapter 1 n. 130.

47. Lambert 1960, 104; *qiptu* (loan, credit) 147 f.

48. Prov. 19,17: NT Math. 6,4 cf. 6.

49. Aesch. *Lib. Bearers* 792 f.

50. P. Thieme, "Studien zur indogermanischen Wortkunde und Religionsgeschichte," *Berichte der Sächsischen Akademie der Wissenschaften zu Leipzig,* Phil.-Hist. Klasse 98,5 (1952) 62–76.

51. *Anth.Pal.* 6,152,3 f; 6,238,5 f.

52. CEG 227; 275.

53. CIL I²2, 1531 = *CLE* 4, *donu danunt . . . orant se voti crebro condemnes.*

54. K. Ehlich in S. Döpp, Hg., *Karnevaleske Phänomene in antiken und nachantiken Kulturen und Literaturen* (Trier, 1993), 293 f.

55. Greek *ploutos* (riches) originally meant grain, to be stored in the subterranean treasury *(thesauros);* in the myth, Plutos is the son of Demeter the grain-goddess, and the god of the underworld is called Pluton.

56. See also Widengren 1969, 288.

57. Canopos Decree of Ptolemy III, 239–38 B.C., *OGI* 56, 8 f., 19 f.

58. Acts 20,35. The opposite asymmetry is stated by Thucydides 2,97,4 in reference to those Thracians who had the power "to take rather than to give."

59. Cf. invitations without expectation of *antapodosis:* Luke 14,12; equal recompense for different labor: Matth. 20,1–16; the prodigal son and the dishonest stewart: Luke 15,11 ff; 16,1–9; giving away riches: Mark 10,21. "If you have money, do not lend at interest, but give [to him] from whom you will not get them [back]"—this is the version of the Gnostic Gospel of Thomas (95) which becomes "don't turn from him who asks you to borrow" in Matthew (5,42), whereas Luke has "give to everyone who ask you, and don't claim back from him who takes your belongings" (6,30). *Didache* 1,5, combining Luke 6,30 and Acts 20,36, even proclaims: "Woe to him who takes." The fifth section of the Lord's prayer, Mt. 6,12, usually translated as "forgive us the

225

wrong we have done," has the word *opheilemata* which primarily means "debts" and can be understood: "as we renounce the debts owed to us"; the traditional interpretation is upheld by rabbinic material, see *ThWbNT* V 565. Jesus' model is the behavior of children begging from their parents. Compensation *(amoibe)* is also denied in the ethics of Marcus Aurelius: "If you have done good, and somebody has had good done to him, what else do you desire?" (7,73).

60. Quran, *Sura* 9,111.

61. See Chapter 1 at n. 36. The following discussion is largely parallel to the sociobiology debate (see Chapter 1 n. 34), but takes success rather in the sense of goods acquired than of multiplication of genes.

62. Dawkins 1976.

63. This goes back to Rapoport-Chamnah 1965; cf. R. Axelrod and W. D. Hamilton, "The Evolution of Cooperation," *Science* 211/4489 (1981) 1390–1396; D. R. Hofstadter, *Scientific American* (May 1983) 14–20; Axelrod 1984–1988.

64. See Dawkins 1976, 199 f. for the grudger's strategy. But see the objections raised by Boyd-Lorberbaum 1987.

65. P. J. Hamilton Grierson, "The Silent Trade," in D. Dalton, ed., *Research in Economic Anthropology* III (Greenwich, Conn. 1980) 1–74; A. Price, "On Silent Trade," ibid. 75–96; R. Hennig, "Der stumme Handel als Urform des Aussenhandels," *Weltwirtschaftliches Archiv* 11 (1917) 265–278; D. Veerkamp, "Stummer Handel. Seine Verbreitung, sein Wesen," (Ph.D. diss., Göttingen, 1956); A. Giardino, "Le merci, il tempo, il silenzio. Ricerche su miti e valori sociali nel mondo greco e romano," *Studi Storici* 27 (1986) 277–302; *RlAss* s.v. "Markt."

66. Hdt. 4,196.

67. Pomp. Mela 3,60; Plin. *n.h.* 6,88; Amm. Marc. 23,6,68; most detailed Eustathius, *In Dionys.Perieg.* 752, who also refers to Herodotus.

68. On a different quality of giving, *do ut abea*s, see at n. 134.

69. Diagoras (5th century) in Diog. Laert. 6,59, Cic. *Nat.Deor.* 3,89 = Diagoras Melius, Theodorus Cyrenaeus ed. M. Winiarczyk (Leipzig, 1981), T 36/37.

70. See Lambert 1960, 75.

71. Cassandra in Aesch. *Ag.* 1168 f.

72. Hdt. 1,90,2 cf. 4; on the stages of the historical tradition see Burkert, "Das Ende des Kroisos. Vorstufen einer Herodoteischen Geschichtserzählung," in *Catalepton, Festschr. B. Wyss* (Basel, 1985), 4–15.

73. For the formulation in *Atrahasis,* see at n. 43.

74. Lysias 30,18.

75. *Il.* 24,425 f.

76. Epictetus 2,23,5.

77. See above at nn. 54–55.

78. See e.g. I. Paulson in I. Paulson, A. Hultzkrantz, and K. Jettmar, *Die Religionen Nordeurasiens und der amerikanischen Arktis* (Stuttgart, 1962), 67–100.

79. Lys. *Or.* 30, cf. Burkert 1985, 226.

80. Aristoph. *Eccl.* 779–783.

81. Tert. *Apol.* 13,6.

82. Aesch. *Fr.* 161 *TrGF.*

83. See the sarcastic argumentation in Hippocr. *Aer.* 22, II 80 L. It is clear that the rich should get rich recompense from the gods, because of their sacrifices; when it comes to the poor, both sides remain unsatisfied.

84. Hes. *Erga* 336 f.: *kad' dynamin,* cf. Xen. *Mem.* 1,3,3; 4,3,16.

85. Porph. *abst.* 2,15 = Theophrastus Fr. 584 A, line 145–153 Fortenbaugh; 2,16 = Theopompus *FGrHist* 115 F 344.

86. Servius *Aen.* 2,116, regarding Iphigeneia's sacrifice: *et sciendum in sacris simulata pro veris accipi.*—E. Lane, ed., *Corpus Monumentorum Religonis Dei Menis* I, Leiden 1971, nr. 50.—Herakles Melon: Pollux 1,30 f. For substitution sacrifice see Chapter 2.

87. Cf. Latte 1920–21, 285 f. = 1968,25 f; I Sam. 15,22; Jesayah 1,11–17; cf. Prov. 21,27; 22,11.

88. Cf. W. Schuller, ed., *Korruption im Altertum* (Munich, 1982).

89. Hes. Fr. 361 (Quoted by Plato *Resp.* 390e; parody in Ovid *Ars am.* 3,653 f.); Plat. *Resp.* 364d, e.

90. *Il.* 9,497.

91. Hom. *Hymn. Dem.* 367–369, cf. Richardson 1974, 270–275.

92. Esp. Plato *Leg.* 905d-907b.

93. Plato *Tht.* 176b. In later Platonism, sacrifice could be vindicated by a magical interpretation of it as a means of getting "attached to gods" *(synaphthēnai theois),* Sallustios 16 cf. 14, 2 f.

94. Lebrun 1980, 92 ff., 121 ff; H. G. Güterbock in W. Röllig, ed., *Altorientalische Literaturen* (Wiesbaden, 1978) 227. Aesch. *Lib. Bearers* 255–257; cf. *Seven* 174–181, 301–320: "which better site than this will you get" (304 f.).

95. I owe the text to Wyatt MacGaffey, Haverford. Cf. Joel 2,14: Jahweh should leave "blessing enough for grain-offering and drink-offering."

96. *Atrahasis* III iv 35, Lambert-Millar 1969, 58 f., Dalley 1989, 33; *Gilgamesh* XI 156 ff., Dalley 114.

97. H. G. Güterbock, *Kumarbi* (Istanbul, 1946) 21.

98. Lambert 1960, 148 f.

99. Complete destruction of war booty occurs in Hebrew *hrm,* but also with the Celts, Caesar *b.g.* 6,17,3–5, cf. U. E. Hagberg in Linders and Nordquist 1987, 77–81.

100. Hdt. 7,54,3 reflects upon the question that came up when Xerxes threw a golden bowl into the Hellespont. Was this a dedication to the Sun God (which would go the wrong way), or a gift to the Sea (which he had flogged before)?

101. Hdt. 3,41 f.

102. See Burkert in *Hérodote et les peuples non grecs.* Entretiens sur l'antiquité classique XXXV (Geneva, 1990) 18, comparing Hdt. 4,61,2.

103. Gen. 15,11.

104. See R. K. Yerkes, *Sacrifice in Greek and Roman Religions and Early Judaism* (London, 1953); Burkert 1983.

105. On *ʿolah* in Israel, see A. Hultgård in Linders and Nordquist 1987, 83–91. On Moloch sacrifice, see Chapter 2 at n. 75–77.

106. Burkert 1992a, 20.

107. Cf. Burkert 1979, 41–43; for Mesopotamia, see *RlAss* VII 1–12 s.v. Libation; Ch. Watanabe, "A Problem in the Libation Scene of Ashurbanipal," in Prince Takahito Mikasa, ed., *Cult and Ritual in the Ancient Near East* (Wiesbaden, 1992) 91–104; Ugaritic and Hebrew *nsk,* HAL 664, cf. *ThWbNT* VII 529–537.

108. Mark 14,3–10 and parallels.

109. Meissner 1920/25, II 81–90; Oppenheim 1964, 106 f., 191 f; Ringgren 1973, 81–89; H. Altenmüller, s.v. Opfer, Opferumlauf, *Lexikon der Aegyptologie* IV (1982) 579–584; 596 f; W. Helck s.v. Tempelwirtschaft, ibid. VI (1986) 414–420.

110. Akkadian *ešru, AHw* 257; Hebrew *ʿašer,* e.g. at the sanctuary of Bethel, *Gen.* 28,22; Greek *dekate,* especially connected with Apollo; see H. W. Parke, "A Consecration to Apollo," *Hermathena* 72 (1948) 82–114.

111. Detailed descriptions of the cult at the temple of Anu at Uruk are in Thureau and Dangin 1921, 61–118.

112. Dt. 14,22 f., 'Law of the tithe.'

113. Latte 1960, 215 f.

114. *ER* V 554; cf. 555 on China.

115. Aristoph. *Plut.* 594–597 with schol.

116. Mt. 10,5–15 cf. Mark 6,8–11, Luke 9,2–5.

117. III Ep. of John 7.

118. An expression equivalent to "setting up" is used in Akkadian, *AHw* 209 s.v. *elû,* cf. *HAL* 785 s.v. *ʿlh.* But oriental temples needed food above all to feed their dependents.

119. I Kings 7,13–50.

120. See n. 31.

121. Sallustios 16,1 (cf. above at n. 38) makes sacrifice an *aparche* of life, as hair sacrifice is an *aparche* of one's body; cf. the concept of *hostia animalis,* Trebatius in Macrob. *Sat.* 3,5,1–4: *in quo sola anima deo sacratur.* But evidently life cannot be transferred, only destroyed. Israelites called blood "life" or "soul" *(nephesh),* Lev. 17,11; Dt. 12,23; this can be taken and poured out at the altar.

229

122. Hes. *Theog.* 535 cf. 556 f. Cf. Gladigow 1984. The element of trickery in sacrifice has been stressed by M. Horkheimer and Th. W. Adorno, *Dialektik der Aufklärung* (Frankfurt, 1981) 67–76. Cf. above at n. 86.

123. See especially Meuli 1946 and Burkert 1983.

124. See also Fouts and Budd 1979, 370; Bygott 1979, 454; De Waal 1989, 209.

125. See Baudy 1983; Gladigow 1984; cf. Lanternari 1976, 196.

126. Schieffelin 1980.

127. See at n. 13.

128. Ethiopians: *Il.* 1,423 f; *Od.* 1,22–26; Phaeacians: *Od.* 7,201–206.

129. That they usually "eat" the smoke is said in the unorthodox version of *Il.* 8,550–552, preserved in Plat. *Alk.* II, 149de.

130. Lev. 17,2 f; cf. Meuli 1975, 938; Burkert 1992b, 173 f.

131. Burkert 1992b, 174. For the basic concept of animal sacrifice presupposed here, and for details see Meuli 1946; Burkert 1983.

132. Hdt. 1,105,1 *doroisi te kai litesi;* in other words, *do ut abeas,* see n. 134.

133. See Chapter 2 at n. 21.

134. Harrison 1922, 7; 1927, 134–138.

135. Namtar the Plague God is pacified through cult in *Atrahasis,* Dalley 1989, 24. *Febris* (fever) has a temple at Rome, Val. Max. 2,5,6; Cic. *N.d.* 3,63; Wissowa *RE* VI 2095 f.

136. Aesch. *Seven* 699–701.

137. Jameson et al. 1993, 45, inscription B line 12 f., cf. pp. 63–67.

138. Cf. e.g. Aesch. *Pers.* 219; 523: "gifts for Earth and for the dead." Cf. A. Henrichs, "Namenlosigkeit und Euphemismus: Zur Ambivalenz der chthonischen Mächte im attischen Drama," in H. Hofmann and A. Harder, eds., *Fragmenta dramatica* (Göttingen, 1991) 161–201.

139. See B. Janowski, "Erwägungen zur Vorgeschichte des israelitischen ŠᴱLAMÎM-Opfers," *Ugarit-Forschungen* 12 (1980) 231–259; Burkert 1983, 9,41.

140. See Chapter 2.

141. Petzl 1994, VII n. 2.

142. B 90 = Fr. XL Kahn. Cf. Seaford 1994, 220–232.
143. B 1, cf. Kirk, Raven, and Schofield 1983, 117–122.
144. Plato *Phd.* 72 bc.
145. Plato *Tim.* 42e.
146. Lorenz 1973; Vollmer 1994.

7. The Validation of Signs

1. This is not the place to tackle the intricacies of the modern science of semiology. Eco 1976, 16 defined sign as "everything that, on the grounds of a previously established social convention, can be taken as something standing for something else," which would exclude the biological signs, which obviously work without social convention. In the wake of poststructuralism, the very concept of sign is taken to be outdated, cf. Eco 1984.

2. Cf. Sommer 1992.

3. Matth. 16,3—a passage missing in basic manuscripts, hence usually considered a later interpolation; the canonical gospels refer to the fig tree as a sign for approaching summer, Mark 13,28, Matth. 24,32, Luke 21, 29.

4. Burkert 1985, 111–114.

5. The term for sign is *ittu* in Akkadian, *'ot* in Hebrew. Greek had, besides *sema/semeion*, the word *teirea* especially for heavenly signs, whence the mythical seer got his name, Teiresias.

6. The most extensive study is still A. Bouché-Leclerq, *Histoire de la divination dans l'antiquité* I-IV (Paris, 1879–82); see also W. R. Halliday, *Greek Divination* (London, 1913); A. Caquot, M. Leibovici, *La Divination* (Paris, 1968); J. P. Vernant, ed., *Divination et rationalité* (Paris, 1974); R. Bloch, *La Divination dans l'antiquité* (Paris, 1984); "Actes du IIe Colloque international du C.E.R.G.A. sur 'Oracles et mantique en Grèce ancienne,'" *Kernos* 3 (1990); R. Bloch, *La Divination* (Paris, 1991); M. Sordi, ed., *La profezia nel mondo antico* (Milan, 1993). For Akkadian texts, see Borger 1967–75 III 95–99; for Hittites, A. Kammenhuber, *Orakelpraxis, Träume und Vorzeichenschau bei den Hethitern* (Heidelberg, 1977); for Etruscans, C. O. Thulin, *Die etruskische Disziplin* (Göteborg, 1905–9); in general, U. Ritz, *Das Bedeutsame in den Erscheinungen. Divinationspraktiken in traditionalen Gesellschaften* (Frankfurt, 1988).

7. See Cicero, *De divinatione* 2,26 *(genus artificiosum—naturale),* cf. 1,11 f; 1,34, with the commentary of A. S. Pease, *M. Tulli Ciceronis De Divinatione Libri Duo* (1920–23, repr. Darmstadt, 1963). Servius

Aen. 6,190 distinguishes *auguria oblativa* (signs that present themselves) and *impetrativa* (signs produced on purpose).

8. This expression is peculiar to the author, see *ThWbNT* VII 241–257.

9. Hdt. 8,137–139.

10. Hdt. 9,91.

11. Leaves of the oak of Dodona, *Od.* 14,328; 19,297; water oracle: Paus. 7,21,13; for Akkadian river omens see F. Nötscher in *Orientalia* 51/4 (1930) 121–146.

12. Romulus: Ennius *Ann.* I 78 ff, cf. *RE* I A 1091; Kalchas: Hom. *Il.* 1,71 f; Akkadian: J. Hunger, "Babylonische Tieromina nebst griechisch-römischen Parallelen," *Mitteilungen der Vorderasiatischen Gesellschaft* 1909,3; one series has been edited and translated by F. Nötscher in *Orientalia* 51/54 (1930) 176–179.

13. The story of Mosollamos, Ps.-Hekataios *FGrHist* 264 F 21 = Iosephus *C.Ap.* 1,201–204.

14. Burkert 1992a, 46–53.

15. Herzfeld 1985, 247–258.

16. See H. Diels, *Beiträge zur Zuckungsliteratur des Okzidents und Orients* I/II; *Abh.* (Berlin, 1907–8, repr. Leipzig, 1970).

17. This was a formulation of Paracelsus, who wrote *de signatura rerum*, see Theophrast von Hohenheim, gen. Paracelsus, *Sämtliche Werke* I 2 (Berlin, 1928), 397–400.

18. See Chapter 1 at n. 87.

19. For families of seers see Burkert 1992a, 43–46.

20. Cf. Lorenz 1973; Ditfurth 1976.

21. Ptol. *Tetr.* 1,2.

22. G. Glotz, *L' Ordalie dans la Grèce primitive* (Paris, 1904); *HDA* III 1016–1021; H. Nottarp, *Gottesurteilsstudien* (Munich, 1956).

23. On "war as an ordalic procedure" in the ancient Near East see Liverani 1990, 150–159; in Roman legend the most famous example was the battle of *Horatii* and *Curiatii*, Livy 1,24, cf. *RE* VIII 2322–2327.

24. Hammurapi's *Laws* §2; 132, *ANET* 166; 171; *Middle Assyrian Laws* A §25, *ANET* 182.

25. See A. Bürge, "Realität und Rationalität der Feuerprobe," *Zeitschrift der Savigny-Stiftung für Rechtsgeschichte* 100 (1983) 257–259. Walking on glowing coals, as ritually done in northern Greece (W. D. Furley, *Studies in the Use of Fire in Ancient Greek Religion,* New York, 1981) and imitated in modern limits-testing groups, is frightening but normally does not cause burns.

231

26. Yasna 43,4; G. Widengren, *Die Religionen Irans* (Stuttgart, 1965), 87 f; cf. Lact. *Inst.* 7,21,3–7.

27. Soph. *Ant.* 264 f. cf. Aristoph. *Lys.* 133–135.

28. See at n. 34.

29. *Num.* 5,11; 21 ff. cf. W. McKane *Vetus Testamentum* 30 (1980) 474–492; Hes. *Theog.* 782–806.

30. See P. Hoskisson, "The *Nishum* 'Oath' in Mari," in G. D. Young, ed., *Mari in Retrospect* (Winona Lake, 1992), 203–210, esp. 206 f, on eating taboo as an oath ceremony; J. Bottéro *ASNSPisa* III 11 (1981) 1005–1068. For Hittites, Ishara "hydropsy" is the goddess of oaths. Cf. Meissner 1920/25, II 290. On the Avestan *Videvdat* 4,54–55, see M. Boyce in *Monumentum H.S. Nyberg* I (Teheran/Liège, 1975), 69–76.

31. See E. Peterson, *Frühkirche, Judentum und Gnosis* (Freiburg, 1959), 334 f.

32. *ER* XV 302; see also G. Lorenz, in F. Hampl and I. Weiler, *Kritische und vergleichende Studien zur alten Geschichte und Universalgeschichte,* Innsbrucker Beiträge zur Kulturwissenschaft 18 (Innsbruck, 1974), 235.

33. Gottfried von Strassburg, *Tristan,* ed. K. Marold, rev. W. Schröder (Berlin, 1977), line 15518–15764, here line 15739 f, transl. with an introd. by A. T. Hatter (Harmondsworth, 1972) 248.

34. Fulcher of Chartres, *PL* 155, 843 f; Raymond d'Aguilers, *PL* 155, 641–643; 646 = Le <Liber> de Raymond d'Aguilers, ed. J. H. and L. L. Hill (1969) 120–124; 128 f; cf. Chr. Auffarth " 'Ritter' und 'Arme' auf dem Ersten Kreuzzug," *Saeculum* 40 (1989) 39–55 esp. 51.

35. See Chapter 1 at n. 93.

36. M. Douglas, *Natural Symbols* (New York, 1973, 3rd ed. 1978), insists that cosmological symbolism usually reflects social conditions.

37. See Burkert 1979, 41 f.

38. Gen. 28,10–22; Burkert 1979, 41 f.

39. See U. Seidl, *Die babylonischen Kudurru-Reliefs* (Fribourg, 1989).

40. Cf. Piccaluga 1974; Gladigow 1992 esp.177–183.

41. Boeotian hipparchs and the tomb of Dirke, Plut. *Gen. Socr.* 578b, cf. Burkert 1983, 188.

42. Paus. 1,28,2.

43. On the function of art as "making special," see Dissanayake 1988, esp. 92–101.

44. See Chapter 1 at nn. 91, 92.

45. See *RAC* s.v. Götterbild.

46. See Chapter 1 at n. 67.

47. See C. P. Jones, "Stigma: Tattooing and Branding in Graeco-Roman Antiquity," *JRS* 77 (1987) 139–155. On initiation marks for men see, for example, C. Calame, *Le Processus symbolique* (Centro Internazionale di Semiotica e di Linguistica: Documents de travail et pré-publications 128/9) (Urbino, 1983) 4 f; for women, Lincoln 1981, 34–49.

48. See Chapter 1 at nn. 111–114.

49. Hdt. 1,74,5; 3,8.

50. Gen. 17,11 (the older version has the "sacrifice of halves" instead, see n. 89); cf. in general *ER* III 511–514; see also Chapter 1 at n. 113; 2 at nn. 50,51.

51. *Erra* 4,56, Dalley 1989, 305; cf. Chapter 2 at n. 41–44; Burkert 1979, 105, 120.

52. The dogma of sacraments as *character indelebilis* was developed by Thomas Aquinas, *Summa theologiae* III quaest. 63, following Augustine, cf. L. J. Pongratz, *Historisches Wörterbuch der Philosophie* I (1971) 984–986.

53. A Christian sect in Russia, the *skopzii*, made castration the real "seal" of the elect; see K. K. Grass, *Die russischen Sekten* II (Leipzig, 1914) 687 ff.

54. An old standard study is Hirzel 1902; see also E. Ziebarth *RE* V 2975–2083; *ThWbNT* V 458–467; *RlAss* II 305–315; *ER* XV 301–305; E. Benveniste, "L'Expression du serment dans la Grèce ancienne," *RHR* 134 (1947–48) 81–94; J. Plescia, *The Oath and Perjury in Ancient Greece* (Tallahassee, 1970); Burkert 1985, 250–254; N. Rollant, "Horkos et sa famille," *LAMA* 5 (1979) 214–304; Faraone 1993.

55. The oath is just "legality to be legalized," *ius iurandum* in Latin.

56. *ER* XV 301.

57. See especially Sommer 1992.

58. Ibid., 66–91, esp. 85.

59. See Dundes 1954.

60. Cyrus in Hdt. 1,153: business in the marketplace is "cheating by oaths." "One must cheat children with dice, grownups with oaths," Lysander said according to Diod. 10,9, or else King Philip according to Ael. *Var.Hist.* 7,12.

61. *Od.* 19,395 f.

62. *Quos me sentio dicere,* formula of devotion in Macrob. *Sat.* 3,9,10.

63. Cf. Chapter 1 at nn. 87–93.

64. This is a normal formula in Egypt, Bonnet 1952, 164, and also in Mesopotamia, see *RlAss* II 307–315 on "oath of king" and "oath of city"; Meissner 1920–1925, II 290 f.

65. *Od.* 14,158 f; 17,155 f; 20,230 f; cf. 19,304.

66. *ANET* 205; Burkert 1992a, 93 f.

67. *Il.* 3,104; 277–279, cf. Burkert, "Homer's Anthropomorphism: Narrative and Ritual," in D. Buitron-Oliver, ed., *New Perspectives in Early Greek Art* (Washington: National Gallery of Art, 1991) 81–91.

68. A puzzling but logical consequence is that a god will take an oath swearing "by himself"; this is a serious act of promise for Jahweh, Deut. 29,9 f., a joke for Callimachus, Fr. 114,5.

69. Above, nn. 67, 65.

70. R. Merkelbach, *ZPE* 9 (1972) 277–285.

71. Bonnet 1952, 164; Stone of Nofer-Abu, Roeder 1915, 58, cf. Chapter 5 n. 85.

72. Aristoph. *Clouds* 397.

73. *AHw* 600; *RlAss* II 314; Meissner 1920/25, II 290 f; cf. J. Pedersen, *Der Eid bei den Semiten* (Strassburg, 1914).

74. Hes. *Erga* 803 f.

75. Cf. Bell 1992, 98 (following Bourdieu): "Ritualization produces this ritualized body through the interaction of the body with a structured and structuring environment."

76. D. Wiseman, "Abban and Alalakh," *JCS* 12 (1958) 129.

77. *Il.* 3,299–301, see n. 67. See also Karavites 1992.

78. Treaty of Ashurnirari V and Mati'ilu, *ANET* 532.

79. N. Oettinger, *Die militärischen Eide der Hethiter* (Wiesbaden, 1976) 21.

80. Livy 1,24,8.

81. *Paroemiographi Graeci* I 225 f; Burkert 1985, 252 f.

82. Treaties from Sfire and the foundation oath of Kyrene, see Faraone 1993; F. Letoublon, "Le Serment fondateur," *Metis* 4 (1989) 101–115; Burkert 1992a, 67 f.

83. Shurpu 3,35, p. 20 Reiner: "oath sworn by slaughtering a sheep and touching its cut-off flesh"; cf. Weinfeld 1990, 187. Hdt. 6,68: Demaratos sacrificed an ox, gave his mother "from the entrails into her hand," and beseeched her to speak the truth.

84. Persians and Greeks in Xen. *Anab.* 2,2,4.

85. Germanic custom, *ER* XV 304.

86. Even the attempt at perjury has this consequence, Hdt. 6,86.

87. Dem. 23,67 f. cf. Dinarch. 47; R. W. Wallace, *The Areopagos Council to 307* B.C. (Baltimore, 1985) 123. A comparable practice is to "cut in halves" and walk through them to make a covenant, known from the Old Testament, Gen. 15,9; Jeremiah 34.18, and the Hittites, see E. Bickerman, "Couper une alliance," *Studies in Jewish and Christian History* I (Leiden, 1976) 1–32; Burkert 1983, 35 at n. 3. More

rational and more drastic is the practice to commit a common crime to ensure loyalty. Athenian oligarchs, plotting their conspiracy, "killed Hyperbolos, thus giving the guarantee of loyalty to each other" (Thuc. 8,73,3); cf. Chapter 1 n. 115. The Catilinarians were accused of having had a cannibalistic feast before their attempt to make a revolution, suppressed by Cicero. Sallust, *Catilina* 22; cf. Chapter 1 n. 113.

88. *Il.* 1,245.

89. Polyb. 3,25,7–9.

90. *RlAss* II 306 (the term is *nasahu*).

91. Hdt. 1,165,3; see also Diod. 9,10,3 (Epidamnos); Callim. Fr. 388,9.

92. Jer. 51,59–64.

93. D.L. 8,22, cf. Iambl. *V.Pyth.* 47; 144; 150; contradicted by Diod. 10,9,1.

94. Matth. 5,34–37.

95. For *Tuppu mamiti* and *ilu mamiti* see *AHw* 599.

96. John Locke, *Epistula de tolerantia/A Letter on Toleration*, ed. J. W. Gough (Oxford, 1968), 135.

235

Bibliography

Aarne, A., and S. Thompson. 1961. *The Types of the Folktale*, 2nd ed. Helsinki. Rev. ed. 1964.

D'Aquili, E. G. 1979. *The Spectrum of Ritual*. New York.

D'Aquili, E. G., and H. Mol. 1990. *The Regulation of Physical and Mental Systems: Systems Theory of the Philosophy of Science*. Lewiston.

Assmann, J. 1992. *Das kulturelle Gedächtnis: Schrift, Erinnerung und politische Identität in frühen Hochkulturen*. Munich.

Atran, S. 1987. "Ordinary Constraints on the Semantics of Living Kinds: A Commonsense Alternative to Recent Treatment of Natural Object Terms." *Mind and Language* 2: 27–68.

Axelrod, R. 1984. *The Evolution of Cooperation*. New York.

van Baal, J. 1971. *Symbols for Communication: An Introduction to the Anthropological Study of Religion*. Assen.

Baldwin, J. D., and J. I. Baldwin. 1981. *Beyond Sociobiology*. New York.

Bammer, A. 1985. "Gibt es eine Autonomie der Kultur?" in Ehalt 1985, pp. 17–26.

———, 1981. *Das Flüstern in uns. Ursprung und Entwicklung menschlichen Verhaltens*. Frankfurt.

Bar-Yosef, O., and B. Vandermeersch. 1993. "Modern Humans in the Levant." *Scientific American* 168/4: 64–70.

Barash, D. *Sociobiology and Behavior*, 2nd ed. New York.

Baudy, G. J. 1980. *Exkommunikation und Reintegration. Zur Genese und Kulturfunktion frühgriechischer Einstellungen zum Tod*. Frankfurt.

————, 1983. "Hierarchie, oder die Verteilung des Fleisches," in B. Gladigow and H. G. Kippenberg, eds., *Neue Ansätze in der Religionswissenschaft*. Munich. (pp. 131–174.)

Becker, E. 1973. *The Denial of Death*. New York.

Bell, C. 1992. *Ritual Theory, Ritual Practice*. New York.

Bickerton, D. 1990. *Language and Species*. Chicago.

Binder, G. 1964. *Die Aussetzung des Königskindes: Kyros und Romulus*. Meisenheim.

Binder, G., and R. Merkelbach, eds. 1968. *Amor und Psyche*. Darmstadt.

Bischof, N. 1985. *Das Rätsel Ödipus: Die biologischen Wurzeln des Urkonfliktes von Intimität und Autonomie*. Munich.

Bloch, M. 1986. *From Blessing to Violence: History and Ideology of the Circumcision Ritual of the Merina of Madagascar*. Cambridge.

————, 1992. *Prey into Hunter: The Politics of Religious Experience*. Cambridge.

Bonnet, H. 1952. *Reallexikon der ägyptischen Religionsgeschichte*. Berlin.

Boon, J. A. 1982. *Other Tribes, Other Scribes: Symbolic Anthropology in the Comparative Study of Cultures, Histories, Religions and Texts*. Cambridge.

Borger, R. 1967–1975. *Handbuch der Keilschriftliteratur* I-III. Berlin.

Bottéro, J., and S. N. Kramer. 1989. *Lorsque les dieux faisaient l'homme: Mythologie mésopotamienne*. Paris.

Bourdieu, P. 1977. *Outline of a Theory of Practice*. Cambridge.

Boyd, R., and J. P. Lorberbaum. 1987. "No Pure Strategy Is Evolutionarily Stable in the Repeated Prisoner's Dilemma Game." *Nature* 327: 58–59.

Brulé, P. 1987. *La Fille d'Athènes*. Paris.

Burkert, W. 1979. *Structure and History in Greek Mythology and Ritual*. Berkeley.

————, 1980. "Griechische Mythologie und die Geistesgeschichte der Moderne," in *Les Etudes classiques au XIXe et XXe siècles: Entretiens sur l'antiquité classique 26*. Vandoeuvres-Geneva. (pp. 159–199.)

————, 1981. "Glaube und Verhalten: Zeichengehalt und Wirkungsmacht von Opferritualen," in *Le Sacrifice dans l'antiquité: Entretiens sur l'antiquité classique 27*. Vandoeuvres-Geneva. (pp. 91–125.)

————, 1983. *Homo Necans: The Anthropology of Ancient Greek Sacrificial Ritual and Myth*. Berkeley. 1983.

————, 1985. *Greek Religion Archaic and Classical*. Oxford.

238

————, 1987a. "The Problem of Ritual Killing," in R. G. Hamerton-Kelly, ed., *Violent Origins*. Stanford. (pp. 149–176.)

————, 1987b. *Ancient Mystery Cults*. Cambridge, Mass.

————, 1991. "Typen griechischer Mythen auf dem Hintergrund mykenischer und orientalischer Tradition," in D. Musti et al., eds., *La transizione dal Miceneo all'alto arcaismo: Dal palazzo alla città*. Rome. (pp. 527–536.)

————, 1992a. *The Orientalizing Revolution*. Cambridge, Mass.

————, 1992b. "Opfer als Tötungsritual: Eine Konstante der menschlichen Kulturgeschichte?" in F. Graf, ed., *Klassische Antike und neue Wege der Kulturwissenschaften*. Basel. (pp. 169–189.)

————, 1993. "Mythos—Begriff, Struktur, Funktionen," in F. Graf, ed., *Mythen in mythenloser Gesellschaft*. Stuttgart. (pp. 9–24.)

————, 1994. *"Vergeltung" zwischen Ethologie und Ethik*. Munich. (Carl Friedrich von Siemens Stiftung: Themen XL)

Bygott, J. D. 1979. "Agonistic Behavior, Dominance, and Social Structure in Wild Chimpanzees of the Gombe National Park," in Hamburg and McCown 1979. (pp. 405–427.)

Cairns, D. L. 1993. *Aidos: The Psychology and Ethics of Honour and Shame in Ancient Greek Literature*. Oxford.

Caldwell, R. 1989. *The Origin of the Gods: A Psychoanalytic Study of Greek Theogonic Myth*. Oxford.

Campbell, J. 1949. *The Hero with a Thousand Faces*. New York.

Caplan, A. L. 1978. *The Sociobiology Debate*. New York.

Castellino, G. R. 1977. *Testi Sumerici e Accadici*. Torino.

Chagnon, N. A. 1988. "Life Histories, Blood Revenge, and Warfare in a Tribal Population." *Science* 239: 985–992.

Chagnon, N. A., and W. Irons, eds. *Evolutionary Biology and Human Social Behavior: An Anthropological Perspective*. North Scituate.

Cheal, D. J. 1988. *The Gift Economy*. London.

Childs, B. S. 1974. *Exodus: A Commentary*. London.

Cook, A. B. 1913–1940. *Zeus. A Study in Ancient Religion* I-III. Cambridge.

Cumont, F. 1931. *Die orientalischen Religionen im römischen Heidentum*. 3rd ed. Stuttgart.

Dalley, S. 1989. *Myths from Mesopotamia*. Oxford.

Dan, J. 1977. "The Innocent Persecuted Heroine: An Attempt at the Surface Level of the Narrative Structure of the Female Fairy Tale," in H. Jason and D. Segal, eds., *Patterns in Oral Literature*. The Hague. (pp. 13–30.)

Dawkins, R. 1976. *The Selfish Gene*. Oxford.

————, 1982. *The Extended Phenotype: The Gene as the Unit of Selection.* Oxford.

Delbos, G., and P. Jorion. 1981. *Le Délit religieux dans la cité antique.* Paris.

Derrida, J. 1967. *L'Écriture et la différence.* Paris.

Dissanayake, E. 1988. *What Is Art For?* Seattle.

v. Ditfurth, H. 1976. *Der Geist fiel nicht vom Himmel: Die Evolution unseres Bewußtseins.* Hamburg.

Dodds, E. R. 1951. *The Greeks and the Irrational.* Berkeley.

Dowden, K. 1989. *Death and the Maiden: Girls' Initiation Rites in Greek Mythology.* London.

Dunbar, R. I. 1988. *Primate Social Systems.* London.

Dumont, L. 1970. *Homo hierarchicus: Religion, Politics and History in India.* The Hague.

Dundes, A. G. 1964. *The Morphology of North American Indian Folktales.* Helsinki.

Durkheim, E. 1965. *The Elementary Forms of Religious Life.* New York.

Ebeling, E. 1931. *Tod und Leben nach den Vorstellungen der Babylonier* I. Berlin.

Eco, U. 1976. *A Theory of Semiotics.* Bloomington.

————, 1984. *Semiotics and the Philosophy of Language.* Bloomington.

Ehalt, H., ed. 1985. *Zwischen Natur und Kultur: Zur Kritik biologistischer Ansätze.* Vienna.

Eibl-Eibesfeldt, I. 1970. *Liebe und Haß: Zur Naturgeschichte elementarer Verhaltensweisen.* Munich.

————, 1976. *Menschenforschung auf neuen Wegen: Die naturwissenschaftliche Betrachtung kultureller Verhaltensweisen.* Vienna.

————, 1986. *Die Biologie des menschlichen Verhaltens.* 2nd ed. Munich.

————, 1987. *Grundriß der vergleichenden Verhaltensforschung.* 7th ed. Munich.

Eigen, M. 1987. *Stufen zum Leben.* Munich.

Éléments orientaux dans la religion grecque ancienne. 1960. Strasbourg Colloquium, May 22–24, 1958. Paris.

Faraone, C. A. 1992. *Talismans and Trojan Horses.* Oxford.

————, 1993. "Molten Wax, Spilt Wine and Mutilated Animals: Sympathetic Magic in Near Eastern and Early Greek Oath Ceremonies." *JHS* 113: 60–80.

Farnell, L. R. 1896–1909. *The Cults of the Greek States* I-V. Oxford.

Fehling, D. 1974. *Ethologische Überlegungen auf dem Gebiet der Altertumskunde.* Munich.

Festugière, A. J. 1976. "Anth'hōn. La Formule 'en exchange de quoi' dans la prière grecque hellénistique." *Revue des Sciences Philosophiques et Théologiques.* 60: 389–418.

Fischer, E. P. 1988. *Gene sind anders.* Heidelberg.

Fleming, Th. 1988. *The Politics of Human Nature.* New Brunswick.

Fogelson, R. D., and R. N. Adams, eds. 1977. *The Anthropology of Power.* New York.

Fouts, R. S. and R. L. Budd. 1979. "Artificial and Human Language Acquisition in the Chimpanzee," in Hamburg and McCown, pp. 375–392.

Fox, R., ed. 1975. *Biosocial Anthropology.* London.

Frankfort, H. 1948. *Kingship and the Gods.* Chicago.

Frazer, J. G. 1898. *Pausanias' Description of Greece* I-VI. London.

Freedman, D. G. 1974. *Human Infancy: An Evolutionary Perspective.* Hillsdale.

———, 1979. *Human Sociobiology: A Holistic Approach.* New York.

Freud, S. 1912/13. *Totem und Tabu.* Vienna. (in *Gesammelte Werke 9,* 1940)

Frye, R. N. 1984. *The History of Ancient Iran.* Munich.

Furlani, G. 1940. *Riti babilonesi e assiri.* Udine.

Gans, E. 1981. *The Origin of Language: A Formal Theory of Representation.* Berkeley.

Geertz, C. 1973. *The Interpretation of Cultures.* New York.

Gernet, L. 1968. *Anthropologie de la Grèce ancienne.* Paris.

Girard, R. 1977. *Violence and the Sacred.* Baltimore.

———, 1986. *The Scapegoat.* Baltimore.

Gladigow, B. 1981. "Kraft, Macht, Herrschaft. Zur Religionsgeschichte politischer Begriffe," in B. Gladigow, ed., *Staat und Religion.* Düsseldorf. (pp. 7–22.)

———, 1984. "Die Teilung des Opfers." *Frühmittelalterliche Studien* 18/1 10–43.

———, 1992. "Audi Juppiter, Audite Fines: Religionsgeschichtliche Einordnung von Grenzen, Grenzziehungen und Grenzbestätigungen," in O. Behrends and L. Capogrossi Colognesi, eds., *Die Römische Feldmeßkunst.* Göttingen. (pp. 172–189.)

Goodall, J. 1971. *In the Shadow of Man.* Boston. Rev. ed. 1988.

———, 1986. *The Chimpanzees of Gombe: Patterns of Behavior.* Cambridge, Mass.

———, 1990. *Through a Window: My Thirty Years with the Chimpanzees of Gombe.* Boston.

Gouldner, A. W. 1960. "The Norm of Reciprocity." *American Sociological Review* 25: 161–178.

Gray, P. J., ed. 1984. *A Guide to Primate Sociobiological Theory and Research*. New Haven.

242

Gregory, C. A. 1980. "Gifts to Men and Gifts to God: Gift Exchange and Capital Accumulation in Contemporary Papua." *Man* 15: 626–652.

Gregory, M. S. et al., eds. 1978. *Sociobiology and Human Nature*. San Francisco.

Grottanelli, C. 1989–1990. "Do ut des?" in *Atti del Convegno Internazionale Anathema: Scienze dell' Antichità: Storia/Archeologia/Antropologia*. 3–4: 45–54.

Grünbaum, A. 1984. *The Foundations of Psychoanalysis*. Berkeley.

Gruppe, O. 1921. *Geschichte der klassischen Mythologie und Religionsgeschichte*. Leipzig.

Hamburg, D. A., and E. R. McCown, eds. 1979. *The Great Apes*. Meno Park.

Hamilton, W. D. 1964. "The Genetic Evolution of Social Behavior." *Journal of Theoretical Biology* 7: 1–52.

———, 1975. "Innate Social Aptitude of Man: An Approach from Evolutionary Genetics," in Fox 1975, pp. 133–155.

Hardy, W. G. 1978. *Language, Thought, and Experience*. Baltimore.

Harrison, J. E. 1922. *Prolegomena to the Study of Greek Religion*. 3rd ed. Cambridge.

———, 1927. *Themis: A Study of the Social Origins of Greek Religion*. 2nd ed. Cambridge.

Hawkes, T. 1977. *Structuralism and Semiotics*. Berkeley.

Head, B. V. 1911. *Historia Numorum*. 2nd ed. Oxford.

Health, A. 1976. *Rational Choice and Social Exchange: A Critique of Exchange Theory*. Cambridge.

Heesterman, J. C. 1985. *The Inner Conflict of Tradition: Essays in Indian Ritual, Kingship, and Society*. Chicago.

Herman, G. 1987. *Ritualized Friendship and the Greek City*. Cambridge.

Herrmann, W. 1960. "Götterspeise und Göttertrank in Ugarit und Israel." *Zeitschrift für Alttestamentliche Wissenschaft* 72: 205–216.

Herzfeld, M. 1985. *The Poetics of Manhood*. Princeton.

Hewlett, B. S., ed. 1992. *Father-Child-Relation: Cultural and Biosocial Contexts*. Berlin.

Hinde, R. 1982. *Ethology: Its Nature and Relation with Other Sciences*. New York.

Hirzel, R. 1902. *Der Eid: Ein Beitrag zu seiner Geschichte*. Leipzig.

Hitzig, H., and H. Blümner. 1896–1910. *Des Pausanias Beschreibung von Griechenland* I-III. Leipzig.

Homans, G. C. 1941. "Anxiety and Ritual: The Theories of Malinowski and Radcliffe-Brown." *American Anthropologist* 43: 164–172.

Hughes, D. D. 1991. *Human Sacrifice in Ancient Greece.* London.

Hutter, M. 1988. *Behexung, Entsühnung und Heilung.* Freiburg.

Jameson, M., D. R. Jordan, and R. D. Kotansky. 1993. *A Lex Sacra from Selinus.* Durham.

Janowski, B., and G. Wilhelm. 1993. "Der Bock, der die Sünden hinausträgt," in B. Janowski et al., eds., *Religionsgeschichtliche Beziehungen zwischen Kleinasien, Nordsyrien und dem Alten Testament.* Freiburg. (pp. 109–169.)

Jason, H. 1984. "The Fairy Tale of the Active Heroine," in G. Calame-Griaule, ed., *Le conte: Pourquoi? Comment?* Paris. (pp. 79–97.)

Jeffery, L. H. 1961. *The Local Scripts of Archaic Greece.* Oxford. Rev. ed. 1990 with supplement by A. W. Johnston. Oxford.

Johnson, M. 1987. *The Body in the Mind.* Chicago.

Karavites, P. 1992. *Promise-Giving and Treaty-Making: Homer and the Near East.* Leiden.

Kautzsch, E. 1922/3. *Die Heilige Schrift des Alten Testaments* I/II. 4th ed. Tübingen.

Kelsen, H. 1982. *Vergeltung und Kausalität.* Vienna.

Kirk, G. S. 1970. *Myth: Its Meaning and Functions in Ancient and Other Cultures.* Berkeley.

Kirk, G. S., J. E. Raven, and M. Schofield. 1983. *The Presocratic Philosophers.* 2nd ed. Cambridge.

Krummen, E. 1990. *Pyrsos Hymnon: Festliche Gegenwart und mythisch-rituelle Tradition als Voraussetzung einer Pindarinterpretation.* Berlin.

Kummer, H. 1971. *Primate Societies.* Chicago.

Lambert, W. G. 1960. *Babylonian Wisdom Literature.* Oxford.

Lambert, W. G. and A. R. Millard. 1969. *Atra-hasis: The Babylonian Story of the Flood.* Oxford.

Lanternari, V. 1976. *La grande festa: Vita rituale e sistemi di produzione nelle società tradizionali.* 2nd ed. Bari.

———, 1989. "La logica dei rapporti tra medicina e valori nelle società tribali," in A. Marazzi, ed., *Antropologia: Tendenze contemporanee.* Milano. (pp. 75–84.)

———, 1988. *Dèi, Profeti, Contadini: Incontri nel Ghana.* Naples.

———, 1994. *Medicina, magia, religione, valori* I. Naples.

Latte, K. 1920/1. "Schuld und Sühne in der griechischen Religion." *Archiv für Religionswissenschaft* 20: 254–298.

———, 1960. *Römische Religionsgeschichte.* Munich.

243

Lazzarini, M. L. 1976. "Le formule delle dediche votive nella Grecia arcaica." *Mem. Acc. Linc.* Ser.VIII/19: 45–354.

―――, 1989–90. "Iscrizioni votive greche," in *Atti del Convegno Internazionale Anathema: Scienze dell' Antichità: Storia Archeologia Antropologia* 3–4: 845–859.

Leach, E. R. 1976. *Culture and Communication.* Cambridge.

Lebrun, R. 1980. *Hymnes et Prières Hittites.* Louvain-la-Neuve.

Lee, R. B., and I. DeVore, eds. 1968. *Man the Hunter.* Chicago.

Levy, R. 1948. *The Gate of Horn.* London.

Lincoln, B. 1981. *Emerging from the Chrysalis: Studies in Rituals of Women's Initiation.* Cambridge, Mass.

―――, 1986. *Myth, Cosmos, and Society: Indo-European Themes of Creation and Destruction.* Cambridge, Mass.

Linders, T. and G. Nordquist, eds. 1987. *Gifts for the Gods.* Upsala.

Liverani, M. 1990. *Prestige and Interest: International Relations in the Near East ca. 1600–1100 B.C.* Padua.

Lorenz, K. 1963. *On Aggression.* New York.

―――, 1973. *Die Rückseite des Spiegels: Versuch einer Naturgeschichte des menschlichen Erkennens.* Munich.

―――, 1978. *Vergleichende Verhaltensforschung: Grundlagen der Ethologie.* Vienna.

Lovin, R. W. and F. E. Reynolds. 1985. *Cosmogony and Ethical Order: New Studies in Comparative Ethics.* Chicago.

Luckenbill, D. D. 1926–27. *Ancient Records of Assyria and Babylonia* I-II. Chicago.

Luhmann, N. 1968. *Vertrauen: Ein Mechanismus der Reduktion sozialer Komplexität.* Stuttgart.

―――, 1977. *Funktion der Religion.* Frankfurt.

―――, 1980. *Gesellschaftsstruktur und Semantik.* Frankfurt.

Lumsden, C. J. and E. O. Wilson. 1981. *Genes, Mind, and Culture: The Coevolutionary Process.* Cambridge, Mass.

―――, 1983. *Promethean Fire: Reflections on the Origin of Mind.* Cambridge, Mass.

Manetti, G. 1987. *Le teorie del segno nell'antichità classica.* Milan.

Marinatos, N. 1993. *Minoan Religion: Ritual, Image, and Symbol.* Columbus, South Carolina.

Marshack, A. 1972. *The Roots of Civilization: The Cognitive Beginnings of Man's First Art, Symbol and Notation.* London.

Mauss, M. 1967. *The Gift: Forms and Functions of Exchange in Archaic Societies.* New York.

Meier, H., ed. 1988. *Die Herausforderung der Evolutionsbiologie.* Munich.

Meissner, B. 1920–25. *Babylonien und Assyrien* I-II. Heidelberg.

Meuli, K. 1946. "Griechische Opferbräuche," in *Phyllobolia: Festschrift Peter Von der Mühll*. Basel. (pp. 185–288.)

———, 1975. *Gesammelte Schriften*. Basel.

Meyer, E. 1962. "Das Gebet des Nabonid." *Sitzungsberichte der Sächsischen Akademie der Wissenschaften zu Leipzig*. phil.-hist.Klasse 107/3.

Milne, P. J. 1988. *Vladimir Propp and the Study of Structure in Hebrew Biblical Narrative*. Decatur, Georgia.

Mol, H. J. 1976. *Identity and the Sacred: A Sketch for a New Social-Scientific Theory of Religion*. New York.

Moore, R. L. and F. E. Reynolds, eds. 1984. *Anthropology and the Study of Religion*. Chicago.

Montagu, A., ed. 1980. *Sociobiology Examined*. Oxford.

Morris, D. 1967. *The Naked Ape: A Zoologist's Study of the Human Animal*. New York.

Nadig, M. 1986. D*ie verborgene Kultur der Frau: Ethnopsychoanalytische Gespräche mit mexikanischen Bäuerinnen*. Frankfurt.

Nock, A. D. 1972. *Essays on Religion and the Ancient World*. ed. Z. Stewart I-II. Oxford.

Noth, M. 1962. *Exodus: A Commentary*. London.

Numbers, R. L. and D. W. Amundsen, eds. 1986. *Caring and Curing: Health and Medicine in the Western Religious Traditions*. New York.

Oppenheim, A. L. 1964. *Ancient Mesopotamia*. Chicago.

Parker, R. 1983. *Miasma: Pollution and Purification in Early Greek Religion*. Oxford.

Petzl, G. 1994. "Die Beichtinschriften Westkleinasiens," *Epigraphica Anatolica*, vol. 22.

Piccaluga, G. 1974. *Terminus: I segni di confine nella religione romana*. Rome.

Pleket, H. W. 1981. "Religious History as the History of Mentality: The 'Believer' as Servant of the Deity in the Greek World," in Versnel 1981, pp. 153–192.

Popp, J. L. and I. De Vore. 1979. "Aggressive Competition and Social Dominance Theory," in Hamburg and McCown 1979, pp. 318–338.

Propp, V. 1968. *Morphology of the Folktale*. 2nd ed. Austin.

Rapoport, A. and N. M. Chamnah. 1965. *Prisoner's Dilemma*. Ann Arbor.

Rappaport, R. A. 1971. "The Sacred in Human Evolution." *Annual Review of Ecology and Systematics*. 2: 23–44.

—————, 1968. *Pigs for the Ancestors: Ritual in the Ecology of a New Guinea People.* New Haven.

—————, 1967. "Ritual Regulation of Environmental Relations Among a New Guinea People." *Ethnology* 6: 17–30.

Reiner, E. 1958. *Aurpu: A Collection of Sumerian and Accadian Incantations.* Berlin.

Reynolds, P. C. 1981. *On the Evolution of Human Behavior: The Argument from Animals to Man.* Berkeley.

Richardson, N. J. 1974. *The Homeric Hymn to Demeter.* Oxford.

Riedl, R. 1985. *Evolution und Erkenntnis.* Munich.

Ringgren, H. 1973. *Religions of the Ancient Near East.* London.

Roeder, G. 1915. *Urkunden zur Religion des alten Ägypten.* Jena.

Rubel, P. G. and A. Rosman, 1978. *Your Own Pigs You May Not Eat.* Chicago.

Ruf, H., ed. 1989. *Religion, Ontotheology, and Deconstruction.* New York.

Sahlins, M. 1970. "The Spirit of the Gift," in J. Pouillon and P. Maranda, eds., *Échanges et communications.* The Hague.

—————, 1976. *The Use and Abuse of Biology: An Anthropological Critique of Sociobiology.* Ann Arbor.

Saler, B. 1993. *Conceptualizing Religion: Immanent Anthropologists, Transcendent Natives, and Unbounded Categories.* Leiden.

Schapp, W. 1953. *In Geschichten verstrickt.* Hamburg.

—————, 1959. *Philosophie der Geschichten.*

—————, 1965. *Wissen in Geschichten.* Wiesbaden.

Schefold, K. 1993. *Götter- und Heldensagen der Griechen in der Früh- und Hocharchaischen Kunst.* Munich.

Schieffelin, E. L. 1980. "Reciprocity and the Construction of Reality." *Man* 15: 502–517.

Schrank, W. 1908. *Babylonische Sühneriten besonders mit Rücksicht auf Priester und Büßer.* Leipzig.

Seaford, R. 1994. *Reciprocity and Ritual: Homer and Tragedy in the Developing City State.* Oxford.

Siegmund, W., ed. 1984. *Antiker Mythos in unseren Märchen.* Kassel.

Sissa, G. 1986. *Le Corps virginal: La Virginité féminine en Grèce ancienne.* Paris.

Slobodkin, L. B. 1992. *Simplicity and Complexity in the Games of the Intellect.* Cambridge, Mass.

Sommer, V. 1992. *Lob der Lüge: Täuschung und Selbstbetrug bei Tier und Mensch.* Munich.

Streck, M. 1916. *Assurbanipal und die letzten assyrischen Könige bis zum Untergang Niniveh's* I-III. Leipzig.

Strommenger, E. 1962. *Fünf Jahrtausende Mesopotamien: Die Kunst von den Anfängen um 5000 v. Chr. bis zu Alexander dem Grossen.* Munich.

Sullivan, C. O., R. S. Fouts, M. E. Hannum, and K. Schneider. 1982. "Chimpanzee Conversations: Language, Cognition, and Theory," in *Language Development II: Language, Thought, and Culture.* London. (pp. 397–428.)

Sullivan, L. E. 1988. *Healing and Restoring: Health and Medicine in the World's Religious Traditions.* New York.

Taub, D. M., ed. 1984. *Primate Paternalism.* New York.

Thureau-Dangin, F. 1921. *Rituels accadiens.* Paris.

van der Toorn, K. 1985. *Sin and Sanction in Israel and Mesopotamia.* Assen.

Trivers, R. L. 1971. "The Evolution of Reciprocal Altruism." *Quarterly Review of Biology* 46: 35–57.

Ulf, C. 1990. *Die homerische Gesellschaft.* Munich.

Vernant, J.-P. 1974. *Mythe et société en Grèce ancienne.* Paris.

———, 1991. *Mortals and Immortals: Collected Essays.* ed. F. I. Zeitlin. Princeton.

Vernant, J.-P. and P. Vidal-Naquet. 1972–86. *Mythe et tragédie en Grèce ancienne* I/II. Paris.

Versnel, H. S. 1990–92. *Inconsistencies in Greek and Roman Religion I: Ter unus. Isis, Dionysos, Hermes. Three Studies in Henotheism. II: Transition and Reversal in Myth and Ritual.* Leiden.

Vogel, C. 1989. *Vom Töten zum Mord: Das wirkliche Böse in der Evolutionsgeschichte.* Munich.

Vollmer, G. 1994. *Evolutionäre Erkenntnistheorie.* 6th ed. Stuttgart.

Waardenburg, J. 1979. "The Language of Religion and the Study of Religions as Sign Systems," in L. Honko, ed., *Science of Religion: Studies in Methodology.* Leiden. (pp. 441–457.)

de Waal, F. 1982. *Chimpanzee Politics: Power and Sex among Apes.* London.

———, 1989. *Peacemaking among Primates.* Cambridge, Mass.

Weinfeld, M. 1990. "The Common Heritage of Covenantal Tradition in the Ancient World," in L. Canfora et al., eds., *I trattati nel mondo antico.* Rome. (pp. 175–191.)

Weißbach, F. H. 1911. *Die Keilinschriften der Achämeniden.* Leipzig.

West, M. L. 1971. *Early Greek Philosophy and the Orient.* Oxford.

Widengren, G. 1969. *Religionsphänomenologie.* Berlin.

Williams, R. 1981. *Culture*. London.

Wilson, E. O. 1975. *Sociobiology: The New Synthesis*. Cambridge, Mass.

———, 1978. *On Human Nature*. Cambridge, Mass.

Wissowa, G. 1912. *Religion und Kultus der Römer*. 2nd ed. Munich.

248

Index

251

Index

253

tale, 56, 66, 78, 112, 126
tattooing, 167
Telemachus, 129
Telesphoros, 36, 50
temple: building, 114; of Jerusalem, 146, 149; system, 147, 151
Terminus, 166
territory, 165; *see also* boundaries
Tertullian, 13 n.46, 143
Thera, 91
Thucydides, 110, 114
tiger, 45
Tillich, P., 7
tithe, 148
trade, silent, 139
tradition, 23, 25
tree, 83; of life, 210 n.28
tripod cauldrons, 149
Tristan, 164
Typhon, 94

Ugarit, 131
universalia of anthropology, 3, 130, 150

validation, 27
van Gennep, A., 74
Vedic. *See* India
Venus statuettes, 26
Vernant, J.-P., 3
Vestal virgins, 44, 76
Villa of Mysteries, 74
Virgil, 52, 106
votive tablets, 135

water, in ordeals, 163
wax, 174
weeping, 86, 88, 96
Wilson, E. O., 9, 10, 12, 18, 42
world tree, 83

Xerxes, 228 n.100

Zeus, 33, 81, 95, 100, 136, 142, 149, 172
Zoroastrian religion, 33

255